THE LEGAL BRAIN

The Legal Brain is an essential guide for legal professionals seeking to understand the impact of chronic stress on their brain and mental health. Drawing on the latest neuroscience and psychology research, the book translates complex scientific concepts into actionable advice for legal professionals looking to enhance their well-being and thrive amidst the demands and stressors of the profession. Chapters cover optimizing cognitive fitness and performance, avoiding or healing cognitive damage, and protecting "the lawyer brain." Whether you are a law student, practicing lawyer, judge, or leader of a legal organization, this book provides valuable insights and strategies for building resilience, maintaining peak performance, and protecting your most important asset – your brain.

Debra S. Austin, JD, PhD, is Professor of the Practice of Law at the University of Denver Sturm College of Law. Dr Austin is a nationally recognized expert in lawyer well-being, with a focus on how to improve performance by enhancing brain health and mental strength.

The Legal Brain

A LAWYER'S GUIDE TO WELL-BEING AND BETTER JOB PERFORMANCE

Debra S. Austin
University of Denver

CAMBRIDGE
UNIVERSITY PRESS

CAMBRIDGE
UNIVERSITY PRESS

Shaftesbury Road, Cambridge CB2 8EA, United Kingdom

One Liberty Plaza, 20th Floor, New York, NY 10006, USA

477 Williamstown Road, Port Melbourne, VIC 3207, Australia

314–321, 3rd Floor, Plot 3, Splendor Forum, Jasola District Centre, New Delhi – 110025, India

103 Penang Road, #05-06/07, Visioncrest Commercial, Singapore 238467

Cambridge University Press is part of Cambridge University Press & Assessment, a department of the University of Cambridge.

We share the University's mission to contribute to society through the pursuit of education, learning and research at the highest international levels of excellence.

www.cambridge.org
Information on this title: www.cambridge.org/9781009484602

DOI: 10.1017/9781009484589

First published 2024

A catalogue record for this publication is available from the British Library

Library of Congress Cataloging-in-Publication Data
Names: Austin, Debra S., author.
Title: The legal brain : a lawyer's guide to well-being and better job performance / Debra S. Austin, University of Denver.
Description: 1e. | Cambridge, United Kingdom ; New York, NY : Cambridge University Press, 2024. | Includes bibliographical references and index.
Identifiers: LCCN 2023048458 (print) | LCCN 2023048459 (ebook) | ISBN 9781009484602 (hardback) | ISBN 9781009484565 (paperback) | ISBN 9781009484589 (ebook)
Subjects: LCSH: Lawyers. | Lawyers–Psychology. | Law–Psychological aspects. | Lawyers–Psychological aspects. | Practice of law–Psychological aspects. | Neurosciences. | Knowledge, Theory of. | Memory (Philosophy)
Classification: LCC K346 .A97 2024 (print) | LCC K346 (ebook) | DDC a340.023–dc23/eng/20231016
LC record available at https://lccn.loc.gov/2023048458
LC ebook record available at https://lccn.loc.gov/2023048459

ISBN 978-1-009-48460-2 Hardback
ISBN 978-1-009-48456-5 Paperback

To Richard, my kind and perseverant orchid. To Phillip, my optimistic and resilient dandelion. To Katherine, the igniter of my flame.

CONTENTS

ACKNOWLEDGMENTS

It takes a tribe to encourage and support a scholar. Many thanks to my high school teachers Glenna Kiser, Scott Sherman, and Terry McEwen; my doctoral professors Bruce Uhrmacher and Nick Cutforth; my mentors and friends Gary Alexander, Peter Huang, Debbie Borman, and Nancy Leong; and my family Dale Pugh, Tracie Mathisen, and Richard and Barbara Austin.

INTRODUCTION

> If we do not transform our pain, we will most assuredly transmit it – usually to those closest to us: our family, our neighbors, our co-workers, and, invariably, the most vulnerable, our children.
>
> —Father Richard Rohr[1]

> Lawyers are inevitably leaders in all positions they hold due to their privilege, power, prestige, and responsibility.
>
> —Randall Kiser[2]

What if you could feel better, be better, and do better? What if the law students or lawyers under your care and supervision could feel, be, and do better?

The legal profession worldwide is suffering from a failure of individual lawyers to thrive. The lawyer well-being crisis is impairing our performance. We must examine our culture, and we can learn from neuroscience and psychology research to address this problem.

Neuro-intelligence is a critical competency in the legal profession because lawyering is a cognitive profession and leading is a cognitive skill.[3] Neuro-intelligence development is centered on an understanding of neuroplasticity – the brain's superpower to constantly rewire with every action, experience, and thought; and neurogenesis – our brain's ability to grow new cells. Our brain is shaped by our daily habits and is influenced by our efforts, successes, stressors, failures, and traumas. Lawyers must process information quickly and accurately, solve complex problems, and demonstrate resilience. A high-functioning brain is essential for lawyers.

I have spent my entire professional life thinking about how to improve learning. I began as a middle school teacher. After law school, I worked at a company training lawyers to do online research.

My undergraduate degree and my PhD are in education, and I have been teaching at the University of Denver Sturm College of Law since 1998, driven by my motive to teach better and help students learn more effectively.

My interest in neuroscience was triggered when the instructor in an anger management class said, "When we get angry, we lose 30 IQ points." I was in that class with my then seventeen-year-old son, and I was taking copious notes. I wanted to help him learn to better regulate his emotions. But when the therapist made that statement, I immediately thought of my work with stressed-out law students. They were often so stressed, they got angry. What if that meant they could not learn as well as when they were not stressed and angry? I contacted the academic researcher responsible for that therapist's statement, and he said it was "mostly a metaphor for what's going on in the brain." I *had* to know what was going on in the brain during stress and anger.

Neuroscience research indicates that the aggregate effects of training to become a lawyer, or of practicing law, under chronically stressful conditions may weaken memory and thinking capacity. Stress might also set the stage for abnormally high rates of anxiety, depression, substance misuse, and suicide risk among law students and lawyers. Exposure to chronic stress can damage brain cells. I learned that *chronically stressful environments can cause brain damage.* And this phenomenon may be the catalyst for the lawyer well-being crisis.

It is startling to hear that there is a lawyer well-being crisis. It is excruciating to think you might be impaired or languishing, and the culture of legal education and law practice may be the root cause. While you are trying to contribute to society, find meaning in your work, develop professionally, and provide for your family, your well-being can get lost in the shuffle.

Lawyers are expected to project strength and competence. If a lawyer is suffering from stress, anxiety, or depression, or if they self-medicate with substances like alcohol, study drugs, or comfort food, they are part of the lawyer well-being crisis. If they are apathetic or burned out, they may be languishing and at risk of becoming impaired. If you know colleagues who are suffering in this way, they are part of the lawyer well-being crisis.

During my early years of research on the impact of stress on cognition, I learned that my first lawyer mentor had died by suicide when he was forty-eight years old. He wrote poetry and played the piano. He was a leader in the local legal community, handled pro bono cases, and spearheaded the program at his church that provided meals for the hungry. He was a workaholic. He remains in my thoughts as I argue that law students, lawyers, and leaders of legal organizations must invest in lawyer well-being to address this crisis.

What happened to my mentor is not common. Most law students and lawyers are likely suffering from languishing – a state of stagnation, emptiness, or despondency. Languishing is not mental illness, but a state of incomplete mental health. When a person is languishing, there are gaps in their emotional, psychological, or social well-being.

What does languishing look like? How can law school or legal practice cause languishing, which threatens to become a slippery slope to illness?

A second-year law student told me that he did not remember anything from his 1L year. He was a former US marine, machine gunner, and squad leader with service experience in the Middle East. He suffered from memory problems during law school.

A lawyer was fired from his job when he called his boss from the emergency room in the midst of a panic attack. He was an accomplished litigator with scores of criminal and civil trials under his belt. He changed professions.

Untreated languishing can devolve into impairment. The reflection below from a languishing law student who is approaching impairment, lightly edited for privacy and length, provides a rich description of the impact of a chronically stressful culture:

> I, unfortunately, did not really get to relax over this break. My weekend job involves shifts that are often late at night. Additionally, I worked on a directed research I was doing for a professor and I started work at a nonprofit that I will be working at while working full time at a law firm this semester. I know what it sounds like – burnout central. But, these are things I need to do to be able to pay for rent and be able to graduate in May, so I do what I have to.

> Here is where my reflection starts – there is so much shame from others when you try to protect your own wellbeing and focus on yourself. I took these last few days off from work in order to rest before I start my work at the law firm and I was told by a friend (in a judgmental way), "wow I wish I could take a few days off." Further, my little brother knows of an opportunity where your proceeds go toward paying off student loans. He insists that I work there. I have told him repeatedly that I am so exhausted and that along with working full time, I also will be doing an externship class, working for the nonprofit and continuing my weekend job. I told him I was too overwhelmed to add anything more to my plate, to which he responded, "I am trying to push you to be better and do more, because you can."
>
> I felt like I have been coming to this breaking point where I am so tired and exhausted, yet no one thinks I am doing enough – like I am enough. It's invalidating and belittling and, really, just makes me feel like I am going insane.
>
> These feelings had me relaying back to our class and what we spoke about – making time to care for ourselves so that we may be healthier, more competent, happier individuals. I remember feeling so excited by the fact that I became more focused on taking care of myself that I did not realize, in reality, there is so much shame in focusing on yourself and putting up boundaries. Focusing on your own well-being comes with many more challenges than I originally even imagined.

If you are a lawyer, a law student, or contemplating law school, you are a person with cognitive chops. You love learning and thinking. But what are you doing to care for your brain, your most important asset?

Hans Selye was a clumsy researcher who worked with rats in a lab. He routinely dropped his rats, followed by a chase and recapture exercise. Salye noticed that being mistreated made his rats sick. An extended exposure to the general unpleasantness of being Salye's lab rats made them ill in ways that the lab rats of other more careful researchers were not. The *culture* in Salye's lab was making his rats sick.[4]

Stress is a ubiquitous feature of legal education and law practice, and the stressors endured by law students and lawyers can result in a significant deterioration in their well-being, including languishing, anxiety, panic attacks, depression, substance misuse, and increased suicide risk.[5] Stress in the profession is making law students and lawyers sick.

Stress harms the body, and especially the brain. Chronic stress, the unceasing kind, arises from a *culture* of overwork, competitiveness, invulnerability, perfectionism, pessimism, isolation, and burnout. And *chronically stressful environments can cause brain damage.*

Legal practice is a cognitive profession, and the legendary stressors in our environment can take a tremendous toll on our cognitive capacity. Stress can weaken and kill brain cells. Research reveals that cognitive performance is diminished during the fight-or-flight response, including impaired concentration, memory, problem-solving, curiosity, motivation, creativity, and math and language processing.[6] This may be due to an overexposure to stress hormones in the hippocampus, the brain structure that processes memory and facilitates emotion.

Professionals relying heavily on optimal cognitive function need to cultivate a healthy hippocampus. Brain scans show hippocampi shrinkage in people experiencing stress, low self-esteem, repeated jet lag, major depression, and posttraumatic stress disorder (PTSD).[7] The hippocampus is extremely vulnerable to damage from stress hormones, and chronically high levels of stress hormones cause degeneration and death of brain cells.[8] *This signifies brain damage.*

The Legal Brain is the culmination of over a decade of research into stress, cognition, and how to optimize brain health and mental strength. Lawyers believe they should be indestructible and unstoppable, but many are overworked, unhappy, and unhealthy.

The risk that a profession can cause brain damage is pretty bad news. But there is good news. *Neuroplasticity proves that every lawyer's brain is a work in progress, and it is never too late to take better care of your cognitive fitness.*

This book translates scientific research into actionable information. It is designed to help law students, lawyers, and leaders of legal organizations understand how to:

- avoid or heal cognitive damage;
- optimize cognitive performance; and

- build, maintain, and protect the most valuable tool in their briefcase – the lawyer's brain.

The rest of the good news is that every beneficial practice you initiate, and every bad habit you curtail, will safeguard your brain as you age, reducing the risk of dementia and Alzheimer's disease.

To adequately care for your brain, you need to develop your neuro-intelligence. *The Legal Brain* is your neuro-intelligence manual:

- Chapter 1, "The Impaired Lawyer," describes the global lawyer well-being crisis and establishes that mental and physical health impairments can weaken performance and diminish well-being. It shows that lawyers struggle with anxiety, depression, burnout, substance misuse, and suicide risk at rates that are higher than the rest of the population.
- Chapter 2, "The Spectrum from Languishing to Flourishing," outlines the continuum of mental health.
- Chapter 3, "The Lawyering Culture," summarizes the key features of law school and legal practice cultures that undermine lawyer well-being.
- Chapter 4, "The Lawyer's Brain," introduces the triune brain structure and describes important parts of the emotional and thinking brains. These areas of the brain work together to facilitate learning, memory, developing expertise, and habit formation.
- Chapter 5, "Memory, Knowledge, and Building Expertise," examines how memory is formed and expertise is established by explaining how the lawyer's brain learns, remembers, and recalls information.
- Chapter 6, "Motivation, Reward, and Developing Habits," differentiates intentional learning from automated habit formation. It illuminates how the brain's motivation and reward system entrenches our habits, both good and bad.
- Chapter 7, "The Impact of Stress," reveals the damaging influences of stress and trauma and how they weaken our brain's health and function.
- Chapter 8, "The Influence of Self-Medication," demonstrates how various substances of abuse can impair cognition.
- Chapter 9, "The Importance of Fuel," explores how diet can improve or impede brain health.

- Chapter 10, "Optimizing Brain Health," provides research-based recommendations for maintaining a healthy brain.
- Chapter 11, "Enhancing Mental Strength," offers a series of practices that augment mental strength.
- Chapter 12, "Developing an Action Plan for the Neuro-intelligent Lawyer," delivers the tools to formulate a customized action plan for improving brain health and mental strength.
- Chapter 13, "The Neuro-intelligent Legal Organization," summarizes research-based well-being recommendations, examines burnout, describes leveraging energy styles and neurosignatures, and explains what legal organizations can do to support lawyer and law student well-being.
- Finally, the Conclusion challenges lawyers to consider their positions as leaders in society, the impact of developing neuro-intelligence, and the broader implications for their profession, their loved ones, and their work in the law, public policy, and business.

Each chapter has a "Summary" section followed by a section on "The Science." Lawyers will be able to learn the basics by reading "The Summary," and those who want a richer explanation can explore the research in "The Science" section.

The information provided in *The Legal Brain* is applicable to both law students and lawyers, but for the sake of simplicity moving forward, I will refer to lawyers and the lawyer's brain.

First, Chapter 1 asks how did the legal profession get here? Lawyers make important contributions to society, but do we do so while impaired? Data from research on lawyer well-being indicates the answer may be "yes."

NOTES

1 Richard Rohr, "Suffering: Week 1 Summary," October 14–19, 2018, https://cac.org/suffering-week-1-summary-2018-10-20.

2 Randall Kiser, Soft Skills for the Effective Lawyer (Cambridge University Press, 2017), 226.

3 Debra S. Austin, "Drink Like a Lawyer: The Neuroscience of Substance Use and Its Impact on Cognitive Wellness," 15 *Nev Law J* (2015), 826, at 829.

4 Robert M. Sapolsky, Why Zebras Don't Get Ulcers (Holt, 2004), 7–12.

5 Lawrence S. Krieger, "Institutional Denial about the Dark Side of Law School, and Fresh Empirical Guidance for Constructively Breaking the Silence," 52 *J Leg Educ* (2002), 112; Nancy Levit and Douglas O. Linder, The Happy Lawyer: Making a Good Life in the Law (Oxford University Press, 2010), 6–8.

6 Rick Hanson, Buddha's Brain: The Practical Neuroscience of Happiness, Love, & Wisdom (Brilliance, 2009), 52–60; John Medina, Brain Rules: 12 Principles for Surviving and Thriving at Work, Home, and School (Pear Press, 2008), 178; David Perlmutter and Alberto Villoldo, Power Up Your Brain: The Neuroscience of Enlightenment (Hay House, 2011), 61; John J. Ratey, Spark: The Revolutionary New Science of Exercise and the Brain (Little, Brown Spark, 2008), 67–71.

7 Talitha Best and Louise Dye, "Good News Story: Nutrition for Brain Health," in Nutrition for Brain Health and Cognitive Performance (CRC Press, 2015), 4; Sapolsky, *supra* note 4, at 221.

8 Larry R. Squire et al. (eds.), Fundamental Neuroscience (4th ed., Academic Press, 2012), 804; Eric R. Kandel et al. (eds.), Principles of Neural Science (5th ed., McGraw Hill, 2013), 1320.

1 THE IMPAIRED LAWYER

> To be truly free, we must choose beyond simply surviving adversity, we must dare to create lives of sustained optimal well-being and joy. In that world, the making and drinking of lemonade will be a fresh and zestful delight, a real life mixture of the bitter and the sweet, and not a measure of our capacity to endure pain, but rather a celebration of our moving beyond pain.
>
> —bell hooks[1]

In Linkin Park's aching anthem "One More Light," the chorus mourns, "[W]ho cares if one more light goes out."[2] Lead singer Chester Bennington took his own life on July 20, 2017, a day that should have been the fifty-third birthday of his friend and fellow musician Chris Cornell, who had committed suicide on May 18, 2017. Both musicians were creating new music and performing on tours delighting their fans, yet both had a history of depression and addiction.[3] In popular culture, we tend to think that anxiety, depression, and substance abuse are afflictions of creative artists who pour out their histories and hardships on canvas and stage. Failure to thrive is not limited to artists, and there are many ways to extinguish a person's light.

THE SUMMARY

The extreme socialization process of becoming a lawyer may snuff out the ideals, goals, and values of enthusiastic new law students. The intense workload, the expectation of 24/7 connectivity, and the lack of work–life balance in legal practice might suffocate the lawyer trying mightily to help clients achieve their goals. These characteristics of the law school and legal practice cultures can have devastating consequences for the well-being of law students and lawyers.

The pressure during law school can devolve well-adjusted students into anxious and depressed zombies, and it happens as early as the first semester.[4] Compared to other graduate student populations, they are less fulfilled and they handle the culture of intense competition by binge-drinking more often and using more marijuana than other graduate students. Fatigue, apprehension of failure, and increased anxiety and depression can result.

The culture of legal practice is not an improvement due to the steep billable hour requirements and responsibility for client outcomes. Lawyers suffer from anxiety and depression at higher rates than the general population, and they are at the greatest risk of suicide among professionals, behind only those in the medical field. Alcohol misuse is a significant problem, with one study finding that 20% of lawyers are problem drinkers and another revealing that 46% of male and 60% of female attorneys abuse alcohol. Lawyers in the first ten years of their career have the most problematic drinking habits.

The lawyering culture, featuring extreme stress, intense competition, and overwork, can drive lawyers to succumb to mental and physical health problems. Neuroscience and psychology research explains how the damage happens and provides recommendations to help lawyers recover their well-being and cognitive capacity.

THE SCIENCE

AMERICAN LAW STUDENTS AND LAWYERS

Students enter law school with the dream of contributing to social justice enterprises, reform endeavors, entrepreneurial ventures, and legislative and administrative law efforts. They become leaders in the legal system, politics, governance, business, finance, nonprofit management, news media, entertainment, and philanthropy. But many cannot escape the personal damage that is done by legal education and law practice cultures.

Law students are among the "most dissatisfied, demoralized, and depressed" of all graduate students in the United States.[5] These students do not start their legal education with these problems. Students often begin law school with higher-than-average mental health and life satisfaction indicators, but during the 1L year, many students experience an increase in anxiety and depression.[6] "Something distinctly bad is happening to the students in our law schools," states law professor and researcher Lawrence Krieger, and igniting the lawyer well-being crisis is one consequence.[7]

The stresses of attending law school are well known. Law schools define student success in terms of grades, class rank, and selection for work on law journals. Students are introduced to "these prizes" as early as orientation, creating an acute pressure to compete.[8] Students surveyed about their prevailing impressions of their 1L year cited exhaustion, anxiety, and stress. They were particularly worried about final exams, their grades, and the potential for failing out of law school.[9] While some students may enjoy law school, many state that the workload, competition, and grades create significant stress.[10] Douglas Litowitz argues that rather than a transformative educational experience, law school is a "hazing ritual" that traumatizes and breaks people: "When I say that law school *breaks* people I mean that almost nobody comes out of law school feeling better about themselves, although many come out much worse – caustic, paranoid, and overly competitive."[11]

Law professors describe students as the walking wounded, gradually becoming insecure and disheartened. The context in which law students are educated prompts a "single-minded focus on competitive achievement."[12] Students become fixated on grades as the only means to credential their legal career, marginalizing the importance of learning legal skills and developing domain expertise. Those who cannot meet their grade point average objectives can become disengaged.

Stressed-out law students may choose to self-medicate in order to cope with stress. In a 2014 study of over 11,000 students from fifteen different law schools, researchers discovered that:

- 53% had consumed sufficient alcohol to become drunk within the past thirty days, compared to 39% of other graduate students;

- 43% had participated in binge-drinking once in the previous two weeks, compared to 36% of other graduate students, while 22% had been binge-drinking twice in that time period, compared to 21% of other graduate students;
- 25% had used marijuana in the past year, compared to 14% of other graduate students, and 14% had used marijuana in the past month, compared to 7% of other graduate students;
- 12% were prescribed anxiety medications, 12% antidepressants, 13% stimulants, and 15% pain medication; and
- 14% used medications without a prescription, with stimulants being used the most by 9% of respondents.[13]

In addition:

- 37% of the students screened positive for anxiety,
- 17% were suffering from depression, and
- 27% were dealing with an eating disorder.[14]

Between July 2014 and February 2015, seven law students and one law professor committed suicide.[15]

In May 2014, students at Yale Law School were surveyed and 70% of the 296 respondents reported experiencing mental health issues during law school. While 80% of the respondents considered seeking treatment, only 50% actually received help, even though they reported that their academic performance and personal relationships were impaired due to their mental health challenges.[16]

The mental health and substance use issues of law students do not improve when they enter law practice. In a 2015 study of 12,825 attorneys practicing in nineteen states, 23% experienced stress, 19% had anxiety, and 28% suffered from depression. This research also revealed that 20.6% of these employed lawyers could be classified as problem drinkers, compared to 11.8% of other highly educated professionals. Lawyers working in law firms and those in the first ten years of legal practice experienced the highest levels of problem alcohol use. Of participants who had reported using other substances in the prior twelve months, 16.9% used tobacco, 15.7% sedatives, 10.2% marijuana, 5.6% opioids, and 4.8% stimulants. However, for the lawyers in the group that used these substances, the weekly use of stimulants was 74.1%, sedative use was 51.3%, tobacco 46.8%, marijuana 31%, and opioids 21.6%.[17]

Among professionals, lawyers rank fourth in suicide rates, behind dentists, pharmacists, and doctors, and many recent lawyer suicides are linked to depression.[18] Females in the legal profession rank second in suicide rates, behind female first responders.[19]

Recognizing a lawyer well-being crisis, the American Bar Association (ABA) formed a National Task Force on Lawyer Well-Being.[20] The comprehensive task force report, *The Path to Lawyer Well-Being: Practical Recommendations for Positive Change*, was released on August 14, 2017.[21] The report acknowledges the legal profession's mental health and substance use problems and promotes making changes to the cultures in which law students are educated and lawyers practice law.[22]

The Path to Lawyer Well-Being provides five key themes to inspire action to improve the lawyer well-being crisis. The legal profession must:

1. identify stakeholders and reduce toxicity in the profession;
2. eliminate the stigma associated with help-seeking behaviors;
3. emphasize that well-being is part of a lawyer's duty of competence;
4. educate lawyers, judges, and law students on lawyer well-being issues; and
5. take steps to change how law is practiced, instilling greater well-being in the profession.[23]

The Path to Lawyer Well-Being provides general recommendations for all stakeholders and then offers specific recommendations for judges, attorney regulators, legal employers, law schools, bar associations, professional liability carriers for lawyers, and lawyer assistance programs.[24] These universal recommendations emphasize taking responsibility for the crisis, destigmatizing lawyer well-being problems and efforts to get help, providing well-being training to all stakeholders by experts in the field, mentoring aging and suffering lawyers, and discussing suicide risk and prevention.[25]

The Path to Lawyer Well-Being provides three reasons to address the lawyer well-being crisis: to enhance the effectiveness of legal organizations; to improve the professional and ethical behavior of lawyers; and to help individual lawyers flourish. Well-being is defined as the continuous effort to thrive in each of the physical, emotional, intellectual, occupational, social, and spiritual domains of their lives.[26] The report appeals to leaders within each stakeholder group, urging a shift from neglect to action and a transformation of the culture.[27]

The Path to Lawyer Well-Being recommends that law schools:

- identify organizational practices that may contribute to well-being problems and assess changes that can be made;
- educate the faculty on well-being issues in the legal profession;
- provide a well-being curriculum to students;
- survey student well-being anonymously;
- promote student resources that address mental health and substance use disorders;
- facilitate networks to support students in recovery; and
- discourage alcohol-centered social events.[28]

The Path to Lawyer Well-Being recommends that legal employers:

- provide professional development on lawyer well-being issues;
- establish organizational infrastructure, policies, and practices to promote lawyer well-being; and
- establish leadership standards and incentives to promote lawyer well-being.[29]

Research conducted since the release of *The Path to Lawyer Well-Being* demonstrates that well-being in the legal profession has not yet improved. A mid-2020 study examined stress, substance misuse, and attrition. Participants were recruited from three attorney organizations: the State Bar of California, the California Young Lawyers Association, and the Washington, DC Bar. Data from 2,863 lawyers (51% female) showed:

- Overwork is a problem, with 67% of both women and men reporting heavy workloads, typically over forty hours per week.
- Women were more overcommitted than men, and women had to exert more effort than men to receive workplace rewards.
- A significantly higher number of women than men engaged in risky drinking (55.9% of women and 46.4% of men) and hazardous alcohol consumption (34.0% of women and 25.4% of men).

- More women (25%) than men (17.4%) had considered leaving the legal profession due to burnout or mental health concerns.
- Younger lawyers are two to four times more likely to report moderate or high stress compared to older attorneys.

The study suggested that law schools should better prepare law students for the demands of practice, and stakeholders in the legal profession should develop training, resources, and mitigation strategies for lawyers in practice.[30]

To assess the impacts of the COVID-19 pandemic on legal practice, the ABA deployed the Practice Forward ABA Member Survey between September 30 and October 11, 2020. Over 4,200 ABA members completed the survey. Participants were 81% White, 15% people of color, and 4% did not identify their race; 54% were male, 43% female, and 3% nonbinary or did not respond; 6% reported a disability; and about 67% were in private practice. Compared to a year before the study, which was fall 2019, participants reported:

- feeling overwhelmed by all their responsibilities (46% overall, 38% of men, and 60% of women);
- having trouble taking time off from work (43% overall, 37% of men, and 57% of women);
- feeling the day never seems to end (41% overall, 32% of men, and 57% of women);
- experiencing stress from their work (40% overall, 34% of men, and 52% of women); and
- thinking it would be better to stop working (33% overall, 31% of men, and 37% of women).[31]

The 2020 National Asylum Attorney Burnout and Secondary Traumatic Stress Survey, which collected data from 718 asylum lawyers, revealed the strain caused by representing low-income clients in an evolving area of law under continuous adverse government and public scrutiny. These lawyers reported high rates of burnout and secondary traumatic stress, with the highest levels occurring among female lawyers, lawyers of color, and solo practitioners.[32]

Lawyers practicing immigration and asylum law are working in a system described by this study as highly dysfunctional, racist, and unjust. These lawyers are exposed to victims of trauma and their work has been under greater public scrutiny in recent years.[33]

Burnout can occur in work environments with the following characteristics:

- excessive workloads;
- high stress and low financial and/or emotional rewards;
- little to no respect or sense of community;
- inequity; and
- conflict between organizational objectives and individual values.

Secondary traumatic stress (STS) is "the natural consequent behaviors and emotions resulting from knowing about a traumatizing event experienced by a significant other – stress resulting from helping or wanting to help a traumatized or suffering person."[34] Symptoms of STS are similar to those of PTSD and include sleep problems, fatigue, hypervigilance, irritability, anger, difficulty with concentration, and avoiding clients and their situations.[35]

The study found that female-identifying asylum lawyers experienced more symptoms of burnout and STS than male-identifying asylum attorneys. These results are consistent with other studies and may be due to bias, discrimination, and sexual harassment. The study also found that lawyers who identified as other than White/Caucasian (39 percent of the participants) experienced higher rates of burnout than those who identified as White/Caucasian. Three racial/ethnic groups reported higher rates of STS: Middle Eastern/North African, Asian/Pacific Islander, and mixed-race participants.[36]

The study recommends that law schools take the lead in training law students to be aware of the impacts of stress, trauma, and burnout and learn how to practice self-care. It highlights the work being done in clinical education on developing strategies to maintain well-being. And it recommends that legal organizations consider how they can better support lawyer wellness as a means to provide the most effective client representation and help individual lawyers "carve out a sustainable career."[37]

As bar associations and law firms better understand how costly untreated mental health and substance use issues are for their attorneys, they will embrace resources and training to help their lawyers recover.[38] Costs to firms include absenteeism, attrition, and lawyer disciplinary actions.[39]

Investments in lawyer wellness save money as every dollar spent on their well-being saves $3.27 in medical costs and $2.73 by reducing absenteeism.[40] Clients will also benefit from improved lawyer well-being, as lawyer misconduct often involves substance use, depression, or both and results in high percentages of disciplinary and malpractice claims.[41]

According to Patrick Krill, "The law has always been a magnet for hard-working, self-reliant, and competitive people who often prioritize success and accomplishment far above personal health or wellbeing. On top of that, stress, unhappiness and imbalance abound, while unhealthy coping skills such as excessive drinking are the cultural norm."[42]

While numerous surveys of law students and lawyers have shown high rates of mental distress, Professor Yair Listokin and Lawyer Raymond Noonan argue that collecting survey information from voluntary respondents is not the gold standard of empirical research. They reviewed data from the annual National Health Interview Survey, administered by the US Centers for Disease Control, involving 100–200 lawyers per year, which showed that lawyers who participated in this survey did not experience higher rates of mental illness than similarly educated professionals, but they did consume alcohol at twice the rate of other professionals. "Lawyers drink problematic amounts of alcohol at rates well in excess of their similarly educated peers." The review also found that alcohol misuse is getting worse especially for lawyers under forty years of age. Finally, they state that their findings do not indicate that "mental illness is not a problem in the legal profession."[43]

At a symposium on mental health and the legal profession, researchers Katherine M. Bender, David Jaffe, and Jerome Organ presented findings from a spring 2021 survey of over 5,000 law students from thirty-nine law schools. They found that binge-drinking rates were down from a 2014 survey they had conducted. They discovered that from 2014 to 2021:

- marijuana use in the previous thirty days had increased from 14% to 25%;
- anxiety had increased from 21% to 40%;

- depression had increased from 18% to 33%;
- frequency of suicidal thoughts had increased from 20% to 33% over their lifetime; and
- 11% had seriously considered suicide in the past twelve months, compared to 6% in 2014.[44]

LAWYERS FROM AROUND THE WORLD

Studies on lawyer and law student well-being are limited to Americans up to this point. Research indicates that lawyers who practice in countries other than the United States suffer in similar ways.

The International Bar Association (IBA), established in 1947, has a membership of over 80,000 lawyers, 190 bar associations and law societies, and 200 law firms in over 170 countries. It published *Mental Wellbeing in the Legal Profession: A Global Study* in October 2021.

The *Mental Wellbeing* report indicates that there is a "global crisis in lawyer mental wellbeing."[45] It acknowledges that legal practice is intellectually stimulating and rewarding, but sustained levels of high demands, including extreme workloads, high billable hour goals, intensified client expectations, and unsupportive workplace environments, expose lawyers to negative health consequences. The problems with lawyering culture, which lead to lawyer languishing and impairment, are similar all around the world.[46]

From July through December of 2020, the IBA conducted two global surveys: the IBA Survey of Individuals and the IBA Survey of Institutions. It collaborated with Acritas, a marketing research company, to make the online surveys available in English and Spanish. Both quantitative and qualitative data were collected from anyone in the legal profession not just IBA members. Over a period of five months, responses were received from 3,256 individuals and 186 institutions from 124 jurisdictions. The respondents were 56% female, 15% ethnic minority, and 3% disabled lawyers. The geographical areas represented were 42% Asia Pacific, 34% Europe, 11% North America, 9% Latin America, 7% Africa, and 2% Arab regions.[47]

Individual lawyers responded to another survey, the World Health Organization Mental Wellbeing Index (WHO-5), a five-item, validated self-assessment that spans a two-week period. A WHO-5 score below 52 percent indicates that a health professional should screen the respondent for depression and other mental health disorders. To provide perspective, scores from the 2012 European Quality of Life Survey ranged from 70.1% for Denmark to 53.7% for the Republic of Serbia. The average score for the IBA Survey of Individuals was 51%, with the lowest scores reported by women (47%), ethnic minorities (47%), lawyers with a disability (45%), and younger lawyers – twenty-three to thirty-nine years old (43%). These scores all fall below the 52% threshold of WHO-5 that calls for a mental health assessment. These data suggest a connection between mental well-being and issues with diversity, equity, and inclusion.[48]

Overall, 35 percent of respondents reported their work had a negative or extremely negative impact on their mental well-being. The most significant adverse factors were stress and workload. Other problems in lawyering culture include long hours, competing demands, inability to take breaks, unrealistic time pressures, unclear expectations, lack of feedback and support, and harassment or bullying.[49] These workplace problems result in lawyers who feel unable to perform (32%), feel unable to cope (32%), look for another job (31%), make a mistake (26%), nearly make a mistake (24%), and take time off (20%). The impact on lawyers' health included fatigue (57%), disrupted sleep (57%), anxiety (56%), emotional upset (44%), depressed thoughts (41%), negative physical health (31%), suicidal thoughts (6%), and self-harm (2%).[50]

While 82 percent of legal institutions stated that mental well-being is a priority, individual respondents reported that their workplaces were somewhat or highly ineffective at dealing with cultural problems that harm their mental well-being, such as lack of support (67%), harassment and bullying (66%), lack of feedback (58%), unclear expectations (57%), long hours (53%), unrealistic time pressures (48%), inability to take breaks (44%), and competing demands (36%).[51]

Individual lawyers are keen to see improvements in their workplace culture. They would like to see increased awareness of and openness around issues of well-being, as well as a culture that centers on mutual respect and restricts poor behavior. They would like more resources to be devoted to professional support, such as therapy and mentoring, and wellness programs and social activities. They want better work–life balance; more opportunities for remote work; more effective workload allocation; and enhanced health benefits, vacations, sabbaticals, and parental leave.[52]

The *Mental Wellbeing* report concludes that market forces are driving legal practice into an unsustainable position worldwide, jeopardizing the mental well-being of individual lawyers, the recruitment of new members into the profession, the future of legal organizations, and the profession's response to the issues of societal diversity and equality.[53]

The *Mental Wellbeing* report proposes the following IBA Mental Wellbeing Principles for the Legal Profession:

1. Mental well-being matters because lawyer impairment is a global crisis.
2. Struggling with mental well-being is not a weakness.
3. Raising awareness is critical to eliminating stigma and improving lawyer well-being.
4. Commitment to regular assessment, and sustainable and systemic change, is imperative to address the crisis. Leaders must reform cultures and model healthy behaviors.
5. Collaboration on the development and adoption of policies that promote and protect mental well-being must be a priority.
6. Open dialogue and communication are necessary to support new well-being policies, foster systemic change, recognize and learn from mistakes, and create work environments that optimize mental well-being.
7. The focus must be on the structural and systemic aspects of the lawyering culture that are problematic for lawyer mental well-being (the competitive culture that promotes unsustainable workloads and billable hour goals; sexism, racism, bullying, and harassment; lack of mental well-being support, and poor management training, especially regarding professional growth and development), not on enhancing the resilience of individual lawyers.

8. The profession must acknowledge intersectionalities and recognize that issues of diversity, equity, and inclusion may be at the center of mental health struggles for lawyers with disabilities or who are younger, female, or ethnic minorities. These intersectionalities and issues must be understood and addressed.
9. Helpful practices must be shared, disseminated, and perpetuated to create healthy ways of working in the post-pandemic legal profession.
10. All constituents must continue to grapple with and discuss mental well-being issues, as well as learn from lawyer well-being experts and groups.[54]

A 2023 working paper of the National Bureau of Economic Research has revealed gaps in gender well-being in 167 countries. Compared to men, women reported experiencing more negative moods and fewer positive mood events; poorer mental and physical health and worse sleep; and less satisfaction with the state of democracy, the economy, and the availability of public services.[55]

The literature review in this paper cites recent research evidence of women feeling more "anxious, depressed, downhearted, tense, lonely, frustrated, sad" and experiencing greater distress and more restless sleep compared to men. Women are said to suffer from lower self-esteem, higher pulse rates, and more chronic pain compared to men, and the gender well-being gap appears as early as the start of adolescence. Research suggests some of the common reasons for the gender gap across numerous countries include gender inequality, access to fewer resources, lack of power, and exposure to violence.[56]

"We hypothesize that women express greater negative affect and lower positive affect on experiential dimensions of wellbeing because in their daily lives they face a world that, even today, is patriarchal – structured by men, for men."[57]

In its Global Gender Gap Report 2023, the World Economic Forum reviewed the progress of efforts to close the gender gap across four dimensions: economic participation and opportunity; educational attainment; health and survival; and political empowerment. It has been tracking these dimensions for 122 countries since 2006, and currently includes 146 countries. Rated on a scale of 1–100, a country's score represents the distance covered toward parity. The global score for 2023 is 68.4%, with an improvement of only 0.3% from the previous year. If progress continues at its current rate, it will take 131 years to reach full global gender parity.[58]

The scores of the top ten countries in the 2023 report are:

1. Iceland – .912
2. Norway – .879
3. Finland – .863
4. New Zealand – .856
5. Sweden – .815
6. Germany – .815
7. Nicaragua – .811
8. Namibia – .802
9. Lithuania – .800
10. Belgium – .796

A sampling of other countries and their scores include:

11. Ireland – .795
15. United Kingdom – .792
18. Spain – .791
20. South Africa – .787
21. Switzerland – .793
23. Denmark – .780
26. Australia – .778
27. Chile – .777
30. Canada – .770
33. Mexico – .765
40. France – .756
43. United States – .748
60. Poland – .722
66. Ukraine – .714[59]

This research on gender indicates that people identifying as women may need more well-being support than those identifying as men.

We cannot afford the light of one more lawyer to be extinguished. Research discoveries in the fields of neuroscience and psychology can guide the legal profession toward a new paradigm of wellness. Lawyers and leaders in the legal field can learn about how our brains work, what impact stress has on our thinking and memory, how what we eat and drink influence our brain function, and what habits and practices can enhance our well-being and performance.

The cultures of legal education and legal practice are well established and can be slow to change. Leaders must understand how a failure to flourish can harm individual lawyers and jeopardize legal organizations. The profession must move to safeguard the light of individual lawyers and create sustained and optimal well-being for lawyers.

What if you are not impaired by depression or substance misuse? If you are lethargic, unmotivated, or you feel your light barely flickering, are you mentally healthy? Are you languishing? If so, how big a problem is that? The research in Chapter 2 suggests it could be a significant well-being challenge.

NOTES

1 bell hooks, "Moving Beyond Pain," *bell hooks Books*, May 9, 2016, www.bellhooksinstitute.com/blog/2016/5/9/moving-beyond-pain.

2 Brad Delson et al., "One More Light," Linkin Park, *One More Light* album (2017).

3 TMZ, "Linkin Park Singer Commits Suicide by Hanging," July 20, 2017, www.tmz.com/2017/07/20/linkin-park-singer-chester-bennington-dead-commits-suicide.

4 Peter H. Huang and Corie L. Rosen, "The Zombie Lawyer Apocalypse," 42 *Pepp L Rev* (2015), 727.

5 Abigail A. Patthoff, "This Is Your Brain on Law School: The Impact of Fear-Based Narratives on Law Students," 391 *Utah L Rev* (2015), 424.

6 Lawrence S. Krieger, "Institutional Denial about the Dark Side of Law School, and Fresh Empirical Guidance for Constructively Breaking the Silence," 52 *J Legal Educ* (2002), 113.

7 Ibid., at 114–115.

8 Nancy Levit and Douglas O. Linder, The Happy Lawyer: Making a Good Life in the Law (Oxford University Press, 2010), 125.

9 Andrew J. Mcclurg, 1L of a Ride: A Well-Traveled Professor's Roadmap to Success in the First Year of Law School (2nd ed., West Academic, 2013), 368–389. (These were students of Cecil C. Humphreys School of Law, University of Memphis.)

10 Rebecca Nerison, Lawyers, Anger, and Anxiety: Dealing with the Stresses of the Legal Profession (American Bar Association, 2010), 68.

11 Douglas Litowitz, The Destruction of Young Lawyers: Beyond One L (University of Akron Press, 2005), 10, 19, 30.

12 William M. Sullivan et al., Educating Lawyers: Preparation for the Profession of Law (Jossey Bass, 2007), 31.

13 Jerome M. Organ, David B. Jaffe, and Katherine M. Bender, "Suffering in Silence: The Survey of Law Student Well-Being and the Reluctance of Law Students to Seek Help for Substance Use and Mental Health Concerns," 66 *J Legal Educ* (2016), 116, at 123–124, 127–129, 133–134.

14 Ibid., at 136–138.

15 Ibid., at 117.

16 Jessie Agatstein et al., FALLING THROUGH THE CRACKS: A REPORT ON MENTAL HEALTH AT YALE LAW SCHOOL (Yale Law School Mental Health Alliance, 2014), www.law.yale.edu/system/files/falling_through_the_cracks_120614.pdf. (The total student population of Yale Law School was 650 students at the time of this study.)

17 Patrick R. Krill, Ryan Johnson, and Linda Albert, "The Prevalence of Substance Use and Other Mental Health Concerns among American Attorneys," 10 *J Addict Med* (2016), 46.

18 Rosa Flores and Rose Marie Arce, "Why Are Lawyers Killing Themselves?" *CNN*, January 20, 2014, www.cnn.com/2014/01/19/us/lawyer-suicides.

19 CBS News, "These Jobs Have the Highest Rate of Suicide", June 30, 2016, www.cbsnews.com/news/these-jobs-have-the-highest-rate-of-suicide (summarizing results from the 2012 Centers for Disease Control and Prevention study on suicide rates by occupational group).

20 Bree Buchanan et. al., THE PATH TO LAWYER WELL-BEING: PRACTICAL RECOMMENDATIONS FOR POSITIVE CHANGE (American Bar Association, 2017), 1, www.americanbar.org/content/dam/aba/images/abanews/ThePathToLawyerWell-beingReportFINAL.pdf.

21 Ibid.

22 Ibid., at 7, 12.

23 Ibid., at 2. (These core steps are detailed at 10–11.)

24 Ibid., at 4–6.

25 Ibid., at 12–21.

26 Ibid., at 8–9.

27 Ibid., at 12.

28 Ibid., at 35–40.

29 Ibid., at 31–34.

30 J. Anker and P. R. Krill, "Stress, Drink, Leave: An Examination of Gender-Specific Risk Factors for Mental Health Problems and Attrition among Licensed Attorneys," 16 *PLoS ONE* (2021), e0250563, https://journals.plos.org/plosone/article?id=10.1371/journal.pone.0250563.

31 Stephanie A. Scharf and Roberta D. Liebenberg, PRACTICING LAW IN THE PANDEMIC AND MOVING FORWARD: RESULTS AND BEST PRACTICES FROM A NATIONWIDE SURVEY OF THE LEGAL PROFESSION (American Bar Association, 2021), www.americanbar.org/content/dam/aba/administrative/digital-engagement/practice-forward/practice-forward-survey.pdf.

32 Lindsay M. Harris and Hillary Mellinger, "Asylum Attorney Burnout and Secondary Trauma," 56 *Wake Forest L Rev* (2021), 733, at 736–737.

33 Ibid., at 743.
34 Ibid., at 744–745.
35 Ibid., at 746.
36 Ibid., at 774–779.
37 Ibid., at 799–806.
38 Jarrod F. Reich, "Capitalizing on Healthy Lawyers: The Business Case for Law Firms to Promote and Prioritize Lawyer Well-Being," 65 *Vill L Rev* (2020), 361, at 396.
39 Ibid., at 396–400.
40 Ibid., at 408.
41 Michael E. McCabe, Jr., "Lawyer Alcoholism and Substance Abuse Frequent Causes for Lawyer Discipline," McCabe, www.ipethicslaw.com/lawyer-alcoholism-and-substance-abuse-frequent-causes-of-discipline; D. B. Marlowe, "Alcoholism, Symptoms, Causes & Treatments," in STRESS MANAGEMENT FOR LAWYERS, 104–130 (Amiram Elwork ed., 2nd ed., Vorkell Group, 1997) (cited in M. A. Silver, SUBSTANCE ABUSE, STRESS, MENTAL HEALTH AND THE LEGAL PROFESSION (New York State Law Assistant Trust, 2004), www.nylat.org/documents/courseinabox.pdf).
42 Ibid.
43 Yair Listokin and Raymond Noonan, "Measuring Lawyer Well-Being Systematically: Evidence from the National Health Interview Survey," 18 *J Empir Leg Stud* (2021), 4, at 6, 18.
44 David Jaffe, Katerine M. Bender, and Jerome Organ, "It Is Okay to Not Be Okay," 60 *U Louisville L Rev* (2022), 441.
45 IBA Presidential Task Force, MENTAL WELLBEING IN THE LEGAL PROFESSION: A GLOBAL STUDY (International Bar Association, 2021), 13.
46 Ibid., at 19.
47 Ibid., at 22–29.
48 Ibid., at 9, 24, 30.
49 Ibid., at 32, 37.
50 Ibid., at 39–40.
51 Ibid., at 41–43.
52 Ibid., at 44.
53 Ibid., at 54.
54 Ibid., at 10, 12–17.
55 David G. Blanchflower and Alex Bryson, "The Gender Well-Being Gap," National Bureau of Economic Research Working Paper 31212, May 2023, at 2–3.
56 Ibid., at 5–7.
57 Ibid., at 21.
58 World Economic Forum, GLOBAL GENDER GAP REPORT 2023 (World Economic Forum, 2023).
59 Ibid., at 11.

2 THE SPECTRUM FROM LANGUISHING TO FLOURISHING

Industry cannot flourish if labor languish.

—Calvin Coolidge[1]

Although some lawyers are impaired by mental illnesses such as anxiety, depression, and substance abuse, many more may be suffering from a state of incomplete mental health known as languishing.

Mental health is described by the World Health Organization (WHO) as "a state of mental well being that enables people to cope with the stresses of life, realize their abilities, learn well and work well, and contribute to their community. It is an integral component of health and well-being that underpins our individual and collective abilities to make decisions, build relationships and shape the world we live in."[2]

Mental health is assessed on a continuum, ranging from languishing to flourishing. Languishing has been described as feeling uninspired, joyless, and lacking the power to function at full capacity. And languishing may increase your risk of mental illness, such as a major depressive episode, generalized anxiety, panic attacks, or substance use disorder.[3]

THE SUMMARY

Research indicates that a segment of the lawyer population is impaired by mental illness, such as anxiety, depression, substance misuse, or suicide risk. A much higher number of lawyers likely fall on the languishing end of the mental health spectrum. If you are languishing, you may be at a higher risk of sliding into impairment. Research on languishing may help you assess your well-being and consider interventions designed to improve it.

THE SCIENCE

The spectrum of languishing to flourishing was first described by social psychologist Corey L. M. Keyes, a professor at Emory University.[4] Professor Keyes found in a 1995 survey of 3,032 adults, aged 25–74 years, that 17.2% were flourishing; 56.6% were moderately mentally healthy; 12.1% were languishing; and 14.1% had suffered a major depressive episode in the prior twelve months.

Keyes described flourishing as the presence of mental health, and languishing as the absence of mental health. For Keyes, being mentally healthy requires three components:

- Emotional well-being – the presence of positive emotion, such as enthusiasm and joy, and the absence of negative mood, such as sadness or distress;
- Psychological well-being – a perception of strong life satisfaction; and
- Social well-being – the capacity for positive functioning in life.

Positive functioning incorporates:

- Psychological well-being – the capacity for strong satisfaction with life – which comes from a combination of self-acceptance, positive relationships, personal development, purpose, environmental mastery, and autonomy; and
- Social well-being, which is:
  - Social coherence – viewing society as meaningful and understandable,
  - Social actualization – believing society offers the potential for growth,
  - Social integration – being accepted by and belonging to the community,
  - Social acceptance – accepting most aspects of society, and
  - Social contribution – feeling confident in the capacity to contribute to society.

Professor Keyes stated that another way to think about the continuum is that to be flourishing is to enjoy complete mental health, and to be languishing is to be burdened with incomplete mental health.

To experience flourishing, an individual is "filled with positive emotion" and "functioning well psychologically and socially." To be languishing is to live life in quiet despair, feeling empty, hollow, or stagnant. Mental illness leads to negative moods; anhedonia, which is the inability to derive pleasure from life; and malfunctioning.

Lawyers may suffer from several obstacles to mental strength, including a lack of self-awareness, perfectionism, imposter syndrome, social comparisons, trained pessimism, the inability to regulate emotions, and inauthenticity from a failure to understand or leverage their temperament and personality strengths. Features of the lawyering culture may augment these obstacles, leading to lawyer languishing.

SELF-AWARENESS

In his book *Soft Skills for the Effective Lawyer*, attorney and researcher Randall Kiser devotes an entire chapter to the duty of lawyers to become self-aware by committing to "detached self-assessment and self-improvement."[5] In order to adequately assess legal skills and mental strength, lawyers must be able to evaluate honestly what they know and don't know, and what impediments hinder their performance and self-development. Kiser quotes Professor K. Anders Ericsson: "The journey to truly superior performance is neither for the faint of heart nor the impatient. The development of genuine expertise requires struggle, sacrifice, and honest, often painful self-assessment."[6]

Self-discerning lawyers must assess and develop their skills throughout their careers. Common obstacles to mental strength include perfectionism, imposter syndrome, social comparisons, trained pessimism, and failure to leverage emotion regulation, temperament and personality strengths, and energy sources.

PERFECTIONISM

Perfectionists hold themselves to idealistic standards, or they attempt to meet the unreasonable expectations of others. Factors that can contribute to perfectionism include receiving early praise for high grades or strong athletic performance, rather than for the effort exerted; a need to feel accepted in an important group; overemphasis on external rewards such as money and popularity; or childhood trauma where stellar performance helped to curtail abuse.

The risks of perfectionism include mental health issues, physical health problems, early death, and suicide. Other drawbacks for perfectionists are self-defeating behaviors such as procrastination and avoiding activities where they might fail. A 2017 study of college students revealed that perfectionists were less engaged, suffered from weaker self-regulation, and were less accomplished than other students.[7]

In her book *Dare to Lead*, Brene Brown states that perfectionism is not the key to success. Research shows it is correlated with missed opportunities, anxiety, depression, and addiction. The fear of making mistakes, being criticized, and not meeting people's expectations impairs achievement. She argues that perfectionism is self-destructive because perfection is an unattainable goal that does not exist.[8]

IMPOSTER SYNDROME

People with imposter syndrome suffer from self-doubt. They feel unworthy of a grade, promotion, or position because they distrust their competence or expertise. They lack confidence and may attribute success to luck, rather than to hard work and experience.

Self-doubt saps the mental strength that is necessary to meet goals. It can lead to negative thoughts, low self-esteem, and adverse behavior, which can cause mistakes and result in a self-fulfilling prophecy. Thoughts and emotions influence each other, and worrying can trigger fear, anxiety, and depression.[9]

SOCIAL COMPARISONS

Competitive work or learning environments can increase social comparisons. Social media fuels social comparisons by making transparent the most positive aspects of others' lives, for example, their most successful cooking endeavor, their splashiest party, and their most sumptuous vacation. These highly curated windows into the experiences of others can make it seem like everyone else can have it all and that most people are highly successful in their pursuit of the good life.

Upward social comparison is when you focus on people who appear to be superior, happier, healthier, or wealthier than you. It can damage self-worth and promote jealousy and depression. Downward social comparison is focused on those who are less fortunate than you are. It might improve short-term self-esteem, but ultimately causes sympathy and concern.[10]

TRAINED PESSIMISM

Lawyers are trained for pessimism. This training begins with issue spotting in law school and continues in practice when lawyers identify and worry about all the potential problems that might befall a client. They utilize worst-case scenarios and critical thinking to identify and solve problems for clients. The practice of pessimistic thinking likely contributes to the success of lawyers, but it can seep into a lawyer's personal life and contribute to anxiety, depression, or languishing.[11]

EMOTION REGULATION

Research in psychology demonstrates that emotions help professionals focus, make decisions, enhance memory, provide vital social cues, and embrace change.[12] Emotions indicate the presence of a threat or a reward. It is important to understand emotions and how to leverage them.[13]

In *Soft Skills for the Effective Lawyer*, Randall Kiser discusses the tendency of lawyers to ignore or suppress emotions, which he describes as emotional numbing. Legal education stresses that analytical thinking requires the absence of emotion, but research indicates that strong performers are aware of their emotions, and they leverage them to facilitate authentic and empathic relationships.

When lawyers are unaware of or suppress their emotions, they lack emotion regulation skills and may experience intensified negative feelings. They are also less able to experience positive emotions. The result is a lawyer who feels inauthentic and alienated, incapable of building trust with colleagues and clients, while also suffering from weakened personal relationships with family and friends.[14]

One reason why lawyers might suppress emotion is because their brains develop to sharply focus on dealing with threats to ensure survival. For lawyers, threat evaluation is a major part of representing clients. Negativity bias is protective because it helps us determine whether something is wrong. Fear and anxiety make us vigilant. Disgust, anger, and pain help us avoid or escape danger. "We are not meant to be happy, or even content. Instead, we are designed simply to survive and reproduce, like every other creature in the natural world. In fact a state of contentment is positively discouraged by Nature because it would lower our guard against possible threats to our survival."[15]

Rewards such as food, shelter, safety, and the presence of a partner or tribe yield pleasure and positive emotions, but these are more fleeting than negative emotions. The result is a state of continuous dissatisfaction and reward-seeking.[16]

Emotion regulation involves initiating or inhibiting actions, or modifying responses, triggered by emotions. The way we interpret emotions impacts our thinking, decision-making, and the actions we take. A well-regulated lawyer will take time to assess outcomes. A negative emotional trigger sets the fight-or-flight response in motion. Emotion regulation modifications provide some time between trigger and response.[17]

Emotion regulation strategies help us objectively assess a situation, stay calm under pressure, and respond in a way that is aligned with our core values. We apply self-control to create a pause between feelings and reactions to enable a measured response.[18]

Emotions are experienced as feelings – the conscious perceptions of the involuntary responses of the body to emotional triggers. The first emotion regulation tactic is emotion literacy. This is the practice of noticing and naming your emotions. The six primary emotions are sadness, fear, anger, disgust, surprise, and joy. However, there are many nuances of human emotion, and a tool such as Plutchik's Wheel of Emotion can help lawyers recognize emotion intensity. For example, grief is more intense than sadness, but pensiveness is less so.

Naming your emotions can help you identify triggers and process your emotions more effectively.[19]

Another proactive approach is to dedicate time for self-compassion each day to enhance emotion regulation skills. Practices such as gratitude, mindfulness, meditation, and relaxation enhance the capacity to take a pause after experiencing an emotional trigger, thereby promoting optimism. These calming practices help slow down our automatic reactions, allowing for intentional responses.[20]

ENERGY AND THE INTROVERT–EXTROVERT SPECTRUM

A major aspect of lawyer self-awareness is to appreciate where you fall on the introvert–extrovert spectrum of temperament.

In her seminal book on introverts, *Quiet*, author and former lawyer Susan Cain argues that while society values extroverts – folks who are social, verbal, appealing, and action-oriented – some 30–50 percent of us are introverts. Cain describes the Extrovert Ideal – an oppressive standard of desirable extroverted behaviors, such as self-confidence and conviviality, that is often demanded of introverts who are sensitive, thoughtful, cerebral, and innovative.[21]

Cain points out that the Extrovert Ideal and bias against introverts causes them considerable psychological distress. Yet contributions from introverts are invaluable. She lists the following accomplished introverts: Warren Buffett, Frederic Chopin, Albert Einstein, Mahatma Gandhi, Sir Isaac Newton, Rosa Parks, Eleanor Roosevelt, J. K. Rowling, Steven Spielberg, Dr. Seuss, and Vincent van Gogh.[22]

Carl Jung coined the terms introvert and extrovert and described these temperament types in terms of the stimulation they derive from the inner or outer world. Introverts are energized by the inner world of ideas and emotions. They thrive while reading, researching, thinking, and writing. Extroverts are energized by the outside world of people and experiences. They flourish during activity and action.[23]

Introverts and extroverts differ when it comes to the amount of outside stimulation they require to function well. Extroverts need a great deal of arousal, generally from interaction with other people. Introverts need to limit their exposure to others. Extroverts recharge with social interaction, while introverts are depleted by it.

Extroverts are assertive, prefer talking and thinking on their feet, and crave the company of others. At work, they are comfortable with multitasking, risk-taking, conflict, and quick decision-making. They can make rash decisions or blurt out things they might not intend to. They are often motivated by external rewards such as money and status.

Introverts are adept listeners and prefer to think before they talk and express themselves well in writing. They practice solo-tasking and tend to work slowly and deliberately. They dislike small talk and conflict. They prefer the company of close family, friends, and colleagues. They thrive on deep discussions with their small circle of select people. They are recharged by solitude and are not usually motivated by external rewards.[24]

Introversion and extroversion are aspects of temperament we are born with, although people are also shaped by their experiences. People can learn, stretch, and grow over time, and no one is purely an introvert or extrovert. We all exhibit, and can excel at, both introverted and extroverted skills. You are more of an extrovert if you are most interested in the external world, become energized by socializing, and feel depleted after too much time alone. You are more of an introvert if you are most interested in ideas, become energized by solitude, and feel depleted after socializing, even if you find it enjoyable.[25]

Extroverts and introverts differ in the way their nervous systems respond to stimulation. The nervous system is made up of the senses, which receive information, and the brain, nerves, and spinal cord, which process information and initiate responses. There is more dopamine in the brains of extroverts than those of introverts. Dopamine is a neurotransmitter that motivates us, especially extroverts, to seek external rewards such as money, promotions, and high-profile projects. Acetylcholine is a transmitter that is more active in the brains of introverts. It motivates them to seek internal rewards such as ideas, insights, meaningful conversations, and purposeful work projects. All these neurotransmitters drive decisions by extroverts and introverts toward the rewards they find most satisfying.

The information-processing pathway differs between extroverts and introverts. The extrovert's pathway is short, straightforward, relies on short-term memory, and is externally focused. The introvert's pathway is longer, more complex, involves long-term memory, and is internally focused. Introverts are deep thinkers who take longer to respond due to their brain's longer processing pathway.[26]

Leveraging your energy style allows you to feel authentic, function well, and optimize productivity. When you identify your temperament style, you are aware of what energizes you and what depletes you. You can create the conditions for optimal flow, and you can advocate for support.

To determine your introverted or extroverted temperament, consider logging your activities for a few days. *What activities energize or invigorate you? What activities deplete or drain you?*

To support the most effective work environment, introverts need solitary spaces, time when they can work uninterrupted, and the capacity to communicate in writing and after reflection. Extroverts need to interact with others, communicate in person, and cultivate a brainstorming partner.[27]

Shyness is not the same as introversion. Shyness is extreme self-consciousness and fear of judgment, embarrassment, or rejection. Rather than resisting social interaction due to a need to recharge, shy people are concerned about being assessed by others as odd, unattractive, unintelligent, or unlikeable. They feel evaluated, critiqued, and shamed by others. Shyness is painful and can ignite the fight-or-flight stress response.[28]

Social anxiety is a disabling type of shyness. It is excessive concern about embarrassing or humiliating oneself.[29] Up to 13 percent of Americans suffer from social anxiety, and they may experience severe anxiety or panic attacks in anticipation of social situations.[30]

Some people are both introverts and shy or socially anxious. One model maps the introvert–extrovert spectrum on the horizontal axis and the anxious–calm spectrum on the vertical axis. This reveals four personality types: calm extroverts, anxious or impulsive extroverts, calm introverts, and anxious introverts.[31]

In her book about introverted lawyers and law students, *The Introverted Lawyer*, Professor Heidi K. Brown discusses how the widely deployed Socratic method of discussing cases in law classes can create a judgmental and competitive classroom culture that can shame or humiliate introverted, shy, or socially anxious law students. As a result, professors and other students might assume these quieter law students are unprepared or less intelligent than their extroverted peers. Introverted students are likely to be more prepared than extroverted students; they simply cannot demonstrate their knowledge at a rapid-fire pace.[32]

In legal practice, a bold and aggressive extrovert who is adept at self-promotion may be rewarded more frequently than a quiet dogged introvert who plumbs the precedent and crafts the most effective argument. Both kinds of strengths are needed to successfully represent clients; thus, strategies to recognize and value the assets introverts bring to the table should become a priority for legal organizations.[33]

Introverts are capable of giving exceptional extroverted performances for work that is especially meaningful and important to them, for their loved ones, or for anything they highly value. And extroverts can leverage strengths associated with introverts. The Free Trait Theory states that although we are born with a certain temperament, we can perform out of character in the service of core personal projects. The Free Trait Theory explains why introverts can shine in occupations that value the Extrovert Ideal.[34]

To help you understand how the Free Trait Theory impacts you:

- Determine where you fall on the introvert–extrovert spectrum. *What energizes you? What depletes you?*
- Use Susan Cain's method to recognize your core personal projects:
  a. *What work do you gravitate to?*
  b. *What do you envy about others?* This may reveal what you desire.
  c. *What did you love as a child?* You might have been more self-aware at the time.
- Ask yourself: *Do I act out of character in the service of a core personal project? What free trait skills do I deploy in the service of core personal projects?*[35]

PERSONALITIES AND STRENGTHS ARE SHAPED BY TRANSMITTERS AND HORMONES

In addition to our introvert or extrovert temperaments, our personalities also differ by how active certain transmitters and hormones are in our brains.

In her book *The Brain-Friendly Workplace*, neuroscientist Friederike Fabritius explains the work of Helen Fisher, PhD, who discovered four neurosignatures based on the actions of the neurotransmitters dopamine and serotonin and the hormones estrogen and testosterone. When Dr. Fisher compared the results of personality assessments with activity in these brain systems, she found that MRI results linked high activity in each of the dopamine, serotonin, estrogen, and testosterone systems to a particular group of personality traits. Therefore, Dr. Fisher's personality tests have been validated by neuroscience.

Everyone has all four brain systems; so our personalities reflect a combination of these chemicals and a spectrum of behaviors. It can be helpful to consider how active dopamine, serotonin, estrogen, and testosterone are in individual lawyers' brains.

People with a high-dopamine neurosignature are optimistic, curious, creative, and future-oriented. They cope well with change, love to explore, and travel easily. They often bring humor, fun, and inspiration to their work. They can be impulsive and easily bored. They thrive with autonomy, creative freedom, and interesting projects.

People with a high-serotonin neurosignature are reliable, loyal, detail-oriented, and careful. They respect authority, follow the rules, and seek stability. They prefer orderly and consistent environments. They can become incapacitated with worry, anxiety, and rumination over what others think of them. They thrive with regular routines, security, and a dependable system of steady increases in responsibilities and promotions.

People with high estrogen levels are empathetic, intuitive, and value cooperation and inclusion. They excel at lateral thinking, which involves considering problems from multiple perspectives, making innovative connections, and assessing long-term consequences of decisions. Money and status are less important than the purpose and impact of their work. They are diplomatic, insightful, and have strong verbal and writing skills. They prioritize making connections and building community. They seek a healthy work–life balance. While we may assume that all high-estrogen people are female, research shows only 72% of women, but also 28% of men, have high-estrogen neurosignatures.

Under stress, people with high-estrogen neurosignatures can worry and succumb to self-criticism. They can become indecisive or overwhelmed. They can ruminate, the activation of a loop of high-intensity problem-solving, and indulge in gossip and back-stabbing. Because they concentrate on the big picture, they can be systems-blind, losing focus on important details.

People with high testosterone levels are independent, outspoken, and direct. They enjoy competition, debate, and exercising power. They are self-directed and prefer autonomy in their work. They are linear systems thinkers, using logic to proceed step by step using a system's rules to solve problems. They value analytical reasoning and achievement. They can be so driven that they fail to care for their physical or mental health. At menopause, when estrogen levels decline and testosterone is more influential, women often become more confident and assertive.

Under stress, people with high-testosterone neurosignatures can resort to bullying, power trips, and angry outbursts. They can be mind-blind, oblivious to the feelings of others. They are risk-takers and drive competitive and stressful work environments. They can be impatient, impulsive, or aggressive.

Using the Fisher Temperament Inventory available online, lawyers can increase their self-awareness of their particular neurosignature.[36]

LANGUISHING AND LONGEVITY

Languishing can impact life span. Professor Keyes later reexamined the data from the 1995 study, along with data from the National Death Index, and determined that the absence of positive mental health – languishing – can increase the probability of all-cause mortality for both women and men. Fewer than 1% of the participants who were flourishing in 1995 died in the following ten-year period, whereas 5.5% of the nonflourishing ones had died. The likelihood of death had increased by as much as 62 percent in ten years for participants who were not flourishing, which represented 8 out of 10 American adults.[37]

A prepandemic analysis of thirty years of data from the Global Burden of Disease Studies, ranging from 1900 to 2019, sought to examine the impact of mental disorders on disease burden. Mental disorders accounted for 654.8 million cases in 1990, and 970.1 million in 2019, which is an increase of 48.1 percent. The two most common disorders among all people were anxiety and depression. Most common among females were anxiety, depression, and eating disorders, while ADHD and autism spectrum disorders were more common among males. Disability-adjusted life-years (DALYs) represent the number of years lost to poor health, disability, or early death. Globally, the DALYs swelled from 80.8 to 125.3 million between 1990 and 2019, which was an increase of 44.5 million.[38]

The COVID-19 pandemic has exacerbated mental health problems. The WHO has reported that there was a 25 percent increase in anxiety and depression worldwide due to stress, uncertainty, social isolation, financial difficulties, and grieving people lost to the pandemic. Women suffered more than men during the pandemic, and young people were gravely impacted and prone to self-harming behaviors and suicide risk. In addition, individuals with preexisting health issues were more likely to develop mental health problems than those without.[39]

Canadian law school administrators have discovered that pandemic learning has caused law students to report consistent concerns over the state of their deteriorating mental health, struggles with social isolation, extreme overwork, online learning fatigue, and thoughts of suicide for those who had never experienced suicidal ideation previously.[40] It is likely that some law students and lawyers devolved from a state of languishing to become impaired during the pandemic.

Languishing puts one at risk of developing mental health problems, and it shortens lifespan. Individuals and institutions should invest in improving people's mental strength. This requires personal and organizational awareness of the risks of languishing and mental illness. It also involves personal and professional development and the acknowledgment that people are different in some key ways. To address languishing, we can learn from the literature devoted to the other end of the mental health continuum, flourishing.

POSITIVE PSYCHOLOGY AND FLOURISHING

The other end of the mental health spectrum from languishing is flourishing. An entire subfield of psychology is devoted to the study of flourishing.

The field of positive psychology was initiated in 2000 by Professors Martin Seligman and Mihaly Csikszentmihalyi to study the conditions under which individuals flourish and communities thrive. They were interested in studying the mental strength and attributes that protect people against mental illness.[41] Professor Seligman has described the five elements that result in well-being and, in doing so, developed the PERMA well-being framework. To flourish, a person must experience:

- Positive Emotion – happiness and life satisfaction;
- Engagement, deep involvement in life activities;
- Rewarding Relationships, strong connections to other people;
- Meaning, participation in and service to an endeavor that is larger than oneself; and
- Accomplishment, mastery or proficiency that is pursued for its own sake.[42]

Some lawyers suffer from mental illnesses such as anxiety, depression, or substance use disorder. Others are languishing, enduring a state of incomplete mental health.

The ABA report *Path to Lawyer Well-being* tells us that the reasons the profession needs to address the well-being crisis are to enhance the effectiveness of legal organizations, improve the professional and ethical behavior of lawyers, and support the flourishing of individual lawyers. In order to flourish, lawyers must thrive in the physical, emotional, intellectual, spiritual, occupational, and social domains of their lives.

The well-being domains are further explained:

- "Physical Domain – Striving for regular physical activity, proper diet and nutrition, sufficient sleep, and recovery; minimizing the use of addictive substances; seeking help for physical health when needed.
- Emotional Domain – Recognizing the importance of emotions; developing the ability to identify and manage our own emotions to support mental health, achieve goals, and inform decision-making; seeking help for mental health when needed.
- Intellectual Domain – Engaging in continuous learning and the pursuit of creative or intellectually challenging activities that foster ongoing development; monitoring cognitive wellness.
- Spiritual Domain – Developing a sense of meaningfulness and purpose in all aspects of life.

- Occupational Domain – Cultivating personal satisfaction, growth, and enrichment in work; financial stability.
- Social Domain – Developing a sense of connection, belonging, and a well-developed support network while also contributing to our groups and communities."[43]

This book provides an argument, via an examination of neuroscience and psychology research, that explains *why* lawyers should attend to the well-being domains.

Before we can identify ways of enhancing individual lawyer's brain health and mental strength, we need to examine the core characteristics of the lawyering culture that trigger languishing or impairment. How did we get here?

NOTES

1 Calvin Coolidge Presidential Foundation, "Have Faith in Massachusetts," January 7, 1941, https://coolidgefoundation.org/resources/have-faith-in-massachusetts.

2 Pan American Health Organization and World Health Organization, "Mental Health," www.paho.org/en/topics/mental-health#:~:text=The%20World%20Health%20Organization%20(WHO,to%20his%20or%20her%20community%E2%80%9D.

3 A. Grant, "There's a Name for the Blah You're Feeling, It's Called Languishing," *New York Times*, April 19, 2021.

4 C. Keyes, "The Mental Health Continuum: From Languishing to Flourishing in Life," 43 *J Health Soc Behav* (2002), 207.

5 Randall Kiser, Soft Skills for the Effective Lawyer (Cambridge University Press, 2017), 42–87, at 87.

6 Ibid., at 46.

7 Amy Morin, 13 Things Mentally Strong Women Don't Do (William Morrow Paperbacks, 2020), 33, 37–38, 41–43.

8 Brene Brown, Dare to Lead: Brave Work. Tough Conversations. Whole Hearts (Random House, 2019), 79–80.

9 Morin, *supra* note 7, at 77, 82–86; Tara Swart et al., Neuroscience for Leadership: Harnessing the Brain Gain Advantage (Springer, 2015), 206.

10 Morin, *supra* note 7, at 13–16.

11 Martin E. P. Seligman et al., "Why Lawyers Are Unhappy," 23 *Cardozo L Rev* (2001), 33, at 39, 41.

12 See Richard D. Lane et al., "Neural Correlates of Levels of Emotional Awareness: Evidence of an Interaction between Emotion and Attention in the Anterior Cingulate Cortex," 10 *J Cogn Neurosci* (1999), 529.
13 Madhuleena Roy Chowdhury, "Emotion Regulation: 6 Key Skills to Regulate Emotions," *Positive Psychology*, August 13, 2019, https://positivepsychology.com/emotion-regulation.
14 Kiser, *supra* note 5, at 47–48.
15 Dr. Rafa Euba, YOU ARE NOT MEANT TO BE HAPPY SO STOP TRYING! (Crux, 2021), xii–xiv, 9–11.
16 Ibid.
17 Chowdhury, *supra* note 13.
18 Ibid.
19 Ralph Adolphs and David J. Anderson, THE NEUROSCIENCE OF EMOTION: A NEW SYNTHESIS (Princeton University Press, 2018), 6; Chrystal Raypole, "How to Use an Emotion Wheel to Get in Touch with All Your Feels," *Healthline*, September 30, 2020, www.healthline.com/health/emotion-wheel; Chowdhury, *supra* note 13.
20 Chowdhury, *supra* note 13.
21 Susan Cain, QUIET: THE POWER OF INTROVERTS IN A WORLD THAT CAN'T STOP TALKING (Crown, 2012), 3–5.
22 Ibid., at 5–6.
23 Hana Ayoub, "Introverted or Extraverted? How to Leverage Your Energy Style," *Shine*, September 7, 2016, https://advice.theshineapp.com/articles/introverted-or-extraverted-how-to-leverage-your-energy-style.
24 Cain, *supra* note 21, at 11.
25 Introvert, Dear, "Introvert/Extrovert Test, 2022," https://introvertdear.com/introvert-extrovert-test-quiz.
26 Holley Gerth, THE POWERFUL PURPOSE OF INTROVERTS (Revell, 2020), 18–21.
27 Ayoub, *supra* note 23.
28 Heidi K. Brown, THE INTROVERTED LAWYER: A SEVEN-STEP JOURNEY TOWARD AUTHENTICALLY EMPOWERED ADVOCACY (American Bar Association, 2017), 16–17.
29 Cain, *supra* note 21, at 111, 190.
30 Brown, *supra* note 28, at 18.
31 Cain, *supra* note 21, at 12.
32 Brown, *supra* note 28, at 27–29.
33 Ibid., at 33–34.
34 Cain, *supra* note 21, at 209–210.
35 Ibid., at 218.
36 Friederike Fabritius, THE BRAIN-FRIENDLY WORKPLACE: WHY TALENTED PEOPLE QUIT AND HOW TO GET THEM TO STAY (Rowman & Littlefield,

2022), 9–11, 13–14, 28–29, 32–39; Open-Source Psychometrics Project, "Fisher Temperament Inventory," https://openpsychometrics.org/#:~:text=Fisher%20Temperament%20Inventory%3A%20The%20FTI,associated%20with%20specific%20neuro%2Dchemicals.

37 C. Keyes and E. Simoes, "To Flourish or Not: Positive Mental Health and All-Cause Mortality," 102 *Res Pract* (2012), 2164.

38 GBD 2019 Mental Disorders Collaborators, "Global, Regional, and National Burden of 12 Mental Disorders in 204 Countries and Territories, 1990–2019: A Systematic Analysis for the Global Burden of Disease Study 2019," 9 *Lancet Psychiatry* (2022), 137–150; World Health Organization, "Disability-Adjusted Life-Years (DALYS)," www.who.int/data/gho/indicator-metadata-registry/imr-details/158#:~:text=One%20DALY%20represents%20the%20loss,such%20as%20cataract%20causing%20blindness).

39 WHO, "COVID-19 Pandemic Triggers 25% Increase in Prevalence of Anxiety and Depression Worldwide," March 2, 2022, www.who.int/news/item/02-03-2022-covid-19-pandemic-triggers-25-increase-in-prevalence-of-anxiety-and-depression-worldwide.

40 R. Jochelson, "Students Face Acute Mental Health Needs during Pandemic Learning," *Slaw*, December 2, 2021, www.slaw.ca/2021/12/02/students-face-acute-mental-health-needs-during-pandemic-learning.

41 Martin E. P. Seligman and Mihaly Csikszentmihalyi, "Positive Psychology: An Introduction," 55 *Am Psychol* (2000), 5, 7.

42 Martin E. P. Seligman, Flourish: A Visionary New Understanding of Happiness and Well-Being (Atria, 2012).

43 Bree Buchanan et al., The Path to Lawyer Well-Being: Practical Recommendations for Positive Change (American Bar Association, 2017), 9, www.americanbar.org/content/dam/aba/images/abanews/ThePathToLawyerWell-beingReportFINAL.pdf.

3 THE LAWYERING CULTURE

> Change is hard, but delaying what's right is toxic. Today we can remember just how much we have to do and realize the ability each of us has to see and alter the systems around us.
>
> —Seth Godin[1]

> When a careerist culture meets a digital revolution that allows unlimited access to work, something's got to give. And in America, that something tends not to be work demands but is instead the human soul. The rise of digital technology requires us, as a culture, to re-examine what it means for work to be humane.
>
> —Tish Harrison Warren[2]

The intense socialization of law school is where students are introduced to the pressures that dehumanize the lawyering culture. The law school environment, featuring intense competition, isolation, and alienation, undermines well-being and can transform students into dispirited zombies.[3] The hierarchical law firm ecosystem has been commodified to focus on profits, where the billable hour and overwhelming workload weaken lawyer wellness. The common denominator in the lawyering culture is chronic stress.

THE SUMMARY

Significant features of the law school culture weaken the aspects of wellness for law students outlined in Seligman's PERMA well-being framework. Rather than inspiring positive emotions and the formation of new and robust relationships, the intense workload and stressful learning environment promote negative emotions and deterioration of relationships when students are forced to compete with each other for the few high grades at the top of the grade curve. Engagement and meaning are thwarted by the mandatory grade curve and the frustration and learned helplessness it generates. The dominant culture in legal education is achievement-driven, and Seligman argues that well-being will not be enhanced if achievement is the only thing that is valued in the environment.[4]

For law students to flourish and law schools to thrive, legal education must transform the "culture of dehumanizing competition" into an environment that increases positive emotions, enhances relationships in the law school community, intensifies meaning and engagement in legal studies, and improves well-being along with performance.[5]

The culture of legal practice is not an improvement, with overwork and chronic stress as its key features. Much like the grade curve that drives the competitive learning environment at law schools, the billable hour drives the tradition of overwork in law practice. Stress intensifies; meaning and purpose are lost; social support deteriorates; and negative emotions take over.

THE SCIENCE

Douglas Litowitz believes that most lawyers hated law school and found it to be traumatic and a foundation for increased mental health problems.[6] When asked about their 1L year, most law students reported anxiety, stress, and exhaustion.[7]

In his book about how educational apprenticeships develop professional identity, David Williamson Shaffer argues that professional education should be intentionally designed to transmit the skills, knowledge, identity, and values of the profession. When we learn to think like a professional, we learn to value what successful members of our profession believe are important and meaningful.[8]

Law schools define student achievement in terms of external rewards such as grades, class rank, and invitations to serve on journals, but the grade curve significantly limits the number of students who can be successful in the ways they have been in prior academic programs. Students are introduced to "these prizes" in the early days of law school, and the response is a singular intention to "obtain high grades as a form of credentialing," which can also marginalize the development of domain knowledge and legal skills. Instead of a focus on learning, the objective becomes how to get the A grade.[9]

The *Carnegie Report*, the most recent full-scale analysis on legal education reforms, describes three apprenticeships in legal education: the intellectual apprenticeship, where students acquire a knowledge base; the practice apprenticeship, where students learn practical legal skills; and the professional identity apprenticeship, where students cultivate the attitudes and values of the legal profession. The socialization process of legal education instills in law students the ideals that the legal profession deems important and meaningful, and the primary value is an intense focus on competitive achievement. The grade curve and competitive classroom climate shape the professional identity of law students and contribute to the decline in their well-being.[10]

The Foundations for Practice: The Whole Lawyer and the Character Quotient describes the results of a survey of more than 24,000 lawyers, practicing in all fifty states between 2014 and 2015, about their expectations for lawyer behavior. The report calls for law schools to develop programs that increase the character quotients in law students. It recommends that law schools teach:

- character attributes, including courtesy, respect, tact, humility, sensitivity, tolerance, compassion, and diplomacy; and
- self-care and self-regulation skills such as positivity and managing stress, exhibiting flexibility, adaptability, and resilience when dealing with challenging circumstances and the capacity to make decisions under pressure.[11]

The report's character attributes, self-care, and self-regulation skills map on to Professor Seligman's PERMA well-being framework in this way:

- Positive Emotions
  - Positivity and energy
  - Stress management
- Engagement
  - Intellectual curiosity

  - Resourcefulness
  - Flexibility and adaptability
  - Resilience
- Rewarding Relationships
  - Positive professional relationships
  - Work cooperatively and collaboratively as part of a team
  - Sensitivity, tolerance, and compassion
  - Humility, patience, and diplomacy
- Meaning
  - Self-awareness of strengths, weaknesses, preferences, boundaries, and sphere of control
  - Ownership of work
  - Passion for work
- Achievement
  - Commitment to excellence.[12]

THE BUSINESS CASE FOR LAWYER WELL-BEING

Social responsibility consultant Scott Curran states that "everything you see happening in the world, whether it's in philanthropy, whether it's social innovation ... it's all driven by lawyers."[13] Lawyers have significant social responsibilities, but they have a negative social reputation. The ABA *Path to Lawyer Well-Being* report acknowledges that helping lawyers thrive will likely improve their professional and ethical behavior.

Professor Jarrod F. Reich states that "there exists a strong correlation between the legal profession and lawyer distress that can no longer be ignored," in his article that makes the business case for prioritizing lawyer well-being.[14] Professor Reich begins his article with the harrowing story of a forty-two-year-old Los Angeles law firm partner who was so overwhelmed by workload and exhaustion that he committed suicide by shooting himself in his law firm's parking lot. This is a heartbreaking example of the loss of a husband and a son to the well-being crisis.[15] Gabe MacConnaill's light was forever extinguished by the extreme stressors of law practice culture.

Professor Reich explains that some features of the law firm model enhance the likelihood of lawyer dissatisfaction, mental health problems, and substance misuse. The commodification of legal practice, privileging annual profits over all other objectives, has contributed to widespread lawyer distress. Mental health problems have an impact on the ethical behavior of lawyers. Around 40–70 percent of disciplinary proceedings and malpractice actions involve depression and/or substance abuse.[16]

THE ROLE OF COMPETITION AND CHRONIC STRESS

In a 2015 study of nearly 8,000 lawyers, researchers discovered that lawyer well-being was best when their internal values and the psychological needs of autonomy, competence, and relatedness to others were met. Lack of autonomy, scarcity of social relatedness, and focus on external rewards contributed to mental health and substance use problems.

Law practice has devolved from a calling that served a community to a commodified game replete with stress and an oppressive workload, devoid of purpose other than generating profits. Law firm culture often clashes with lawyer values, leaving lawyers gravely dissatisfied. The most significant aspect of lack of autonomy is the heavy reliance on the billable hour to measure lawyer productivity. "Law firms in general are undermining their lawyers' internal values and motivations that foster subjective well-being in favor of prioritizing the external values and motivations that correlate to emotional distress."[17]

Dr. Kelly McGonigal, a health psychologist and lecturer at Stanford University, states that "stress is what arises when something you care about is at stake."[18] It is difficult to imagine what key accomplishments of the law school or legal practice cultures – the external rewards of high grades and firm partnership – that are not at stake.

When an environment strictly limits the number of available external rewards, the people in that culture exist in a chronically stressful zero-sum atmosphere. As such, the main characteristic of the lawyering culture – persistent stress – is propelled by competition for those prizes. This is a culture of scarcity that establishes the notion that only a few law students or lawyers can be truly successful. The continuous fear over failure creates an environment of chronic stress.

Legal education is part of a competitive education marketplace that captivates students, parents, and employers who shop for educational products. This has been fueled by the *U.S. News & World Report* rankings, which use a widely criticized methodology that can create a misleading narrative about the quality of legal education. Rankings determine who is allowed to study to be a lawyer, how law students are assessed by employers, and what practice areas are available to them. Ranking systems determine who counts and who is noticed, and who is not. They shape patterns of exclusion in education, professions, and politics, and they dictate how we define good education, healthcare, and any other social institutions.[19]

Ranking individual students is a practice devised to evaluate "an individual's potential, to assess their performance, and to control their behavior." Standardized tests have been used to rank students, soldiers, and employees in factories and office buildings. "By classifying, creating hierarchies of ability and performance, and establishing what is 'normal' and what is not, disciplinary practices turn people into objects amenable to transformation."[20] Law student transformation is established with the embrace of a "single-minded focus on competitive achievement."[21]

Law schools justify ranking students with the claim that ranking assists large law firms during their hiring processes. Institutions designed around the ranking and sorting of people often suffer from an inability to innovate.[22] Legal education has been criticized for being slow to innovate and change. Law schools recognize the imperative to train lawyers to think critically and solve problems in innovative ways, but while they have adapted some programs to add value and control costs, they have not abandoned their competitive assessment model.[23]

Ranking students inevitably pits them against one another, where for one student to be successful, another must lose out. The competition "stokes panic and a desperate sense that every student is on his or her own, left to hack a solitary path through a dangerous educational jungle."[24]

Law firms also feature a significant social hierarchy, with partners at the top and associates at the bottom. In any organization, the Power

Distance Index describes "the steepness of the hierarchy and the emotional distance between those who have power and those who do not."[25] The higher the power distance score, the steeper the hierarchy.

Dutch psychologist Geert Hofstede established the idea of power distance to describe how people fit into and feel about a country or culture. Research has revealed that people at the bottom of a social hierarchy would rather have power and resources more evenly distributed, but people at the top of the hierarchy do not want to lose the power and wealth they enjoy. Income inequality is one of the metrics that can be used to assess the power distance in a country or company.[26]

The power distance index is measured on a scale of 1–100, with higher scores indicating the steepest hierarchies. According to *Hofstede Insights*, the power distance scores of a few countries are ranked from high to low: Russia (93), Mexico (81), China (80), France (68), the United States (40), Canada (39), Australia (38), Germany (35), the United Kingdom (35), Switzerland (34), Finland (33), Norway (31), Sweden (31), New Zealand (22), Denmark (18), Israel (13), and Austria (11).

In countries like Austria, Israel, and New Zealand, with low power distance scores, citizens and employees believe in and expect equal rights. The mindset is egalitarian; communication is participative; control is unpopular; and power is decentralized.

In mid-range power distance countries such as the United States, Canada, and Australia, citizens and employees more readily accept that power and resources are unevenly distributed. Inequality is approved by both leaders and followers. In cultures with steep hierarchies, the few people or families at the top enjoy a concentration of wealth, power, and privilege. People who do not sit atop the steep hierarchies endure a constant social threat of expulsion, such as flunking out of law school or losing a job for not billing enough hours. These social structures feature extreme stress and the potential for cheating and corruption.[27]

The *World Happiness Report* asks approximately 1,000 participants from each country to assess their current satisfaction with life on a scale of 1–10. The happiness rankings are based on a three-year average of the life evaluation scores, increasing the sample size for stronger estimates. The top twenty countries in 2023, followed by their life evaluation scores, are (1) Finland, 7.804; (2) Denmark, 7.586; (3) Iceland, 7.530; (4) Israel, 7.473; (5) the Netherlands, 7.403; (6) Sweden, 7.395; (7) Norway, 7.315; (8) Switzerland, 7.240; (9) Luxembourg, 7.228; (10) New Zealand, 7.123; (11) Austria, 7.097; (12) Australia, 7.095; (13) Canada, 6.961; (14) Ireland, 6.911; (15) the United States, 6.894; (16) Germany, 6.892; (17) Belgium, 6.859; (18) Czechia, 6.845; (19) the United Kingdom, 6.796; and (20) Lithuania, 6.763. Mexico is thirty-sixth, 6.330; China is sixty-fourth, 5.818; and Russian Federation is seventieth, 5.661.[28]

It is hard not to notice the connection between social fairness and happiness. Countries that are more egalitarian and feature flatter hierarchies have higher happiness scores. Eight of the top ten happiest countries have low power index scores: Finland (33), Denmark (18), Iceland (30), Israel (13), the Netherlands (38), Sweden (31), Norway (31), Switzerland (34), Luxembourg (40), and New Zealand (22).

A number of companies have experimented with forced ranking of employees in an attempt to improve performance: General Electric, Lending Tree, AIG, and Microsoft. The most striking example of a failed forced ranking was when Microsoft required every department to "declare a certain percentage of employees as top performers, then good performers, then average, then below average, then poor." The evaluation cycle was every six months, so the emphasis for employees became performance review rather than product design. The focus was on short-term thinking; there was a failure to collaborate; innovation was debilitated; and forced ranking became the most destructive initiative at Microsoft. The ranking of employees drove them to compete with each other, rather than with other technology companies.[29]

Lawyers must work on solutions to society's most complex problems. Psychologist Joy Paul Guilford has developed the theory of convergent and divergent thinking. Convergent thinking is the identification of a single answer to a problem. Divergent thinking is the development of as many potential solutions as possible that address a challenge. The American education system incentivizes convergent thinking and marginalizes divergent thinking, via its obsessions with standardized testing and the sorting and ranking of students.[30]

Standardized testing promotes the idea that most problems have one correct answer, promoting memorization and convergent thinking. This culture of education fails to develop motivation, creativity, risk-taking, and divergent problem-solving. Instead, the system favors the selection and ranking of a few winners in a narrowly tailored game of education. Every stage in the education system weakens intrinsic motivation, and the cost of rewarding only those few successful students at the top of the hierarchy is the persistent demotivation of all the other students. Top students strive to attend highly ranked universities to secure their place among the elite. The decisions and policies promoted by such students, who become society's leaders and were empowered by an educational system designed around exclusion, reflect a lack of empathy for, or capacity to work with, people outside their circle of privilege.[31]

Cognitive abilities become compromised under punishing levels of stress. Individuals suffer from diminished physical and mental health, and the costs to organizations include reduced innovation and productivity. Extreme competition is antisocial because self-interest kills creativity and impairs the capacity to connect and cooperate with others.[32]

One of the higher prices we pay for our long love affair with competitive cultures is that we attempt to confront extreme challenges without the skilled means for resolving them. Our social progress is stalled because our problems are complex and our means of addressing them are crude, rigid, and ineffective. That our political standoffs are embarrassing and mostly acts of performative theater is bad enough, but the damage to creative thinking about solutions to critical problems is the bigger cost. In the looming face-off between government, business, and society, a competitive mindset can frame the contest, but doing so destroys all the potential for working toward practical solutions to world-endangering crises. The problem is not a failure of imagination but the lack of courage to relinquish fantasies of winning in exchange for social progress and sustainability.[33]

The costs to legal organizations due to lawyer languishing and mental illness include disciplinary actions and malpractice complaints, absenteeism and presenteeism, and attrition. Some 40–70 percent of discipline and malpractice problems involve substance misuse, depression, or both. Absenteeism represents the number of hours or days of missed work due to employee illness. Presenteeism involves unproductive or underproductive time an employee spends at work while languishing. Lawyer attrition rates are high with about 44% of associates leaving firms within three years and 75% within five years. The cost of replacing an associate is 1.5–2 times their annual salary, in the range of $200,000–$500,000.[34]

THREE WELL-BEING FRAMEWORKS

Endangering the light of each individual lawyer comes at a cost to legal organizations. Yet many legal organizations expect individual lawyers to secure their own well-being. The literature provides several important models of individual well-being: flourishing, PERMA, and *The Path to Lawyer Well-Being* domains. These models can serve as guides for both individuals and organizations, as innovative leaders develop policies that promote lawyer well-being.

The flourishing model, developed by Professor Keyes, proposes that being mentally healthy requires:

- Emotional Well-being – the presence of positive affect, such as delight and pleasure, and the absence of negative affect, such as unhappiness or grief;
- Psychological Well-being – a perception of strong life satisfaction via self-acceptance, purpose, autonomy, personal development, environmental mastery, and positive relationships; and
- Social Well-being – the capacity for positive functioning in life through coherence (viewing society as meaningful and understandable), actualization (society offers the potential for growth), integration (being accepted by and belonging to the community), acceptance (accepting most aspects of society), and contribution (belief they are contributing to society).[35]

The PERMA framework, devised by Professor Seligman, holds that well-being involves:

- Positive Emotion and satisfaction with life;
- Engagement and deep involvement in significant activities;

- Rewarding Relationships and connections with people;
- Meaning and service to an important endeavor; and
- Accomplishment, mastery, or proficiency in an area of expertise.[36]

Lawyer well-being requires that lawyers thrive in the following *Path to Lawyer Well-Being* domains:

- Physical – regular physical activity, proper diet and nutrition, sufficient sleep and recovery, and minimal use of addictive substances; seek help for physical health when needed;
- Emotional – recognize the importance of emotions; develop the ability to identify and manage emotions to support mental health, achieve goals, and inform decision-making; seek help for mental health when needed;
- Intellectual – engage in continuous learning and the pursuit of creative or intellectually challenging activities that foster ongoing development; monitor cognitive wellness;
- Spiritual – develop a sense of meaningfulness and purpose in all aspects of life;
- Occupational – cultivate personal satisfaction, growth and enrichment in work, and financial stability;
- Social – develop a sense of connection, belonging, and a well-developed support network while also contributing to our groups and communities.[37]

THE POTENTIAL OF NEURO-INTELLIGENCE

The conventional wisdom in the lawyering culture is that you must work long and hard to be successful, forgoing many of life's pleasures and subordinating your well-being. The scientific proof supports a counterargument, that if you invest time on well-being, you will perform better and more efficiently than if you used those hours to work. You will also heal and grow a healthier brain – your primary work tool. You will protect your own light.

The International Bar Association's *Mental Wellbeing in the Legal Profession: A Global Study* reveals that lawyers support transforming the lawyering culture. They seek change in the culture that undermines their well-being, including unreasonable workloads, long hours, inability to take breaks, unrealistic time pressures, and harassment or bullying.[38] They want resources and support for therapy and mentoring, work–life balance, remote work, effective workload allocation, and enhanced health benefits, vacation, and parental leave.[39]

The *Mental Wellbeing* report emphasizes that the responsibility for improving lawyer well-being does not fall solely on individual lawyers. Leaders and organizations must address the structural and systemic aspects of the lawyering culture that jeopardize lawyer mental well-being, particularly stress, workload, and diversity, equity, and inclusion issues.[40]

Leaders of organizations and individual lawyers need to cultivate neuro-intelligence to understand *why* the lawyering culture causes the harm that it does and how to effectively support lawyer well-being. In order to optimize brain function, enhance mental strength, and improve well-being, the first step is to learn about key areas of the brain and the ways in which they support cognition.

NOTES

1 Seth Godin, "Too Long Delayed," June 19, 2020, https://seths.blog/2020/06/too-long-delayed.
2 Tish Warren Harrison, "How to Fight Back against the Inhumanity of Modern Work," *New York Times*, October 16, 2022.
3 Peter H. Huang and Corie L. Rosen, "The Zombie Lawyer Apocalypse," 42 *Pepp L Rev* (2015), 758.
4 Martin E. P. Seligman, FLOURISH: A VISIONARY NEW UNDERSTANDING OF HAPPINESS AND WELL-BEING (Atria, 2012), 231.
5 Huang and Rosen, *supra* note 3, at 771; Debra Austin, "Positive Legal Education: Flourishing Law Students and Thriving Law Schools," 77 *Md L Rev* (2018), 649, at 670–671.
6 Douglas Litowitz, THE DESTRUCTION OF YOUNG LAWYERS: BEYOND ONE L (University of Akron Press, 2005), 19, 30.
7 Andrew J. Mcclurg, 1L OF A RIDE: A WELL-TRAVELED PROFESSOR'S ROADMAP TO SUCCESS IN THE FIRST YEAR OF LAW SCHOOL (2nd ed., West Academic, 2013), 386–389.
8 David Williamson Shaffer, HOW COMPUTER GAMES HELP CHILDREN LEARN (Macmillan, 2016), 12, 105.
9 Nancy Levit and Douglas O. Linder, THE HAPPY LAWYER: MAKING A GOOD LIFE IN THE LAW (Oxford University Press, 2010), 125.

10 William M. Sullivan et al., EDUCATING LAWYERS: PREPARATION FOR THE PROFESSION OF LAW (Jossey-Bass, 2007), 28, 31–32.
11 Alli Gerkman and Logan Cornett, "Foundations for Practice: The Whole Lawyer and the Character Quotient," AccessLex Institute Research Paper No. 16-04 (2016), 1, at 30, 33, https://iaals.du.edu/sites/default/files/reports/foundations_for_practice_whole_lawyer_character_quotient.pdf.
12 Ibid., at 30, 33; Seligman, *supra* note 4, at 14–20.
13 Rebecca Blair, "Helping Nonprofits Grow," 38 *Am Law* (2016), 44, at 44.
14 Jarrod F. Reich, "Capitalizing on Healthy Lawyers: The Business Case for Law Firms to Promote and Prioritize Lawyer Well-Being," 65 *Vill L Rev* (2020), 361, at 374–375.
15 Joanna Litt, "Big Law Killed My Husband: An Open Letter from a Sidley Partner's Widow," *American Lawyer*, November 12, 2018.
16 Reich, *supra* note 14, at 364, 366, 373–374.
17 Ibid., at 382–383, 387–388, 391.
18 Kelly McGonigal, THE UPSIDE OF STRESS: WHY STRESS IS GOOD FOR YOU (AND HOW TO GET GOOD AT IT) (Avery, 2016), xxi.
19 Wendy Nelson Espeland and Michael Souder, ENGINES OF ANXIETY: ACADEMIC RANKINGS, REPUTATION, AND ACCOUNTABILITY (Russell Sage, 2016), 11, 16–17, 105–106, 179, 201.
20 Ibid., at 21, 177.
21 Sullivan et al., *supra* note 10, at 31.
22 Barbara Glesner Fines, "Competition and the Curve," 65 *UMKC L Rev* (1997), 879, at 886–887; Lani Guinier, Michelle Fine, and Jane Balin, BECOMING GENTLEMEN: WOMEN, LAW SCHOOL, AND INSTITUTIONAL CHANGE (Beacon Press, 1997), 17–19.
23 Blake D. Morant, "The Continued Evolution of American Legal Education," 51 *Wake Forest L Rev* (2016), 245, at 245–246, 55–58.
24 Margaret Heffernan, A BIGGER PRIZE: HOW WE CAN DO BETTER THAN THE COMPETITION (PublicAffairs, 2014), 28, 36.
25 Ibid., at 92.
26 Organizational Psychology Degrees, "Power Distance: Definition and Examples," www.organizationalpsychologydegrees.com/faq/what-is-power-distance.
27 Hofstede Insights, "Country Comparison Tool," www.hofstede-insights.com/country-comparison-tool.
28 World Happiness Report 2023, "World Happiness, Trust and Social Connections in Times of Crisis," https://worldhappiness.report/ed/2023/world-happiness-trust-and-social-connections-in-times-of-crisis.
29 Heffernan, *supra* note 24, at 180–183; Kurt Eichenwald, "How Microsoft Lost Its Mojo: Steve Ballmer and Corporate America's Most Spectacular Decline," *Vanity Fair*, August 2012, www.vanityfair.com/news/business/2012/08/microsoft-lost-mojo-steve-ballmer.

30 Heffernan, *supra* note 24, at 32–33.
31 Ibid., at 32–33, 35, 37, 39, 46.
32 Ibid., at 86–87, 92–98.
33 Ibid., at 321.
34 Reich, *supra* note 14, at 396–400.
35 C. Keyes, "The Mental Health Continuum: From Languishing to Flourishing in Life," 43 *J Health Soc Behav* (2002), 208–209.
36 Martin E. P. Seligman, Flourish: A Visionary New Understanding of Happiness and Well-Being (Atria, 2012), 109.
37 Bree Buchanan et al., The Path to Lawyer Well-Being: Practical Recommendations for Positive Change (American Bar Association, 2017), 9, www.americanbar.org/content/dam/aba/images/abanews/ThePathToLawyerWell-beingReportFINAL.pdf.
38 IBA Presidential Task Force, Mental Wellbeing in the Legal Profession: A Global Study (International Bar Association, 2021), 32, 37.
39 Ibid., at 44.
40 Ibid., at 10, 12–17.

4 THE LAWYER'S BRAIN

> In the face of overwhelming odds, I'm faced with only one option. I'm going to have to science the shit out of this.
>
> —Mark Watney, played by Matt Damon, in *The Martian*[1]

Our brain evolves continuously from birth to death. Neuroplasticity is the brain's capacity to reshape its neural circuitry in response to every experience, action, and thought. Until 1998, scientists believed the brain you were born with was the brain you were stuck with. But research has revealed that the human brain can grow new brain cells, called neurons, in the hippocampus (the brain's memory processor) and olfactory bulbs (responsible for smell), over the entire lifespan. This process is called neurogenesis.

Our brains have some 80–100 trillion neurons, and each neuron has hundreds to thousands of connections to other neurons. These neural networks grow and expand with every thought, act, and experience. It is possible to optimize neurogenesis and neuroplasticity in the human brain, but it takes some background knowledge to understand *why* certain lifestyle practices are important to brain maintenance.

THE SUMMARY

The brain has two superpowers: (1) continuous development, which is the capacity to rewire itself based on everything you think, learn, and do, called neuroplasticity; and (2) neurogenesis, which is the birth of new brain cells in our memory-processing hippocampus. The brain requires many of the body's resources to function: 25% of our food calories and blood flow, and 20% of our oxygen.

The brain has three functional areas: the primitive brain, the emotional brain, and the thinking brain. This book discusses how the emotional and thinking brains work together to help us learn and think and develop our habits.

Information flows throughout the brain, and from the brain to the body, via brain cells called neurons. Each person's brain has a unique network of brain cells because each of us leads different lives. Information is transmitted as an electrical impulse within the neuron, which shifts to a chemical messenger, called a neurotransmitter, to jump from neuron to neuron. The architecture of the thinking brain's neural networks is called the connectome, and each brain is a work in progress for the entire lifespan. We can make choices that empower our brain, or decisions that harm our brain. With the right information, one can self-hack the brain to change its structure and function, improving its capabilities.

THE SCIENCE

The brain changes throughout our life, and we can empower it with good habits, or harm it with bad habits. To understand how, one needs to develop neuro-intelligence (NQ). Lawyers are aware of general intelligence (IQ) and emotional intelligence (EQ), but most do not have a background knowledge of NQ.[2] NQ starts with an understanding of brain basics.

BRAIN BASICS

The human brain weighs a mere three pounds, yet it requires 20% of the oxygen we breath, consumes 25% of the calories we eat, and utilizes 25% of the body's blood flow. It is the size of a coconut and the consistency of butter for carnivores, or that of tofu for vegans and vegetarians.[3] It evolved from the spine upward into three functional areas, known as the triune brain. The three brain regions can be described as primitive, emotional, and thinking brains.[4]

In her book *The Sharp Solution: A Brain-Based Approach for Optimal Performance*, Heidi Hanna uses the human hand to help us imagine the triune brain structure.[5] The primitive brain sits right above the spine, and if you examine the open palm of your hand, this is the area just above the wrist. It includes the brain stem and cerebellum and facilitates many of the body's automated survival functions such as breathing, heartbeat, and digestion.[6] The primitive brain is not the focus of this book. The brain regions that are integral to cognition and the neurobiology of performance are the emotional and thinking brains.

To envision the emotional brain, fold your thumb across your hand to create the number four. Your thumb now represents your emotional brain, resting above the primitive brain and sitting deep inside your skull. The emotional brain manages memory, emotions, hunger, circadian rhythm, and addiction. Vital components of the emotional brain are the hippocampus, amygdala, thalamus, nucleus accumbens (NA), and ventral tegmental area (VTA).[7]

Close your fingers over your thumb to make a fist and visualize how the thinking brain wraps around the emotional brain. The thinking brain, also known as the cerebral cortex, governs executive functions, reasoning, and higher-order thinking. If the wrinkled thinking brain were flattened out on a surface, it would be the size of a baby blanket.[8] There are eight bones in the cranium that protect the brain.[9]

The walnut-shaped thinking brain is divided into the left and right hemispheres and four lobes devoted to information processing and the senses: occipital lobe (vision), temporal lobe (hearing and some aspects of memory), parietal lobe (movement, taste, temperature, and touch), and frontal lobe (planning, reasoning, language).[10] The left hemisphere is analytical, logical, detail-oriented, and associated with convergent thinking, the pursuit of a single answer to a problem. The right hemisphere processes information holistically and is creative, intuitive, and associated with divergent thinking, the brainstorming of as many solutions as possible to address challenges.[11]

The outer layer of the thinking brain is gray matter, made up of densely packed brain cells responsible for information processing. The inner layer is white matter that transports information between brain regions.[12] The thinking brain makes up only about 30 percent of your entire brain.[13]

The brain is comprised of two kinds of cells: neurons, which transport information within the brain and from the brain to other parts of the body, and glial cells, which insulate neurons and support their information transport function. About 10% of brain cells are neurons, while 90% are supportive glial cells. The brain's neurons make trillions of connections to create numerous networks.[14]

Neurons are shaped like trees with information-receiving dendrite branches at the top, long axon trunks, and output roots called axon terminals at the bottom. Information travels as an electrical impulse within the neuron and via chemical neurotransmitter between neurons. The tiny gap between neurons is the synapse, and each neuron can connect itself to as many as 10,000 neighboring neurons.[15]

Scientists have identified over a hundred neurotransmitters that facilitate communication between neurons. Neurotransmitters are deployed continuously, facilitating synaptic transmission of information. They leave the axon terminal of the first neuron, move across the synapse, and dock in the dendrite of the adjacent neuron. Each neurotransmitter can attach only to an appropriate receptor on the cell surface of the second neuron. Approximately 80 percent of signaling in the brain is facilitated by two transmitters: glutamate, which stimulates the neurons, and gamma-aminobutyric acid (GABA), which suppresses them. Some of the important transmitters and their key functions are:

- **glutamate** activates brain cells and is involved in learning, memory, and increasing synaptic strength;
- **GABA** quiets neurons, promotes calm, reduces anxiety, and rebalances the nervous system after an episode of stress; it will increase during yoga practice, and depression is linked to low GABA levels;
- **serotonin** regulates mood, emotion, appetite, and sleep; low serotonin is linked to irritability from hunger, and many antidepressants address low serotonin levels;
- **dopamine** focuses attention, inspires motivation, creates meaning, and promotes habit learning as part of the brain's reward system;

- **endorphins** block the sense of pain by docking in opiate receptors and also increase feelings of pleasure; exercise can elevate endorphin levels;
- **oxytocin** promotes social bonds and trust and is released during sex and state of pregnancy;
- **norepinephrine** regulates heartbeat, blood pressure, and mood and arouses attention;
- **acetylcholine** aids in attention, wakefulness, learning, and memory. Low levels of acetylcholine are linked to Alzheimer's disease.[16]

Every lawyer has a unique network of neurons, called the connectome, which reflects their distinctive set of thoughts, experiences, and actions.[17] The brain is a work in progress because the connectome is continuously rewiring itself.[18]

RISKS TO BRAIN HEALTH

There are physical and mental risks to brain health that can cause cognitive deficits.

Aging causes brain tissue loss and degeneration of synapses, which connect neurons. Structural deterioration can begin around the age of thirty, but after the age of forty, the hippocampus can shrink about 5 percent per year. This shrinkage depends largely on genetics, lifestyle, and overall health. The hippocampus is fragile and can be impacted by these health indicators more than any other part of the brain.[19]

Dementia describes symptoms and brain disorders that result in the decline of cognitive function, which includes deterioration of memory, communication, and thinking skills. *Mild cognitive impairment*, characterized by a slight decline in memory, can represent the beginning stage of dementia. Only some people with mild cognitive impairment will go on to develop more severe dementia or Alzheimer's disease.

Alzheimer's disease is the most common form of dementia and affects one in nine Americans over the age of sixty-five years. Its symptoms include memory loss, thinking difficulties, behavioral problems, inability to complete familiar tasks, and eventually loss of ability to live independently. Alzheimer's disease is the sixth leading cause of death in the United States.[20]

A *stroke* occurs when blood flow to some parts of the brain is cut off and oxygen and nutrient supply to brain cells are immediately blocked. Strokes can cause memory loss, cognitive impairment, and permanent brain damage.[21]

Concussion, a type of mild traumatic brain injury, arises from a blow to the head after which the person remains conscious for a period of at least thirty minutes. A loss of consciousness after a head strike signifies a *traumatic brain injury*. Symptoms of concussion include memory loss, headaches, vision problems, fatigue, and mood changes. Multiple concussions can lead to chronic traumatic encephalopathy (CTE), most often experienced by veterans and football players.[22]

Anxiety is the most common mental health issue among American adults. When some brain structures and neural networks are over-stimulated, such as the amygdala and the fight-or-flight response system, anxiety is the result. People who suffer from anxiety can be restless, irritable, and nervous and may endure worry, muscle tension, and sleep disturbances.[23]

Anxiety, along with threat evaluation, fear conditioning, and aggression, is situated in the amygdala. The amygdala senses threat information before the other parts of the brain can and is also extremely sensitive to stress hormones. In anxious people, the amygdala is hyperactive, and stress hormones create greater connections among its neurons, making them more excitable.[24]

Depression often combines chemical imbalances in the brain, along with other factors such as genetics, prescription medications, sleep problems, and work stressors. Changes in the hippocampus, such as shrinkage due to chronic stress, can play a role in depression. The National Institute of Health reports that over 17 million people have had at least one major depressive episode, with symptoms lasting for at least two weeks. The defining feature of depression is anhedonia, also known as dysphoria, which is the inability to feel pleasure. Other characteristics are grief and guilt over deep sadness the person is experiencing. Research shows that the hippocampus is smaller than average in many people with depression.[25]

The neurotransmitters implicated in depression are norepinephrine, serotonin, and dopamine. Depression medications are known to increase the amount of time these transmitters spend in the synapse, helping a depressed person to feel better. People with depression seem to experience stressors at a higher-than-average rate. Stress hormones are typically elevated in people with depression, caused by an overactivated fight-or-flight stress response.[26]

A lawyer's brain can be amplified by stimulating experiences, harmed by illness and poor treatment, and healed with healthy practices. Personal lifestyle choices, environments, and cultures shape the development of a lawyer's brain throughout life. Neurogenesis, the birth of new brain cells, can be stimulated by exercise, learning, and use of some antidepressants, but it can also be suppressed by stress. One of the worst conditions for a lawyer is exposure to chronic stress because chronic stress causes brain damage.

Before delving into the harmful effects of stress in Chapter 7, it is important to understand how cognition works. Two kinds of learning are explained here: the acquisition of knowledge and skills through memory formation, in Chapter 5, and motivation and reward that facilitates habit building, in Chapter 6.

NOTES

1 www.imdb.com/title/tt3659388; "Science the Shit out of This," YouTube, December 26, 2015, www.youtube.com/watch?v=BABM3EUo990.
2 Debra Austin, "Drink Like a Lawyer: The Neuroscience of Substance Use and Its Impact on Cognitive Wellness," 15 *Nev Law J* (2015), 826, at 829.
3 Daniel G. Amen, CHANGE YOUR BRAIN CHANGE YOUR BODY: USE YOUR BRAIN TO GET AND KEEP THE BODY YOU HAVE ALWAYS WANTED (Harmony, 2010), 17–18.
4 Judith Horstman, THE SCIENTIFIC AMERICAN DAY IN THE LIFE OF YOUR BRAIN (Jossey-Bass, 2009), 4–6.
5 Heidi Hanna, THE SHARP SOLUTION: A BRAIN-BASED APPROACH FOR OPTIMAL PERFORMANCE (John Wiley & Sons, 2013), 26.
6 Judith Horstman, THE SCIENTIFIC AMERICAN: BRAVE NEW BRAIN (Jossey-Bass, 2010), 3.
7 Ibid., at 4–5.
8 John Medina, BRAIN RULES: 12 PRINCIPLES FOR SURVIVING AND THRIVING AT WORK, HOME AND SCHOOL (Pear Press, 2009), 102.

9 Eric H. Chudler, The Little Book of Neuroscience Haikus (W. W. Norton, 2013), 113.
10 Rita Carter, Mapping the Mind (University of California Press, 2010), 14.
11 Ibid., at 36; Horstman, *supra* note 6, at 130; Michael S. Sweeney, Brain, The Complete Mind: How It Develops, How It Works, and How to Keep It Sharp (National Geographic Society, 2009), 20.
12 Carter, *supra* note 10, at 14–15.
13 Bessel Van Der Kolk, The Body Keeps the Score: Brain, Mind, and Body in the Healing of Trauma (Penguin, 2015), 55.
14 Rita Carter, The Human Brain Book (DK, 2019), 69.
15 Sweeney, *supra* note 11, at 10–11; Joseph Ledoux, Synaptic Self: How Our Brains Become Who We Are (Penguin, 2003), 47; National Geographic Society, Your Brain: A User's Guide (National Geographic Society, 2012), 27.
16 Carter, *supra* note 10, at 29; Horstman, *supra* note 4, at 8; John J. Ratey, Spark: The Revolutionary New Science of Exercise and the Brain (Little, Brown, 2013), 37; Sweeney, *supra* note 11, at 15.
17 Sebastian Seung, Connectome: How the Brain's Wiring Makes Us Who We Are (Mariner Books, 2012), xiii.
18 Horstman, *supra* note 6, at 7.
19 Sanjay Gupta, Keep Sharp: Build a Better Brain at Any Age (Simon & Schuster, 2021), 67–68.
20 Ibid., at 71; Kristen Willeumier, Biohack Your Brain: How to Boost Cognitive Health, Performance and Power (William Morrow, 2020), 45–46.
21 Willeumier, *supra* note 20, at 47–48.
22 Ibid., at 46–47.
23 Ibid., at 47.
24 Robert M. Sapolsky, Why Zebras Don't Get Ulcers (Holt, 2004), 7–12, at 322–323.
25 Willeumier, *supra* note 20, at 47; ibid., at 272–273, 276.
26 Sapolsky, *supra* note 24, at 278–280, 291, 294.

5 MEMORY, KNOWLEDGE, AND BUILDING EXPERTISE

> Sixty minutes of thinking of any kind is bound to lead to confusion and unhappiness.
>
> —James Thurber[1]

Lawyering requires life-long learning. Learning involves the acquisition of new information, and memory is how that information is stored in the brain. Cognition integrates consciousness, attention, intelligence, memory, and the acquisition of knowledge and skills. The top two-thirds of the triune brain, the emotional brain, and the thinking brain, collaborate to support cognitive capacity and the development of expertise.

The effectiveness of cognitive function depends upon the quality of communication between neurons and overall brain health. Lawyers with neuro-intelligence understand how the brain processes information and how learning and memory function to facilitate their work.

THE SUMMARY

The thinking and emotional brains work together to help lawyers develop expertise, through a process called memory consolidation. Information enters the thinking brain through the senses, such as the eyes and ears, and travels from the eyes or ears to the memory-processing hippocampus. Newer memories are stored in the network of brain cells that loop between the thinking brain and the hippocampus in the emotional brain. Stable memory, a lawyer's hard-earned expertise, is recalled from the connectome, which is a unique architecture of neurons in the thinking brain. Chapter 10 covers practices that optimize brain health and empower cognitive capacity.

THE SCIENCE

Expertise is the development of a knowledge base and skill set that is fully stabilized in the brain. The process of acquiring expertise is memory consolidation. Fragile memory traces are converted into durable memories in the three-step memory consolidation process, which include encoding, storing, and retrieving.[2]

Learning involves a complex interaction between the emotional and the thinking brains. The knowledge acquisition process begins with encoding when new information enters the thinking brain via the senses. The occipital lobe processes visual information; the temporal lobe handles sound; the frontal lobe manages language; and the parietal lobe deals with movement, touch, or taste data. These sensory memory traces move from the lobes of the thinking brain to the emotional brain, where the thalamus focuses the brain's attention, screens and sorts the information, and sends it to the hippocampus. The information travels back to the thinking brain, to the sensory lobe of its origin, then returns to the hippocampus in the emotional brain, forming a loop.[3]

Information travels along this thinking-emotional brain circuit via neurons and neurotransmitters. Neurons fire along the route, with increasing sensitivity and likelihood that they will fire again along the same path, in a process called long-term potentiation (LTP). Canadian psychologist Donald Hebb stated that neurons that "fire together wire together," describing the process of neural network building.[4]

The hippocampal neurons start to encode the information for permanent storage along chains of firing neurons. This temporary synaptic interaction, which lasts an hour or two, is called early LTP. If the information is reviewed or revisited, it is strengthened when the same neurons fire together more often, and thus late LTP occurs. Consolidation makes temporarily stored fragile information more stable for later retrieval by reinforcing the neural connections in the information circuit between the hippocampus in the emotional brain and the lobes of the cerebral cortex, the thinking brain.[5]

When law students prepare for class by doing the assigned reading, they begin the memory consolidation process as new information enters their brains as memory traces. When they listen, participate, and take notes during class, the information is firing again along the newly established neural networks. If they prepare an outline for an exam or practice hypothetical problems in their study group, these activities augment memory consolidation by further establishing the wired networks of their brain cells. All these activities help knowledge become stable in long-term memory, which enhances retrieval for performance on the exam, via LTP. The information is retrieved or recalled from the hippocampus–cerebral cortex or the emotional–thinking brain loop.

Analyzing, synthesizing, outlining, drafting, and arguing in a mock setting all strengthen synaptic connections in the neural networks of a lawyer's brain. Information travels in the emotional–thinking brain circuit from as few as two years to as long as a decade, gradually evolving from a fragile to a stable memory. Scientists believe this journey takes place largely during sleep, making adequate sleep one of the most important activities a lawyer can improve on to enhance brain function.[6]

Once the consolidation process is complete, the hippocampus terminates its relationship with the sensory lobes of the thinking brain. Now a lawyer's expertise resides in the neural networks of their brain's cerebral cortex.[7] The neural network, unique to each lawyer because it was constructed from individual experiences, actions, and thoughts, is called the connectome. Law students recall information for exams from the emotional–thinking brain loop. When representing and counseling clients, lawyers combine recall of stable information from their thinking brain (connectome) and retrieval of newer information from their emotional–thinking brain circuit.

Aging involves a decline in the speed with which neurons receive and transmit information, a reduction in the number of synaptic connections between neurons, and shrinkage of brain structures that are important for learning and memory.[8] The memory-processing hippocampus is able to grow new cells for our entire life. A study done at the University of Illinois at Chicago has found evidence of new neuron growth in participants between the ages of seventy-nine and ninety-nine years. Participants who scored higher on cognitive tests had a greater number of newly developing neurons than those who scored lower.[9]

To maintain a well-functioning memory consolidation system, the lawyer's brain must have a healthy hippocampus in the emotional brain and a healthy connectome in the thinking brain. Wise lifestyle decisions can slow the rate of brain health decline, and these are detailed in Chapter 10.

Synergy between the thinking and emotional brains is critical to the acquisition of knowledge and skills and the development of expertise. The motivation and reward system, responsible for our habits, also requires interaction between the emotional and thinking brains, albeit via brain structures that differ from the memory consolidation system.

NOTES

1 www.brainyquote.com/quotes/james_thurber_385429.
2 Michael S. Sweeney, Brain, The Complete Mind: How It Develops, How It Works, and How to Keep It Sharp (National Geographic Society, 2009), at 236, 248–252.
3 Rita Carter, The Human Brain Book (DK, 2019), at 60, 66, 156, 158–159.
4 Joseph Ledoux, Synaptic Self: How Our Brains Become Who We Are (Penguin, 2003), at 79.
5 Rita Carter, Mapping the Mind (University of California Press, 2010), at 159–160; Sweeney, *supra* note 2, at 248.
6 Carter, *supra* note 3, at 159; John Medina, Brain Rules: 12 Principles for Surviving and Thriving at Work, Home and School (Pear Press, 2009), at 138, 140–142.
7 Medina, *supra* note 6, at 138; Sebastian Seung, Connectome: How the Brain's Wiring Makes Us Who We Are (Mariner, 2012), at xii–xv.
8 Carter, *supra* note 3, at 44, 214–215.
9 Neuroscience News, "New Neurons Form in the Brain into Tenth Decade of Life, Even in People with Alzheimer's," May 24, 2019, https://neurosciencenews.com/neurogenesis-alzheimers-superagers-14074.

6 MOTIVATION, REWARD, AND DEVELOPING HABITS

> Discipline is choosing between what you want now and what you want most.
>
> —Abraham Lincoln[1]

The memory consolidation system, where knowledge and skills are acquired and expertise is developed, requires collaboration between the thinking and emotional brains. Newer memories are retrieved from the emotional–thinking brain loop, where the information travels between the hippocampus in the emotional brain and the sensory lobes in the thinking brain. Expertise, in the form of fully consolidated memory, is recalled from the knowledge network of neurons in the thinking brain, called the connectome.

The thinking and emotional brains also work together to create our habits. Our lifestyle patterns can creep up on us because the motivation and reward system is very old and mostly automatic. When we understand habit learning, we can also learn how to make lifestyle choices that empower our brain.

THE SUMMARY

The brain has an automated system to keep humans alive by promoting the search for, and remembering the location of, food. It is a motivation and reward system. The main neurotransmitter that drives our motivation and reward system is dopamine, which controls our repeat behavior. Our habits are formed by this system, and modern society offers numerous substances and activities to indulge in, which can become habitual. Beneficial habits include exercise and eating lots of vegetables. Unhealthy habits include drinking too much alcohol, eating too much comfort food, and spending too much time on social media. Our habits often take hold because we use them to soothe our stress, anxiety, and depression. Habits are hard to break because they are established in the networks of our brain cells.

THE SCIENCE

The brain's motivation and reward system, which is activated when we form habits, involves a complicated interface between the emotional and thinking brains. Reward seeking, using food as our example, has six stages:

- incentive, such as the smell of a favorite food;
- desire to obtain that food you believe will bring satisfaction or pleasure;
- motivation – the drive to secure the food;
- action – the activity necessary to procure the food;
- pleasure when the food is enjoyed; and
- learning, which is established in the neural network wiring in the brain when the food is acquired.[2]

The evolutionary purpose of the motivation and reward system is to stimulate eating and procreation to ensure the survival of the human species. The neurotransmitter long associated with reward seeking is dopamine. It plays an important role in drive and motivation, but it is not responsible for the sensation of pleasure.[3]

If the aroma of fresh baked bread wafts from your local bakery, it can stimulate the motivation and reward system. The desire to purchase a loaf is registered in the emotional brain's ventral tegmental area (VTA). The neurons in the VTA produce dopamine, and their long axon trunks reach multiple locations in the thinking and emotional brains. Dopamine is released in

- the thinking brain's prefrontal cortex, which controls executive functions such as planning, reasoning, and judgment; and
- the emotional brain's:
  - amygdala, which evaluates emotional content;
  - hippocampus, which processes memory;

- dorsal striatum, which mediates habit learning; and
- nucleus accumbens (NA), which registers pleasure.[4]

The dopamine instigates motivation and action to obtain the baguette. The pleasure of eating the bread is experienced in tiny hedonic hotspots in the NA, which produce endogenous opioid peptides (EOPs, which include beta-endorphine, enkephalin, and dynorphine) to activate opioid receptors. Dopamine is responsible for the feeling of motivation or seeking, EOPs are responsible for the sensation of pleasure.[5] The bakery acquires incentive salience, particularly robust memory often activated by cravings, for fresh baked goods, which helps create a routine of shopping there for bakery treats. The brain's motivation and reward system, mediated by dopamine, is designed to ensure repeat behaviors and thus develop habits.[6]

This automated motivation and reward system exists to keep us alive. It learns via positive and negative reinforcement to encourage more behaviors that make us feel good and restrict those that make us feel bad. This knowledge is stored in the networks of the emotional brain that operate like muscle memory, so that we don't have to use our thinking brain to acquire calories once we have identified where our food sources are located. Our thinking brain is then available to solve more complex problems.

Food is only one type of reward that engages this system because modern life provides access to plenty of addictive substances and activities.[7] Dopamine is responsible for drive, motivation, seeking, and wanting. In a normal brain, there is a sweet spot for dopamine activation, like the middle of a bell curve. Too far to the left of the curve means there is too little dopamine, and the person can be lethargic. Too far to the right, with too much dopamine exposure, and the person can be irritable. High levels of dopamine in the synapse can cause more motivation for rewards, such as food or drugs, and behaviors, such as gambling, internet usage, video gaming, shopping, TV binging, and overworking.[8] Extensive dopamine exposure results in a disordered reward pathway in the brain, which can lead to addiction.

Rewards in a lawyer's environment that ease discomfort acquire incentive salience, causing the lawyer to notice and be attracted to them and repeatedly desire them. Overindulging in food can be a type of substance misuse. Substances such as alcohol, nicotine, and study drugs can also become habit-forming for lawyers and in some cases lead to addiction. It is even possible to become addicted to work. A detailed discussion of substance misuse and addiction is covered in Chapter 8.

Before we look at self-medication, we must explore the role of stress and trauma in the lawyer's brain. Stress, anxiety, and depression can create conditions where the impaired or languishing lawyer chooses to soothe themself with food, substances, or activities that are harmful to their brain health. These practices can become routines. Habits are imprinted in our brains, as repeat behavior develops neural circuitry.

Stress is often an incentive for self-medication. It impairs our brain function and can weaken both the knowledge acquisition and motivation and reward systems. Chronic stress causes brain damage.

NOTES

1 www.azquotes.com/quote/855206.
2 Jerrold S. Meyer and Linda F. Quenzer, Psychopharmacology: Drugs, The Brain, and Behavior (3rd ed., Oxford University Press, 2019), 291; Dale Purves et al., Principles of Cognitive Neuroscience (Oxford University Press, 2012), 472.
3 Norman Doidge, The Brain that Changes Itself (Penguin, 2007), 106; Barry J. Gibb, The Rough Guide to the Brain (Penguin, 2007), 176.
4 Stephanie D. Hancock and William A. McKim, Drugs and Behavior: An Introduction to Behavioral Pharmacology (8th ed., Pearson, 2018), 104–113; David J. Linden, The Compass of Pleasure: How Our Brains Make Fatty Foods, Orgasm, Exercise, Marijuana, Generosity, Vodka, Learning, and Gambling Feel So Good (Penguin, 2012), 16–18.
5 Robert H. Lustig, The Hacking of the American Mind: The Science behind the Corporate Takeover of Our Bodies and Brains (Avery, 2017), 29, 47.
6 Hancock and McKim, *supra* note 4, at 118–119; Meyer and Quenzer, *supra* note 2, at 291.
7 Judson Brewer, Unwinding Anxiety: New Science Shows How to Break the Cycles of Worry and Fear to Heal Your Mind (Avery, 2021), 31–32, 65–66.
8 Lustig, *supra* note 5, at 47–49.

7 THE IMPACT OF STRESS

> Cognition is just a fancy word for a thought. It's the way you think about what's happening.
>
> —David D. Burns[1]

> Long-term exposure to large doses of cortisol will kill you . . . but slowly.
>
> —Robert H. Lustig[2]

> Any level of stress inhibits performance.
>
> —Judson Brewer[3]

You have learned about the brain's knowledge and habit systems. Those neuro-intelligence basics will help you understand just how toxic stress is for the brain. The rat-fumbling researcher Hans Selye noticed that the discomfort his lab rats suffered made them sick. He used the term *stress* to describe the general unpleasantness his rats experienced when he routinely dropped, chased, and recaptured them during his experiments. The *culture* of his lab was making his rats sick. When law school or legal practice cultures subject students or lawyers to a broad array of incessant stressors, the general unpleasantness is prone to make them sick.

The well-being crisis in the legal profession is likely due to the *stress-saturated cultures* of legal education and law practice. Americans suffer from overwork, and one study has found that 37.8% of professional men and 14.4% of professional women work more than fifty hours per week.[4] Overwork is a habit that students adopt during law school where achievement is defined by grades, class rank, and selection to serve on journals. The practice of overwork becomes amplified when lawyers grapple with demanding client matters, billable hours, the expectation of 24/7 availability, and the drive to become partner. The adversarial zero-sum nature of legal practice adds an additional layer of stress on top of that.

In the fall of 2020, over 4,200 lawyers responded to an ABA survey regarding work and stress. Forty percent reported being stressed by their work; 46% were feeling overwhelmed by their responsibilities; 41% felt like the day never seemed to end; 43% were having difficulty taking time off from work; and 33% felt like it would be better to stop working altogether.[5]

Data from the 2020 International Bar Association's *Mental Wellbeing* report acknowledges that there is a "global crisis in lawyer mental well-being."[6] It reports that while the practice of law is intellectually stimulating and rewarding, sustained levels of high demands expose lawyers to negative physical and mental health consequences. These demands include extreme workloads, high billable hour goals, intensified client expectations, and unsupportive workplace environments.

The problems with the lawyering culture, which lead to lawyer languishing and impairment, are comparable all around the world.[7]

THE SUMMARY

This chapter focuses on how stress causes brain damage. Unrelenting stress is an essential feature of legal education and legal practice. Research shows that chronic stress hurts the brain.

Lawyers suffer from higher rates of anxiety and depression than the rest of the population and rank fourth in professions with the highest number of suicides. Lawyer anxiety, depression, and suicide rates are likely linked to overwork and exposure to toxic chronic stress. We saw in Chapter 4 that anxiety and depression can cause changes in the brain that are related to an overactive fight-or-flight response system. Lawyer languishing, a state of incomplete mental health, may be a precursor to anxiety or depression.

According to Jon Kabat-Zinn, overwhelm is the experience "that our lives are somehow unfolding faster than the human nervous system and psyche are able to manage well."[8] The fight-or-flight stress response is initiated by the nervous system. Designed to promote a short-term action necessary to flee from or fight predators, our stress response system is now routinely activated by modern stressors in our environment. A longer-term activation of our stress response makes us physically and emotionally sick, which damages our brain.

THE SCIENCE

WISDOM OF THE BODY

A lawyer uses both the thinking and emotional brains to process emotion. An emotion is an automatic and unconscious response to an emotional stimulus that results in physical and cognitive changes. Examples of our body responding spontaneously to an emotion include blushing, sweaty palms, and increased heart rate and blood pressure. The six primary emotions are sadness, fear, anger, disgust, surprise, and joy. Emotions are experienced as feelings that are the conscious perceptions of the involuntary responses of the body.[9]

Information travels through the lawyer's brain along two parallel processing routes. First, stimuli, also known as memory traces, enter the thinking brain via the senses and then move to the emotional brain. The quick and dirty route starts in the emotional brain's panic button, the amygdala. The amygdala is alert to threat and opportunity, and it launches the fight-or-flight system in response to danger. On the slower route, information is processed by the hippocampus in the emotional brain, and in the absence of any threat, the fight-or-flight response is overruled.[10]

Walter B. Cannon was a physician, Professor of Physiology at Harvard, and a stress and trauma researcher who coined the term *homeostasis* in 1926. His research on how emotional states impact bodily functions also led him to coin the phrases *fight or flight* and *rest and digest* to describe the two parts of the autonomic nervous system. He theorized that these systems helped the body maintain stability that he called homeostasis. Cannon characterized this homeostatic operation, working to balance the right amount of alertness with relaxation, and anxiety with calm, as the *wisdom of the body*.[11]

The brain works with our body to maintain homeostasis via the autonomic nervous system. Homeostasis can be compared to the heating, ventilation, and air-conditioning (HVAC) system. We use the HVAC system to maintain a comfortable temperature in our home. The autonomic nervous system has a heating half – the sympathetic nervous system – and a cooling half – the parasympathetic nervous system. These were described by Cannon as the fight-or-flight (sympathetic nervous) system and the rest-and-digest (parasympathetic nervous) system. The fight-or-flight arousal system is the body's accelerator, and the rest-and-digest calming system is its brake.[12]

The fight-or-flight system evolved to produce a rapid response when escape from predators was a priority. It is ignited by the threat sensor amygdala, which directs the thalamus to focus attention, and the hypothalamus to inform the pituitary, which in turn instructs the adrenal glands to release stress hormones adrenaline, also known as epinephrine, and glucocorticoids, mainly cortisol. This is the HPA axis: hypothalamus to pituitary to adrenal glands. The amygdala signals the HPA axis to respond to threat by launching a cascade of stress hormones. Stress hormones increase heart rate, raise blood pressure, and elevate blood sugar to provide an energy boost to help the body deal with the threat. At the same time, systems designed to support long-term health, such as digestion and the immune system, are suppressed.[13]

Fight-or-flight activation is meant to help solve short-term problems like the evasive action necessary to escape harm. The wisdom of the body uses the rest-and-digest system to return to homeostasis after the threat has been neutralized. However, there are two kinds of stress: *acute stress*, which is short-lived, for which the fight-or-flight system had evolved; and *chronic stress*, which is long term and caused by serious life challenges such as job loss, financial difficulties, intimate relationship struggles, and arguably legal education and law practice. The body's response to *trauma* is closely related to how it processes chronic stress.

Acute Stress

The short-term stress response evolved to help us with performance and survival. It improves vigilance and directs blood flow to fuel the brain, heart, and muscles. It was meant to be experienced in small doses.

The fight-or-flight acute stress response can help a lawyer focus and enhance performance in a difficult hearing or a demanding negotiation. It also empowers the lawyer's body to participate in a weekend 5k run. Once a challenging task has been resolved, the lawyer's body and brain should return to homeostasis via the rest-and-digest system.

The problem with society today, and with legal education and law practice, is that acute stressors have been greatly reduced, but chronic psychological stressors have increased significantly. Chronic stress can damage your brain, and ultimately kill you.[14]

Chronic Stress

When stress persists for days or weeks, the constant fight-or-flight activation can cause mental disorders such as irritability, anxiety, panic attacks, or depression. The physical effects of chronic stress include breathlessness, dizziness, heart palpitations, chest pain, sweating, chills, abdominal discomfort, muscle tension, and elevated blood pressure. These symptoms indicate an unrestrained fight-or-flight response.

Chronic stress promotes long-term elevation of stress hormones, causing an increased risk of serious health problems, including a compromised immune system, increased appetite and body fat, decreased muscle mass and bone density, diminished libido, and increased anxiety and depression. It can lead to metabolic syndrome – a group of symptoms including increased blood pressure, blood sugar, cholesterol, and triglyceride levels, and body fat around the waist – which raises the risk of diabetes, stroke, and heart disease. Chronic stress has serious impacts on the lawyer's brain as well.[15]

HOW CHRONIC STRESS CAUSES DAMAGE TO THE EMOTIONAL BRAIN

Imagine your emotional brain is like your thumb folded over your palm when you make the number four with your hand. Its structures reside deep inside the brain and are surrounded by the thinking brain, which is the top layer, like your four fingers when they wrap around your thumb to make a fist. The key structures of the emotional brain are the panic button amygdala and the memory-processing hippocampus.

The overactivation of our stress system can have grave consequences on our brain. Lawyers can spend months or years in fight-or-flight overdrive, many believing their work is enhanced by the adrenaline-cortisol rush. The performance upgrade stimulated by the short-term activation of the fight-or-flight system is only effective if the rest-and-digest system regularly returns the brain and body to equilibrium. Under chronic stress, the lawyer's brain never gets a chance to recover and is susceptible to damage caused by extended exposure to stress hormones.

Sensing a threat, the amygdala sounds an alarm by stimulating the release of stress hormones via the HPA axis. During chronic stress, continuous fight-or-flight activation causes iterative damage to the brain. Stress hormones arouse the amygdala, which responds by instigating the production of additional glucocorticoids. The hippocampus is highly susceptible to stress because it has abundant glucocorticoid receptors. Glucocorticoids damage and kill neurons in the hippocampus and weaken synaptic connections.

The hippocampus, normally responsible for calming the amygdala, is suppressed. Under chronic stress, the amygdala is oversensitized, and the hippocampus is compromised. The memory-processing hippocampus is the brain structure most vulnerable to cell death, causing its shrinkage, leading to memory loss and depression.[16]

Because the job of the amygdala is to react to trouble, the lawyer's brain is vulnerable to negativity bias, where the mind can trigger a stress response by simply imagining a threatening situation. Fear of threat can launch the stress response and keep it going. This can happen when a lawyer worries about a short-term task, such as an upcoming hearing, or has anxiety about a long-term goal, such as becoming a partner.

Executive control within the thinking brain is diminished, so it becomes difficult for an anxious lawyer to calm the apprehension of a potential public blunder or career failure when the thinking brain is exposed to chronic stress.

To recap, chronic stress can be caused by either real physical threats or psychological threats such as worrying about the pressures of law school or legal practice. This is an automated process. The lawyer cannot control the brain's involuntary response to chronic stress. The emotional brain is inundated by a constant stream of stress hormones. The memory-processing hippocampus is susceptible to brain cell damage, which can result in memory problems and depression. Stress-infused cultures are likely to cause cognitive dysfunction due to the harm stress hormones cause to the emotional brain.

HOW CHRONIC STRESS CAUSES DAMAGE TO THE THINKING BRAIN

Fight or flight is the body's response system designed to deal with acute stress, which could be physical, adversarial, medical, or psychological. When cortisol is released, the lawyer gets a burst of blood glucose to prevent fainting, their blood pressure increases to prevent shock, and their immune function is suppressed to prevent inflammation. Vigilance and memory are heightened, and blood flow increases to support the action of the muscles, heart, and brain. The fight-or-flight system is designed for brief engagement, in small doses, to successfully handle short-term challenges.

In the thinking brain, stress causes the amygdala and HPA axis to release cortisol and dopamine into the prefrontal cortex (PFC). This impairs rational decision-making, causes impulsivity, and harms the ability to distinguish between immediate or delayed gratification. Dopamine is a transmitter designed to inspire repeat behavior. Dopamine receptors in the thinking brain are fewer than in the emotional brain and are downregulated (shrink in number) with overexposure, attempting to limit the impact.

Together, stress and cortisol decrease the cognitive control of the PFC, making it difficult to resist comfort food and drugs of abuse. Self-medication becomes a health risk for stressed-out lawyers, even if they are trying to break bad habits. The failure of the PFC to manage the drive for stress relief can also lead to substance misuse and addiction. A detailed description of this process is available in Chapter 8.

Chronic stress can also damage a part of the frontal lobe, known as thinning of the PFC. A compromised PFC is a predictor of risk of relapse to self-medicating with food or drugs. When stress hormones damage the thinking brain's PFC neurons, the result is poorer decision-making capacity and the risk of turning to bad habits to provide a respite from stress.[17]

COGNITIVE CAPACITY, LEARNING, AND MEMORY UNDER CHRONIC STRESS

The hippocampus is highly vulnerable to injury from overexposure to stress hormones. It has plentiful glucocorticoid receptors, and stress hormones can damage or destroy the neurons in the hippocampus, along with weakening the synaptic connections. Along with inhibiting other body functions devoted to long-term well-being, such as digestion and immune response, the generation of new brain cells in the hippocampus is also suppressed by chronic stress.

A number of other conditions can also harm the hippocampus, including radiation and starvation. "One of the serial killers that attacks the neurons in the hippocampus is cortisol. The longer your cortisol stays elevated, the smaller and more vulnerable your hippocampus gets, which puts you at risk for depression. This is likely why chronic stress is associated with memory loss."[18]

One study has revealed that adults in midlife with increased levels of stress hormones had reduced brain structure and cognitive function. Data from 2,018 Framingham Heart Study participants, of an average age of forty-eight, showed that those with an elevated cortisol level performed worse on memory and other cognitive tasks than those with average cortisol levels. Participants with higher cortisol levels also had smaller brain volumes.[19]

It should come as no surprise that a compromised hippocampus is not as functional as a healthy one. The impact of stress on the lawyer's cognition includes deterioration in concentration, memory, problem-solving, math performance, and language processing. Motivation is dampened, curiosity is diminished, and creativity is inhibited. Brain scans showed shrinkage of the hippocampi in people experiencing major depression and PTSD. This shrinkage is likely due to hippocampus neurodegeneration caused by overexposure to stress hormones.[20]

TRAUMA

Chronic stress has devolved into trauma for some in the legal field. Mindfulness consultant, author, and lawyer Jeena Cho says, "We need to normalize acknowledging, talking about and getting help for trauma in the legal profession. We need to do this as a community."[21]

Vicarious Trauma

Some legal practices can result in vicarious trauma, also known as compassion fatigue or secondary traumatic stress. Vicarious trauma can be thought of as the cost of caring for others and can be caused by the exposure to trauma victims and their stories. The symptoms of vicarious trauma, many of which mirror chronic stress symptoms, include:

- irritation, impatience, or anger;
- sleep difficulties;
- eating issues;
- jumpiness;
- hopelessness;
- diminished joy, satisfaction, or sense of accomplishment; and
- increased conflict, poor communication or collaboration, withdrawal, and avoiding clients with significant trauma stories.[22]

PTSD and Posttraumatic Stress (PTS)

Law practice and legal education cultures are very often sources of chronic stress, which causes brain damage. Some lawyers experience vicarious trauma because of the clients they serve. But lawyers and law students may also experience stressors outside the work and education context that can exacerbate chronic stress or trauma. Some wider cultural causes include the continued impact of systemic racism and violence on communities of color; misogyny; discrimination; historic weather and wildfire events, enhanced by a warming climate; gun violence in schools, grocery stores, and places of worship; and the degradation of mental and physical health augmented by the challenges of the pandemic.

PTSD is most commonly associated with people who experience military service during violent conflict and with survivors of natural disasters, family violence, or sexual assault. Its symptoms include:

- reexperiencing, such as flashbacks or nightmares;
- avoidance – staying away from certain people, places, or situations;
- hyperarousal, which is heightened vigilance or startling easily; and
- memory loss.

Experts treating trauma victims use PTS to describe the normal and adaptive fight-or-flight response to a stressful, traumatic, or life-threatening event. PTS can trigger some of the PTSD symptoms listed above.[23]

The neurobiology of PTSD and PTS begins with the classic fight-or-flight response. The amygdala immediately and unconsciously processes the threat and activates the HPA axis. Cortisol, the main stress hormone, and glutamate, the brain's main activating neurotransmitter, are released to help mount a response to the threat condition. During the stress response, glutamate contributes to the consolidation of traumatic memory. Excess amounts of both cortisol and glutamate are toxic to the brain, especially the hippocampus and PFC.

Brain imaging of PTSD patients has shown a reduction in the volume of the hippocampus and the PFC. The hippocampus is critical to learning, memory, and calming the fear response of the amygdala. Excess levels of cortisol and glutamate damage brain cells and impair connections between neurons in the hippocampus. The amygdala becomes overreactive, and the PFC, which would normally calm the amygdala, is smaller and less effective in PTSD victims.[24]

Legacy burdens such as childhood hardship, the culture we are surrounded by, and harassment and discrimination related to identity characteristics, such as gender, race, and sexual orientation, can make recovery from trauma difficult when victims normalize them over time.[25] "Trauma produces actual physiological changes, including a recalibration of the brain's alarm system, an increase in stress hormone activity, and alterations in the system that filters relevant information from irrelevant." These brain changes clarify why traumatized people become hypervigilant to threat.[26]

Trauma and High Intelligence

Gifted people may possess unique intensities of emotional and physical responses to stressors. Recent research has revealed that highly intelligent people may have hyperactive emotional and central nervous systems, where the fight-or-flight stress response is initiated. Researchers confirmed the hyper brain/hyper body theory when they surveyed 3,715 American Mensa members with IQ scores at or above 130. The participants were asked to self-report their experiences of both diagnosed and/or suspected mood and anxiety disorders, attention-deficit hyperactivity disorder (ADHD), autism spectrum disorder (ASD), and physiological diseases that include autoimmune disease, environmental and food allergies, and asthma. The Mensa participants had significantly higher rates of all these diseases and disorders than the national average. For example, just over 10% of the US population has been diagnosed with anxiety, while 20% of the Mensa participants suffer from an anxiety disorder.[27]

Environmental Sensitivity

The ways people experience stress or trauma vary widely. "Some people are more easily scared than others; some stay afraid or sad longer than others do."[28]

Dr. Thomas Boyce describes the difference between sensitive children, who are highly susceptible to environmental conditions, and resilient children, who are mostly unflappable, in his book *The Orchid and the Dandelion: Why Some Children Struggle and How All Can Thrive*. He describes sensitive kids as orchids, and resilient kids as dandelions.[29]

A study of 906 adults has shown a range of three sensitivity levels to environmental influences with 31% revealed to be highly sensitive orchids, 40% medium-sensitivity tulips, and 29% resilient dandelions.[30]

Trauma and Cognitive Capacity

Trauma influences how people behave and think, but it also impacts their cognitive capacity. "We have learned that trauma is not just an event that took place sometime in the past; it is also the imprint left by that experience on mind, brain, and body."[31]

Research has examined the association between age at exposure to traumatic events and cognitive functioning in adulthood to determine whether the effects of trauma exposure are more pronounced if the trauma occurred in childhood or later in life. Scientists studied the lifetime trauma exposure of 2,471 participants, aged 28–84 years, in the midlife in the US longitudinal study.

Trauma exposure was defined in that study as "threatening or physically or emotionally harmful events that cause lasting adverse effects on an individual's level of well-being or functional impairment." The researchers studied stressful life events considered the most potentially traumatic, including being sent away from home; parent's drug or alcohol abuse; death of a parent, child, or sibling; divorce; life-threatening illness; physical or sexual assault; losing a home to fire or natural disaster; and combat experience. They also analyzed age at exposure to the trauma.

The cognitive functions examined were executive function and episodic memory. Executive function is the capacity to evaluate options and make decisions using appropriate behavior. Episodic memory is autobiographical personal experience.

Individuals who suffered from traumatic experiences showed significant declines in both executive function and episodic memory nine years after exposure, compared to those with no trauma exposure. Those with the most trauma exposure demonstrated the most deterioration. Participants with trauma exposure as adults showed a larger decline in executive function than those who suffered childhood trauma. The results suggest that trauma in adulthood may be more damaging to later cognitive function and that healing from trauma is possible over time.[32]

EMPOWERING RECOVERY

Short-term stress, chronic stress, and trauma all activate the fight-or-flight response system. Chronic stress and trauma can harm both the emotional and thinking brains when the stress response system is overactivated or incessantly triggered.

Many lawyers spend their lives in fight-or-flight overdrive. This predicament may be fueled by caffeine, comfort food, alcohol, and other substances. Some highly intelligent lawyers are likely to be more susceptible to stress and trauma, and some are likely more vulnerable to toxically stressful environments. Neuroscientists have proven that cognitive performance is diminished during extended fight-or-flight response, but thanks to neuroplasticity, the lawyer's brain can be healed. It is possible for the lawyer to become an "amygdala whisperer" and recover their cognitive function.[33]

A healthy rest-and-digest system can blunt the stress response and improve the body's capacity to return to homeostasis. Lawyers can empower their rest-and-digest system as part of their plan to reduce the impacts of stress. While the fight-or-flight system stimulates arousal, defense, and escape, the rest-and-digest system supports nourishment, procreation, and restored balance after a stress response. The rest-and-digest system slows down the heart rate, lowers blood pressure, promotes digestion and nutrient absorption, and curbs the release of stress hormones. It helps conserve energy, promote relaxation, and produce feelings of contentment.

The rest-and-digest system's ability to control stress hormone levels can help heal both the emotional and thinking brains. Lawyers can cultivate the neurobiology of calm and foster resilience in the face of stress with a series of restorative practices outlined in Chapter 11.[34]

But what happens when the lawyer self-medicates chronic stress? Chapter 8 details how various substances of abuse impact the lawyer's brain.

NOTES

1 David D. Burns, Feeling Great: The Revolutionary New Treatment for Depression and Anxiety (PESI, 2020), 15.

2 Robert H. Lustig, The Hacking of the American Mind: The Science behind the Corporate Takeover of Our Bodies and Brains (Avery, 2017), at 61.

3 Judson Brewer, Unwinding Anxiety: New Science Shows How to Break the Cycles of Worry and Fear to Heal Your Mind (Avery, 2021), at 82.

4 Julian Ford and Jon Wortmann, Hijacked by Your Brain: How to Free Yourself When Stress Takes Over (Sourcebooks, 2013), 18–19.

5 Stephanie A. Scharf and Roberta D. Liebenberg, Practicing Law in the Pandemic and Moving Forward: Results and Best Practices from a Nationwide Survey of the Legal Profession (American Bar Association, 2021), www.americanbar.org/content/dam/aba/administrative/digital-engagement/practice-forward/practice-forward-survey.pdf.

6 IBA Presidential Task Force, Mental Wellbeing in the Legal Profession: A Global Study (International Bar Association, 2021), 13, www.ibanet.org/document?id=IBA-report-Mental-Wellbeing-in-the-Legal-Profession-A-Global-Study.

7 Ibid., at 19.

8 Katie B. Smith, "Stress Got the Best of You?" *Medium*, April 10, 2022, https://medium.com/@katiebsmith/stress-got-the-best-of-you-9b810584a122.

9 Ralph Adolphs and David J. Anderson, The Neuroscience of Emotion: A New Synthesis (Princeton University Press, 2018), at 6.

10 Rita Carter, Mapping the Mind (University of California Press, 2010), at 83.

11 Gayatri Devi, A Calm Brain: How to Relax into a Stress-Free, High-Powered Life (Plume, 2013), 37; Robert M. Sapolsky, Why Zebras Don't Get Ulcers (Holt, 2004), at 12–13.

12 Melanie Greenberg, The Stress-Proof Brain: Master your Emotional Response to Stress using Mindfulness and Neuroplasticity (New Harbinger, 2017), 20.

13 John Medina, Brain Rules: 12 Principles for Surviving and Thriving at Work, Home and School (Pear Press, 2009), at 62–67.

14 Lustig, *supra* note 2, at 60–61.

15 Greenberg, *supra* note 12, at 23–26; Medina, *supra* note 13, at 63–67; Lustig, *supra* note 2, at 61–66; Rita Carter, The Human Brain Book (DK, 2019), at 232; Shawn Talbott, The Cortisol Connection: Why Stress Makes you Fat and Ruins your Health – and What You Can Do about It (Hunter House, 2007), 30–33.

16 Medina, *supra* note 13, at 65–67; Greenberg, *supra* note 12, at 2–24; Rick Hanson, Buddha's Brain: The Practical Neuroscience of Happiness, Love, & Wisdom (Brilliance, 2009), at 50, 52–53, 57; John J. Ratey, Spark: The Revolutionary New Science of Exercise and the Brain (Little, Brown Spark, 2008), at 66–67, 83; Devi, *supra* note 11, at 7.

17 Hanson, *supra* note 16, at 52–60; Ratey, *supra* note 16, at 67–71; Devi, *supra* note 11, at 83–86; Lustig, *supra* note 2, at 64–66.

18 Lustig, *supra* note 2, at 63.

19 Muzaffer Kaser, Barbara Jacquelyn Sahakian, and Christelle Langley, "How Chronic Stress Changes the Brain, and What You Can Do to Reverse the Damage," *Neuroscience News*, March 14, 2020, https://neurosciencenews.com/chronic-stress-reversal-15918.

20 Medina, *supra* note 13, at 178; Sapolsky, *supra* note 11, at 221; David Perlmutter and Alberto Villoldo, POWER UP YOUR BRAIN: THE NEUROSCIENCE OF ENLIGHTENMENT (Hay House, 2011), at 61.

21 Jeena Cho, "One Contributing Factor for the High Rate of Mental Health Issues among Lawyers?" *LinkedIn*, November 7, 2022, www.linkedin.com/posts/activity-6995065784775434240-J_th?utm_source=share&utm_medium=member_desktop.

22 American Counseling Association, "Vicarious Trauma Fact Sheet #9," October 2011, https://www.counseling.org/docs/default-source/trauma-disaster/fact-sheet-9—vicarious-trauma.pdf.

23 Philip Tedeschi and Molly Anne Jenkins, TRANSFORMING TRAUMA: RESILIENCE AND HEALING THROUGH OUR CONNECTIONS WITH ANIMALS (Purdue University Press, 2019), 19.

24 Frank G. Anderson, TRANSCENDING TRAUMA: HEALING COMPLEX PTSD WITH INTERNAL FAMILY SYSTEMS THERAPY (PESI, 2021), 63–68.

25 Ibid., at 185.

26 Bessel Van Der Kolk, THE BODY KEEPS THE SCORE: BRAIN, MIND, AND BODY IN THE HEALING OF TRAUMA (Penguin, 2015), at 2–3.

27 R. I. Karpinski et al. "High Intelligence: A Risk Factor for Psychological and Physiological Overexcitabilities," 66 *Intelligence* (January–February 2018), 8, https://doi.org/10.1016/j.intell.2017.09.001.

28 Adolphs and Anderson, *supra* note 9, at 47.

29 Sam Briger and Seth Kelley (produced and edited the audio of this interview) and Bridget Bentz and Molly Seavy-Nesper (adapted the transcript for this article), "Is Your Child an Orchid or a Dandelion? Unlocking the Science of Sensitive Kids," *NPR Fresh Air*, March 4, 2019, www.npr.org/sections/health-shots/2019/03/04/699979387/is-your-child-an-orchid-or-a-dandelion-unlocking-the-science-of-sensitive-kids.

30 Francesca Lionetti, Arthur Aron, Elaine N. Aron, G. Leonard Burns, Jadzia Jagiellowicz, and Michael Pluess, "Dandelions, Tulips and Orchids: Evidence for the Existence of Low-Sensitive, Medium-Sensitive and High-Sensitive Individuals," 8 *Transl Psychiatry* (2018), article number 24, www.nature.com/articles/s41398-017-0090-6.

31 Van Der Kolk, *supra* note 26, at 21; Medina, *supra* note 13, at 178; Sapolsky, *supra* note 11, at 221; Perlmutter and Villoldo, *supra* note 20, at 61.

32 Kristin S. Lynch and Margie E. Lachman, "The Effects of Lifetime Trauma Exposure on Cognitive Functioning in Midlife," 2 *J Trauma Stress* (2020), https://onlinelibrary.wiley.com/doi/epdf/10.1002/jts.22522.

33 Hanson, *supra* note 16, at 52–60; Ratey, *supra* note 16, at 67–71; Devi, *supra* note 11, at 7, 83–86.

34 Taylor Clark, NERVE: POISE UNDER PRESSURE, SERENITY UNDER STRESS, AND THE BRAVE NEW SCIENCE OF FEAR AND COOL (Little, Brown, 2011), 81.

8 THE INFLUENCE OF SELF-MEDICATION

> Compromised cultures that include stress, adversity, or trauma can increase the likelihood of drug or alcohol use, while positive environmental factors such as parental oversight, involvement in school and social activities, and resilience skills can be protective.
>
> —Jodi Gilman[1]

It's no secret that many lawyers drink too much. The research discussed in Chapter 1 exposed the fact that half of some 11,000 American law students had been drunk within thirty days before the survey, while 43% had been binge-drinking. It revealed that 37% of these students suffered from anxiety and 17% from depression. The study of nearly 13,000 practicing lawyers in the United States uncovered the alarming statistic that drinking is a serious problem for one-fifth of them, and that within this group, 23% experienced stress, 19% had anxiety, and 28% suffered from depression. A smaller study has indicated that women were more overcommitted than men, working harder for workplace rewards, and a significantly higher number of women (55.9%) than men (46.4%) engaged in risky drinking and hazardous alcohol consumption (34.0% of women and 25.4% of men).

A raw and gripping account of the perils of a lawyer's substance misuse was written by Brian Cuban. In his soul-baring memoir *The Addicted Lawyer: Tales of the Bar, Booze, Blow, and Redemption*, Cuban bravely describes how we all feel the powerlessness of our inner child and how some of us experience mental health issues that can lead to substance abuse problems.

Cuban's story helps us comprehend the troubled substance-infused path of some lawyers, and it illuminates various reasons for the well-being crisis that the profession finds itself mired in. He exposes the experiences lawyers face while in active addiction, but then reveals the grace and gratitude of recovery. He shares the stories of many others who suffer from substance misuse disorders and provides numerous resources for those seeking help. It is an inspiring account for those who struggle with substances and those who want to understand this avenue of heartbreak more thoroughly.[2]

Another powerful lawyer biography, *Girl Walks out of a Bar: A Memoir* by Lisa F. Smith, details the misadventures of a high-functioning addict practicing law in New York. Fueled by alcohol, nicotine, and cocaine, Smith describes spending the weekend working on a business proposal for her law firm. When she attempts to leave her building to go to the office on Monday morning, she is gripped by a panic attack and decides that, after ten years of this lifestyle, she needs to get help.

After sending an email to her firm about needing a procedure for a stomach issue, Smith reflects, "I could never let them know what was happening. It wasn't just because I was ashamed, which I was, it was also because of the stigma attached to substance abuse by lawyers. If they found out, overnight I'd go from being viewed as hardworking and smart to weak, defective, and untrustworthy. This was the attitude of the entire industry."[3]

Smith began using substances as a high school student to provide an escape from feeling like she did not belong. She used alcohol and drugs to deal with self-hatred and to have periods of time where she felt happy and relaxed.[4]

As a summer associate attending a law firm's cocktail party, a partner's wife commented that it was noble of the firm to hire a law student from Rutgers, where Smith was on law review. Even a lawyer's spouse can perpetrate hierarchy-based abuse. Smith was consistently confronted with feelings that she would never feel smart enough or worthy of her accomplishments, a common symptom of imposter syndrome and a widespread feature of the lawyering culture. She also suffered from depression. After years as an associate, the competitive legal culture led Smith to leave practicing and switch to the administrative side of big law firms to ease the stress. But her drinking and drug use continued. By the end of her ten-year downward spiral, she was regularly using cocaine to fuel all-night work sessions and churn out work product. And she used alcohol to wind down. Her memoir was published when she had achieved twelve years of sobriety.[5]

THE SUMMARY

Substance use among lawyers is a common way to self-medicate stress, anxiety, and depression and to fuel overwork.

To facilitate an understanding of how substances of abuse work in the brain, it is helpful to grasp the basics of neurotransmission. Information travels through the brain via chains of neurons. This information, starting as an electrical impulse in the brain cell, travels across the gap between neurons by means of chemicals called neurotransmitters. The site of action for substances is at that gap, which is called a synapse.

Different substances cause various changes in the brain. This chapter will cover the impact of antidepressants and how various drugs of abuse influence the synapses of lawyers who use them. These drugs can be divided into substances that stimulate and can fuel overwork, and sedatives that can calm stress and anxiety. All of them impact the brain at the synapse, where communication occurs between neurotransmitters and their receptors.

THE SCIENCE

Anxious, depressed, and stressed-out lawyers may self-medicate with alcohol or other substances. Drugs work by altering the physiology of our body. Some drugs treat disorders, and some are consumed to escape sorrows of life or to produce a high. In order to recognize how drugs work in a lawyer's brain, we must have a deeper understanding of what happens at the site of action, the synapse.

Information moves through the brain, and from the brain to other parts of the body, via an electrochemical process. Recall that brain cells are shaped like trees, with dendrite branches, a long axon trunk, and axon terminal roots. Within the neuron, information is an electrical impulse. It travels from the dendrite branches of the brain cell, through the axon trunk, and out of the axon terminals. To cross the synaptic gap and reach the next brain cell, information travels via neurotransmitters, in a process called synaptic transmission, to the dendrite branches of the next neuron.

Synaptic transmission has four phases: (1) synthesis and storage of the transmitter in the presynaptic neuron, (2) transmitter release, (3) interaction of the transmitter with the receptors of the postsynaptic neuron, and (4) removal of the transmitter from the synaptic gap. Transmitters are inactivated when they are removed from the synaptic gap, either by reuptake into the presynaptic neuron, or by being broken down by enzymes.[6]

For communication to flow between brain cells, transmitters must bind to the receptors on the dendrites of the target neurons. Each transmitter can dock only in a specialized receptor on the dendrite's surface. Receptors recognize the specific molecule shapes of transmitters, or of drugs that mimic transmitters. Transmitters or drugs called agonists attach to receptors and activate them. Those that fit into and bind to receptors, but block activation, are called antagonists.[7]

Receptors respond to abnormally low levels of transmitters by increasing their receptor numbers, and this process of receptor growth is called upregulation. When receptors are persistently activated by the presence of too much transmitter, the neuron responds by reducing the number of receptors, which we call downregulation.[8]

The synapsis is the location where psychoactive drugs create their impact. Lawyers suffer from higher rates of anxiety and depression than the rest of the population. While some rely on medications, others self-medicate with drugs of abuse or food. This chapter will describe how drugs such as antidepressants, alcohol, marijuana, and others work in the lawyer's brain. Chapter 9 will cover the impact of food.

ANTIDEPRESSANTS

Depression is managed in approximately two-thirds of the people who try antidepressants.[9] Because antidepressants are known to reduce anxiety in depressed individuals, they are also being prescribed to treat anxiety unrelated to depression.

Scientists believe that depression is linked to low levels of the transmitter serotonin. All antidepressants increase the utility of serotonin or norepinephrine, or both, in the synapse. Selective serotonin reuptake inhibitors (SSRIs) block the reuptake of serotonin by the neurons that released it, making more serotonin available, and for a longer time, to stimulate the receptors on the postsynaptic neuron. It normally takes several weeks for the lawyer's brain to adapt to the new serotonin levels, but once it does, the lawyer should experience an improvement in anxiety or depression symptoms.

There are several benefits to the use of SSRIs. SSRIs escalate neurogenesis, which is the birth of new brain cells in the hippocampus. They also increase the production of brain-derived neurotropic factor (BDNF), an important protein that stimulates neurogenesis and protects brain cells and the synaptic connections between them. Finally, they prevent stress-related neuron damage and BDNF reduction. The negative side effects of SSRIs include sexual dysfunction and the withdrawal challenges of headaches, diarrhea, and aggression. All SSRIs, except Prozac, can increase suicide risk.

Monoamine oxidase A inhibitors (MAOIs) work by blocking the degradation of serotonin, norepinephrine, and dopamine in the synapse, leaving them available to activate the receptors on the postsynaptic neuron for a longer period of time. MAOIs can have serious side effects including insomnia, weight gain, and elevated blood pressure. They are known to impact all body systems; thus, some foods (certain cheeses, meats, and pickled products) and drugs (cold medications, aspirin, amphetamine, alcohol, cocaine, opioids, and barbiturates) must be avoided due to an increased risk of hypertension or stroke.[10]

SUBSTANCE MISUSE

Self-medicating with drugs of abuse involves the brain's motivation and reward system and thus impacts brain function.

Recall that reward-seeking engages both the thinking and emotional brains. Neuroscientists are in the early stages of understanding the effects of drugs of abuse and addictions, but it is widely believed that most addictive substances hijack the dopamine system and flood the brain with abnormally high levels of dopamine. This extreme activation of the dopamine system, and the intense euphoria that accompanies ingesting drugs of abuse, can become the basis of addiction. Addiction can be defined as continued use of a substance, or performance of a behavior such as gambling or shopping, despite adverse consequences.[11]

The fifth edition of the American Psychiatric Association's *Diagnostic and Statistical Manual of Mental Disorders* (DSM-5) has discontinued use of the terms addiction and addict. Instead it details substance-related disorders involving ten classes of drugs: alcohol, caffeine, cannabis, hallucinogens, inhalants, opioids, sedative-hypnotic and anxiolytic drugs, stimulants, tobacco, and other substances. These substances carry a risk of misuse because they all have the capacity to overactivate the motivation and reward system. "A substance use disorder is characterized by 'a cluster of cognitive, behavioral, and physiological symptoms indicating that the individual continues using the substance despite significant substance-related problems.'"[12]

World over, the combination of smoking, alcohol, and drug use kills 11.8 million people per year. That is more than the number who die from all types of cancer. Over 350,000 people die from overdoses each year. And 1.5 percent of the global disease burden is the result of drug and alcohol addiction.[13]

There are eleven symptom criteria involved in substance use disorder (SUD). Mild SUD is characterized by experiencing two or three symptoms; moderate SUD involves four to five symptoms; and severe SUD is marked by six or more of the following symptoms:

1. craving or strong desire to use the substance;
2. repeated use despite negative impact on home, work, or school responsibilities;
3. repeated use despite creating or exacerbating social or personal relationship problems;
4. repeated use despite interference with life activities;
5. repeated use despite negative consequences, such as legal issues;
6. repeated use in physically dangerous situations such as while driving;
7. ingesting larger amounts of a substance over time or for longer periods than intended;

8. attempts to quit or reduce use;
9. time spent drug-seeking or recovering from use;
10. tolerance; and
11. withdrawal.[14]

In *The Craving Mind*, Professor Judson Brewer describes habit learning as a habit loop that has three steps: trigger, behavior, and reward. Using this process, humans would be able to find food and remember its location for the future. Dr. Brewer argues that we have gone from utilizing this network for survival to killing ourselves with the negative habits we have developed, such as overeating, nicotine usage, and overindulgence in technology. Habit learning meant to ensure our survival has been commandeered by many harmful aspects of modern culture.[15]

ADDICTION TO OVERWORK

Of importance to lawyers is how we can become addicted to performance rewards. This starts early in school when good grades yield praise and attention from parents and teachers. We likely got labeled within the family and our community as smart. And that felt great. We wanted to keep earning good grades so we could keep that praise coming. When we were praised for high achievement, we got a hit of dopamine. Like other addictive behaviors, overwork and grind culture are the result of striving for the rewards of good grades, a high GPA, admission into a desired undergrad or law school, and eventually salary, bonuses, and partnership. The trigger is the task, the behavior is overwork, and the reward is academic achievement or upward trajectory at a law firm.[16]

Reward-seeking, using performance as our example, has six stages:

- incentive, such as a high grade or work bonus;
- desire to obtain that incentive that you believe will bring satisfaction or pleasure;
- motivation – the drive to secure the incentive;
- action – the work necessary to procure the incentive;
- pleasure when the good grade or bonus is received and enjoyed; and

- learning – the brain's wiring that grows stronger when each grade, bonus, or promotion is acquired.[17]

When any substance or behavior overactivates the reward system, the network of brain cells gets stronger, but the sense of pleasure is often reduced. Tolerance occurs when repeated exposure to the same dose of a drug, grade, praise, or bonus produces a diminished effect. Some users respond by increasing the dose. Lawyers addicted to performance rewards might respond by trying to bill more hours or secure more clients. Lawyers addicted to a substance, and experiencing tolerance, may increase the dosage or frequency of use of that substance to try and recreate their earliest high with those substances.[18]

STIMULANTS

Stimulants are substances that can help a person keep working, even when they are tired and should be resting. These stimulants include caffeine, nicotine, amphetamine, and cocaine.

Caffeine

Caffeine is a stimulant commonly consumed in coffee, tea, soft drinks, energy drinks, and chocolate. It is one of the most widely used drugs worldwide. Caffeine can improve cognitive functioning and enhance athletic performance. It is used to reduce fatigue and increase concentration, attentiveness, and energy levels.

Caffeine is anxiogenic, producing anxiety and panic attacks when taken in high doses. It can also interfere with sleep, increase nervousness, and raise blood pressure and respiration rates. Caffeine users can develop tolerance, and withdrawal symptoms include headache, lethargy, drowsiness, anxiety, depression, and cravings.

Caffeine works in the brain by blocking the action of adenosine. It is an antagonist, sitting on the receptor that would normally be occupied by adenosine. Adenosine levels increase throughout the day to make us drowsy and help us fall asleep at bedtime. By blocking the action of adenosine, caffeine helps reduce fatigue. The use of caffeine also increases dopamine, which inspires repeated use, but dopamine levels induced by caffeine are lower than those caused by cocaine or amphetamine.

There is research evidence that caffeine may reduce the risk of neurocognitive disorders such as Alzheimer's and Parkinson's diseases. The positive effects of caffeine are evident at doses from 20 to 200 mg. Doses higher than 300 mg can increase negative impacts, but up to 400 mg is considered safe for healthy adults, but not those who are pregnant.[19]

Energy drinks may boost performance, but recent research suggests they have a negative impact on our heart. Energy drinks have caused improper heartbeat and increased blood pressure in consumers. Researchers have examined the effect of seventeen different energy drinks on cardiomyocytes, the cells that make up heart muscles and that enable the heart to pump blood. The heart cells were studied in vitro, which means they were exposed to energy drinks in a culture dish. Researchers discovered that some energy drinks increased heart rate and the ingredients most suspected for this impact were theophylline, adenine, and azelate.[20]

Coffee, tea, and chocolate (especially dark chocolate) contain antioxidants, which help prevent oxidative damage. Oxidation creates free radicals that hasten aging, stimulate cancer, and rupture plaques, which can cause heart attacks and strokes. People who suffer from Alzheimer's disease show signs of oxidative stress in their brains. Antioxidants bind to and neutralize free radicals and help protect brain cells from damage.

When you feel sluggish, choose coffee, tea, or dark chocolate for beneficial antioxidants and a cognitive boost. The caffeine doses in some coffee, teas, and chocolate are:

- brewed coffee (8 oz) 95–330 mg,
- brewed decaf coffee (8 oz) 3–12 mg,
- black tea (8 oz) 40–74 mg,
- black decaf tea (8 oz) 2–5 mg,
- green tea (8 oz) 25–50 mg, and
- chocolate (8 oz) 0–6 mg.[21]

Nicotine

Nicotine is ingested from smoking or vaping and is a mild stimulant. Research shows that nicotine can improve short-term working and episodic (personal autobiographical events) memory and response time on some memory and fine motor tests.

Nicotine is an acetylcholine agonist, which means it docks in acetylcholine receptors and activates them. It also triggers the release of adrenaline, which stimulates some fight-or-flight symptoms. The result is that nicotine increases heart rate and blood pressure and constricts the blood vessels of the skin. This narrowing causes skin temperature to drop and is likely the reason the skin of smokers and vapers tends to wrinkle and age faster compared to folks who do not smoke or vape. Nicotine inhibits hunger, but it also stimulates the bowels and can have a laxative effect. It also causes the release of dopamine into the brain's reward networks, creating reinforcing effects of smoking or vaping and thus a significant risk of SUD.

Simply put, nicotine is toxic. Low-level nicotine poisoning causes dizziness, weakness, and nausea in nonsmokers or new smokers. Regular nicotine users suffer from increased blood pressure and heart rate, narrowing of blood vessels in the skin, and a decrease in oxygen-transporting capacity of the blood, often causing shortness of breath. Severe nicotine poisoning causes tremors, convulsions, and muscle paralysis, which can cause suffocation and even death.[22]

Amphetamine

Amphetamine and methamphetamine are synthetic drugs similar to a natural substance, ephedrine, found in a herb. While amphetamine has some medical applications, methamphetamine is an illegal street drug.

Amphetamine is prescribed to treat attention-deficit hyperactivity disorder (ADHD) and narcolepsy, and the most commonly known amphetamine medication is Adderall. The causes of ADHD are not well understood, nor is the action of a stimulant in creating calm and improving concentration in people with ADHD. There has been a concern that prescribing stimulants may lead to substance abuse, but research indicates that stimulant therapy for those who need it is protective against the development of SUD involving other drugs.

Methamphetamine causes more heightened effects on the nervous system compared to amphetamine. There are fewer users of methamphetamine than users of other illegal drugs such as cocaine and opioids, and fewer than 15 percent of users will become addicted to meth.

Both amphetamine and methamphetamine cause the release of three neurotransmitters: dopamine, norepinephrine, and serotonin. It is norepinephrine that is likely most responsible for activating the fight-or-flight system and causing alertness and increased heart rate. Above-normal doses are toxic, causing paranoia, hallucinations, and damage to, and the death of, dopamine neurons.[23]

Cocaine

Cocaine is an active chemical derived from the coca plant, a bush that grows in the Andes. It is used for the euphoric effect it produces, as well as to overcome fatigue. Although it has been studied for medicinal purposes, there are no current medical benefits.

Cocaine blocks the reuptake of dopamine, norepinephrine, and serotonin from the synapse, causing those neurotransmitters to activate their receptors for longer than normal. It is a complex drug because it does not impact these three transmitters in the same way. Blocking dopamine reuptake is responsible for the drug's stimulating, reinforcing, and addicting properties. Research shows that many antidepressants block the reuptake of norepinephrine or serotonin, and they neither stimulate users nor cause addictive misuse.

High doses of cocaine can cause restlessness, irritability, and paranoia. Cocaine poisoning can stimulate the fight-or-flight system so profoundly, it can progress to convulsions and cardiac arrest.[24]

SEDATIVES

Sedatives may be used by lawyers who are trying to get relief from stress, numb their anxiety, or escape their work for a few hours. These include alcohol, cannabis (marijuana), and opiates.

Alcohol

Alcohol is the second most used drug in the United States, following caffeine, but it is the most abused. It is one of the oldest and least chemically complicated drugs, yet it has the most complex impact on our nervous system. The main neurotransmitters affected by alcohol include glutamate, GABA, opioids, and dopamine, but it also influences serotonin, norepinephrine, acetylcholine, glycine, and cannabinoids. Because alcohol interacts with so many neurotransmitters, neuroscientist Judith Grisel describes it as promiscuous.[25]

Glutamate is the main activating transmitter in the brain, and GABA is the main calming transmitter. Glutamate and GABA normally work together to maintain homeostasis – the balance between brain cell activation and restraint. These transmitters are so important that the impacts of less glutamate and more GABA help explain alcohol's dramatic effects on emotion, movement, cognition, and memory. Alcohol suppresses glutamate and increases GABA, and the result is sedation, a significant suppression of neural activity and the dysfunction of several brain areas.

A blood alcohol content (BAC) of about .02 percent, which is 20 mg of alcohol per 100 ml of blood, will result in measurable behavioral effects. On average, you can metabolize about .25 ounces of alcohol per hour, but if you have more than one drink (a beer or glass of wine) every two hours, your BAC will rise. Food and water consumption will slow the absorption of alcohol, but carbonated liquids speed it up. The average BAC that produces intoxication is .08%; that triggers vomiting is .15%; that results in loss of consciousness is .35%; and that causes death is .45%.

Alcohol, like other anesthetic drugs, depresses the central nervous system. The signs of alcohol poisoning are slow breathing; loss of consciousness; cold, clammy, pale, or blue skin; and vomiting followed by loss of consciousness. A person suspected of alcohol poisoning should be monitored very carefully to determine the need for medical intervention.

Because alcohol is such a simple molecule, it enters and impacts the brain within minutes of consumption. Alcohol reduces the levels of glutamate in the brain, and it happens at a BAC as low as .03 percent. The areas impacted by glutamate reduction include the cerebral cortex, also known as the thinking brain; the amygdala, hippocampus, ventral tegmental area, and nucleus accumbens in the emotional brain; and the cerebellum in the primitive brain, which is responsible for balance.

Glutamate reduction impairs learning and memory, including long-term potentiation, which is the process wherein new information in the form of fragile memory traces becomes more stable in long-term memory, in other words, the development of expertise. Alcohol is toxic to the memory-processing hippocampus. It significantly reduces the level of glutamate in the hippocampus and hinders the generation of new hippocampal cells. Together these effects are likely responsible for alcohol's negative impact on memory.

When people consume alcohol regularly, the brain responds by upregulating its glutamate receptors. The brain grows more receptors when it experiences a consistent lack of glutamate. When a regular drinker stops drinking, glutamate toxicity can overwhelm the upregulated receptors. It is this toxicity that increases the risk of seizures when chronic users suddenly stop drinking.

Alcohol increases the release of GABA, as well as enhancing its effects. Normally a calming transmitter, the augmentation of GABA is likely responsible for decreasing anxiety, disinhibition, deficits in decision-making, sedation, and loss of coordination during intoxication.

Alcohol enhances natural opioid release, including endorphin, enkephalin, and dynorphin, plus it increases the gene expression rates of these opioid peptides. While dopamine is presumed to enhance the desire to consume drugs and increase the motivation for drug-seeking, opioid release is believed to intensify drug enjoyment and pleasure.

Like most drugs of abuse, alcohol increases dopamine in the reward pathway of the brain. Dopamine enhances the motivation to consume alcohol and reinforces repeated alcohol use. This explains why alcohol is so addictive to some people. Vulnerabilities to alcohol use disorder include family history, anxiety, and stress.

Alcohol and stress have a circular association because while alcohol seems to relieve stress for some people, it is also responsible for elevating three stress hormones: corticotropin-releasing factor (CRF), adrenocorticotropic hormone (ACTH), and glucocorticoids (cortisol). Alcohol use is a stressor that may lead to additional alcohol use. *Alcohol, the most problematic drug for stressed-out law students and lawyers, increases stress hormones.*

There is also a high comorbidity of anxiety and alcohol use disorders. When faced with fear or anxiety, the amygdala is responsible for igniting the stress response by firing up the HPA axis. It is found to be overactive in many people who suffer from generalized anxiety disorder, social anxiety, panic disorder, and PTSD. These folks experience enhanced vigilance and increased risk of alcohol use disorder.

Finally, alcohol increases dopamine transmission in the reward circuitry. Alcohol induced increases during fight-or-flight HPA Axis activation, and increased levels of cortisol from alcohol use make dopamine-mediated alcohol reinforcement even more rewarding in the lawyer's brain.[26]

Alcohol use is a contributor to global disease burden, healthcare costs, and economic losses. Based on MRI studies, prolonged heavy alcohol use, defined as three or more drinks for women and four or more drinks for men in a day, has resulted in volume reduction of the prefrontal cortex and the memory-processing hippocampus.

Researchers were interested in the impact of moderate drinking on brain structure. They examined self-report data about alcohol consumption for a year, along with brain scans at the end of the study, from 36,678 participants (40–69 years) from the UK Biobank. They found that alcohol intake reduced brain volume and structure. In the United Kingdom, consuming just one drink daily was associated with smaller brain volume, in both men and women, compared to people who did not consume alcohol every day. The study limitations included self-reported data about alcohol consumption, only one year of data, a study design that did not inquire about prior alcohol use including alcohol use disorder, and participants were all older and of European ancestry.

Daily alcohol consumption may shrink important brain structures. Replacing alcohol consumption with other ways of stress reduction can be a brain-healthy choice.[27]

Cannabis

Cannabis use is gradually becoming legal across the world, leading users to believe it is a safe substance. Of the over four hundred chemicals present in cannabis, seventy are called cannabinoids because they are unique to the cannabis plant. The most psychoactive cannabinoid is delta-9-tetrahydrocannabinol (THC). Cannabidiol (CBD) is a nonpsychoactive cannabinoid that has been tested for medical applications.

Innovations in cannabis cultivation have gradually led to much higher concentrations of THC in cannabis products. When THC is smoked as marijuana, it is rapidly absorbed into the blood and reaches the brain within a few minutes. The practice of dabbing – inhaling vapors from heating high-concentration THC resin – also results in rapid delivery of THC. Most of the THC is cleared from the brain in about thirty minutes. If THC is ingested as an edible, less than 20 percent reaches the brain and the effects take 60–90 minutes to occur. Because THC is highly fat-soluble, it is stored in fatty tissues and released from the body slowly through feces. THC can remain in the body for two to three weeks after a single dose.[28]

To better understand how THC impacts the body and the brain, scientists discovered two receptors that are activated by THC: CB1 and CB2, as well as the transmitters that naturally activate those receptors: arachidonoyl ethanolamide (AEA) and 2-arachidonoylglycerol (2-AG). The transmitters AEA and 2-AG are known as endocannabinoids because they are produced within the body. When scientists first discovered AEA, they gave it the name anandamide, derived from the Sanskrit word *ananda*, meaning that which brings inner bliss and tranquility.

CB1 receptors are present in the brain and body. They are found in large numbers in the hippocampus (memory processing and storage) and cerebellum (coordination and balance) and in smaller numbers in the cerebral cortex (executive functions), amygdala (fear processing), and hypothalamus (stress hormone signaling as part of the HPA axis). They are also found in reproductive organs, including the uterus, fallopian tubes, placenta, and testes, indicating that endocannabinoid functioning is important to reproduction and fetal development.

CB2 receptors are found in the immune system (activation of CB2 is immunosuppressive), gastrointestinal tract, and bone and fat cells. They are also found, at lower levels than CB1 receptors, in the cerebellum, brain stem (automated functions such as breathing and digestion), and glial cells (insulation for neurons).

We have a system within our brain and other parts of the body that processes the naturally occurring transmitters AEA and 2-AG at the CB1 and CB2 receptor sites. Scientists are still deciphering how these processes work. Cannabinoids that we ingest, such as THC, also activate the CB1 and CB2 receptors all over the brain and body. "Even the opioid system, which is incredibly rich and complex (and is utilized by all narcotics like heroin, OxyContin, and morphine), is nowhere near as densely and widely distributed as the endocannabinoid pathways."[29]

Lawyers and law students may be most concerned with the impact THC has on their cognitive capacity. The effects differ for those who use cannabis infrequently and those who use it chronically. Infrequent users experience slower cognitive processing, loss of concentration, and impaired short-term memory.[30]

Long-term cannabis use impairs learning and working memory well beyond the period that users experience a high.[31] Slower cognitive performance is also an impact experienced by long-term users.[32]

Research has demonstrated additional cognitive impairments, beyond the intoxication period, in learning, memory, attention, and executive function. Researchers have sought to synthesize current evidence on the immediate and residual effects of cannabis use on cognition. They reviewed ten meta-analyses (a review of reviews) that incorporated quantitative examinations of performance of cognitive tasks by over 43,000 adolescent and adult participants in the general population.

Verbal learning and memory (reading or listening and remembering what was learned) were the most impaired during and after cannabis intoxication.

Participants suffered small to moderate negative effects during and after cannabis use in:

- executive functioning (planning, reasoning),
- working memory,

- decision-making, and
- attention and processing speed (especially in heavy cannabis-using youths).

Small deficits in inhibitory processes (suppressing inappropriate responses) and flexibility were also observed.[33]

Other studies have examined the relationship between cannabis and IQ. Approximately 1,000 New Zealanders were recruited for neuropsychological testing at age thirteen prior to cannabis use and then tested again at age thirty-eight. At age thirty-eight, the amount of cannabis use and cannabis dependence were significantly associated with cognitive impairment, including lower IQ, even after controlling for education level.

A recent meta-analysis of seven studies has examined cannabis use in teenagers in the United Kingdom, the United States, Canada, and New Zealand. Eight hundred and eight teens, who started using cannabis before they were eighteen and who had used it weekly for at least six months, were compared to 5,308 nonusers of the same age. All participants took an IQ test prior to any cannabis use, and follow-up IQ testing was done in their late teens while brain development was still occurring. Cannabis users suffered a nearly 2-point IQ decline compared to nonusers in just a few years of adolescence.

Research has shown that cannabis interferes with all aspects of memory processing: encoding information, consolidation of information into long-term memory, and recall. Executive function, which includes planning, considering options, and resisting inappropriate behavior, is impaired in long-term users for two to three weeks after cessation.

A life expectancy study of 6.9 million people living in Denmark from 2000 to 2015 has shown that cannabis use disorder shortened men's lives by 15.7 years and women's lives by 12.2 years. The study also showed alcohol use disorder shortened men's lives by 14.4 years and women's lives by 13.5 years.[34]

A meta-analysis of twelve studies from the United States, the United Kingdom, the Netherlands, France, Denmark, Italy, and New Zealand has indicated that THC concentrations in cannabis products have increased by about 29 percent per year, between 1970 and 2017.

These increases have implications for the health of cannabis users because high THC levels increase the risk of mental health disorders and addiction.

THC is a partial agonist at CB1 receptors, which are concentrated in the habit (reward) and knowledge acquisition networks of brain cells, including the amygdala, hippocampus, thalamus, and cerebellum. Studies show that increasing the dose of THC is accompanied by an increase in intoxication, cognitive impairment, anxiety, and psychotic-like symptoms. Long-term impacts of using high-concentration THC products are associated with increased cannabis use and psychotic disorders.

CBD has a minimal impact on CB1 receptors, but acts on secondary receptors to inhibit the reuptake of AEA (anandamide), an endogenous endocannabinoid. CBD in doses currently available to consumers is not intoxicating, nor does it have a risk of dependency.[35]

Marijuana may be considered a fairly harmless substance, but research indicates that it activates receptors all over our brain and body. Research also reveals that cannabis use impairs cognition, lowers IQ, and shortens lifespan. Because the detrimental cognitive effects of cannabis use persist beyond intoxication, its use may lead to problems with education attainment, school and work performance, and driving. Consider limiting or eliminating cannabis use to better protect learning, memory, decision-making, planning, and reasoning.[36]

Opioids

Narcotic analgesics are the most effective painkillers currently used in medicine. Opiates are naturally occurring constituents of opium, including morphine and codeine. Opioids refer to all opiate-like drugs, including buprenorphine, codeine, fentanyl, heroin, hydromorphone (Dilaudid), Meperidine (Demerol), methadone, oxycodone, and propoxyphene (Darvon).[37]

At lower doses (5–10 mg), respiration is decreased, pain is relieved, pupils are dilated, and drowsiness is increased. Opioids also cause constipation, making them an effective remedy for diarrhea and dysentery. At higher doses, opioids can cause a sense of elation or high.[38]

Exogenous (ingested) opioids exert their action on the body by binding with the receptors designed for endogenous (produced in the body) opioids. These receptors evolved to receive endogenous opioid-like substances known as endorphins (derived from combining endogenous and morphine), endomorphins, enkephalins, dynorphins, and nociceptin. Opioid receptors are widely distributed throughout the brain and spinal cord, impacting pain, stress, mood, learning, motivation, reward, and habit formation.[39]

The brain's motivation and reward system is associated with automated habit learning and addiction. Opioid receptors in the reward system, particularly those along the dopamine pathway between the ventral tegmental area (VTA) and the thinking brain, and between the VTA and the nucleus accumbens, hippocampus, and amygdala in the emotional brain, promote greater dopamine release with opioid use and the risk of repeated use. This system is also responsible for inducing craving by enhancing the salience of people, places, and things related to opioid use. Cravings can be induced by various cues or contexts, such as stress, time of day, money, people, or music.[40]

Repeated opioid use causes tolerance, but the rates vary among people. After prolonged use, relief from pain, or the euphoric high, is not experienced from a routine dose and so higher doses are necessary. Tolerance can lead to dependence when a reduction in use causes withdrawal symptoms. Withdrawal symptoms associated with a reduction in opioid use are probably the most miserable of all drugs, including achiness, nausea, vomiting, and diarrhea. They mimic a very serious case of flu, but last much longer.[41]

Most opioid overdoses and deaths are caused by respiratory depression. Overdose is diagnosed using the opioid triad: depressed respiration, pinpoint pupils, and coma. The administration of opioid antagonist naloxone (Narcan) reverses the effects of opioids within minutes by blocking opioid receptors. If available, naloxone can save an overdose victim.[42]

The opioid abuse and overdose epidemic was fueled when doctors overprescribed opioids to patients. Opioids have become the most widely abused drugs in the United States, and more than one in five Americans take opioids with a prescription or illegally. About four out of five new heroin users are dependent upon prescription painkillers but eventually turn to street drugs that are cheaper and more easily available.[43]

People who use prescription opioids for a short period of time often choose to discontinue use due to sedation, constipation, and cognitive impairment, including difficulties with attention, concentration, memory, and executive decision-making. These effects are common in people with little to no experience using opioids. Experienced users can maintain productive work performance even under the influence of opioids.[44]

Short-term opioid use should be reserved for pain relief for a few days after surgery or injury. Opioids are the second most addictive drugs, after nicotine, and the potential for developing dependence to stave off the horrible symptoms of withdrawal is a significant risk. Rapid tolerance can create a need for higher doses, and the intensity and extent of the withdrawal period is directly proportional to the duration and dosage of the drug.[45]

HEALING OVERCONSUMPTION

In her book *Dopamine Nation*, Dr. Anna Lembke explains the pleasure–pain balance: "Without pleasure we wouldn't eat, drink, or reproduce. Without pain we wouldn't protect ourselves from injury and death. By raising our neural set point with repeated pleasures, we become endless strivers, never satisfied with what we have, always looking for more."[46]

Lembke argues that technology has allowed us to create a society with an abundance of highly rewarding substances and experiences, and we are driven to compulsive overconsumption. Our brains are saturated in dopamine because our dopamine-driven economy has created highly concentrated drugs of abuse, highly processed foods full of fat and sugar, and higher-intensity experiences such as social media and video games.[47]

Whether we are trying to minimize the pain of stress, anxiety, depression, overwork, or simply trying to feel some pleasure, overconsumption causes neuroadaptation when repeated exposure to the drug, food, or technology yields less pleasure due to tolerance, but the pain of withdrawal becomes longer and stronger. "Our hedonic (pleasure) set point changes as our capacity to experience pleasure goes down and our vulnerability to pain goes up."[48]

Flooding the brain with dopamine leads to a downregulation (decrease) of dopamine receptors. Consuming less of a substance or trying to reduce dopamine-mediated experiences leads to lower dopamine release in the brain. The hedonism of overconsumption leads to anhedonia, the inability to experience pleasure of any kind. This makes us vulnerable to a dysphoria-driven relapse, to our drug or experience of choice, in order to simply feel normal.[49]

The good news is that we can heal our brains after overconsumption or SUD. It takes discipline and time away from our drug of choice, but we can reestablish balance in our brain and restore our capacity to feel the pleasures of simple rewards.[50]

Some lawyers may not consume street drugs or nicotine. Some may enjoy alcohol only on occasion. But they might have an issue with food. What happens when we self-medicate with food? We cannot avoid food, but we may need to change our relationship with it.

NOTES

1 Jodi Gilman, "What Happens in the Brain When a Person Becomes Addicted," 57 *Judges Journal* (Winter 2018), 17.
2 Brian Cuban, THE ADDICTED LAWYER: TALES OF THE BAR, BOOZE, BLOW, AND REDEMPTION (Post Hill Press, 2017).
3 Lisa F. Smith, GIRL WALKS OUT OF A BAR: A MEMOIR (SelectBooks, 2016), chapter 1.
4 Ibid., chapter 3.
5 Ibid.
6 James H. Schwartz and Jonathan A. Javitch, "Neurotransmitters," in E. R. Kandel, J. H. Schwartz, T. M. Jessell, S. A. Siegelbaum, A. J. Hudspeth, and S. Mack (eds.), PRINCIPLES OF NEURAL SCIENCE (McGraw Hill, 2014), 289.
7 Jerrold S. Meyer and Linda F. Quenzer, PSYCHOPHARMACOLOGY: DRUGS, THE BRAIN, AND BEHAVIOR (3rd ed., Oxford University Press, 2019), at 30.
8 Ibid., at 30.
9 Barry J. Gibb, THE ROUGH GUIDE TO THE BRAIN (2nd ed., Rough Guides, 2012), 187; Meyer and Quenzer, *supra* note 7, at 621.
10 Carl L. Hart and Charles J. Ksir, DRUGS, SOCIETY & HUMAN BEHAVIOR (17th ed., McGraw Hill, 2018), 170–174; Stephanie D. Hancock and

William A. McKim, Drugs and Behavior: An Introduction to Behavioral Pharmacology (8th ed., Pearson, 2018), at 299–306; Meyer and Quenzer, *supra* note 7, at 621–625.

11 Judson Brewer, The Craving Mind: From Cigarettes to Smart Phones to Love – Why We Get Hooked and How We Can Break Bad Habits (Yale University Press, 2018), 18–19.

12 Meyer and Quenzer, *supra* note 7, at 271.

13 Hannah Ritchie and Max Roser, "Cocaine, Cannabis and Other Illicit Drugs," *Our World in Data*, December 2019, https://ourworldindata.org/illicit-drug-use.

14 Hancock and McKim, *supra* note 10, at 86; Robert H. Lustig, The Hacking of the American Mind: The Science behind the Corporate Takeover of Our Bodies and Brains (Avery, 2017), at 77–78.

15 Brewer, *supra* note 11, at xxv, 3–5, 40.

16 Ibid., at 65–66.

17 Meyer and Quenzer, *supra* note 7, at 291; Purves et al., Principles of Cognitive Neuroscience (Sinauer Associates, 2008), 472.

18 Hart and Ksir, *supra* note 10, at 29–30.

19 Hancock and McKim, *supra* note 10, at 204–210; Meyer and Quenzer, *supra* note 7, at 456–462.

20 Microscope Master, "Cardiomyocytes: Structure, Function, and Histology," www.microscopemaster.com/cardiomyocytes.html#:~:text=Definition%3A%20What%20are%20Cardiomyocytes%3F,of%20blood%20around%20the%20body; Yu-Syuan Luo et al., "Relationships between Constituents of Energy Drinks and Beating Parameters in Human Induced Pluripotent Stem Cell (iPSC)-Derived Cardiomyocytes," 149 *Food Chem Toxicol* (2021), www.sciencedirect.com/science/article/abs/pii/S0278691521000132.

21 Meyer and Quenzer, *supra* note 7, at 456; Debra S. Austin, "Food for Thought: The Neuroscience of Nutrition to Fuel Cognitive Performance," 95 *Or L Rev* (2017), 425, at 458–460, 490–492, https://papers.ssrn.com/sol3/papers.cfm?abstract_id=2808100.

22 Hancock annd McKim, *supra* note 10, at 175–176, 180–183; Hart and Ksir, *supra* note 10, at 235–237.

23 Hancock and McKim, *supra* note 10, at 216–217; Hart and Ksir, *supra* note 10, at 131–140; Meyer and Quenzer, *supra* note 7, at 412–418.

24 Hart and Ksir, *supra* note 10, at 121–129; Meyer and Quenzer, *supra* note 7, at 395.

25 Judith Grisel, Never Enough: The Neuroscience and Experience of Addiction (Random House, 2019), 91.

26 Ibid., at 87–98; Hancock and McKim, *supra* note 10, at 126–127; Hart and Ksir, *supra* note 10, at 195–199, 205–207; Meyer and Quenzer, *supra* note 7, at 308–309, 315–319, 325–335, 338–340.

27 Remi Daviet et al., "Associations between Alcohol Consumption and Gray and White Matter Volumes in the UK Biobank," 13 *Nat Commun* (2022), 1175, www.nature.com/articles/s41467-022-28735-5.

28 Hart and Ksir, *supra* note 10, at 338–339; Meyer and Quenzer, *supra* note 7, at 468–472.

29 Hancock and McKim, *supra* note 10, at 319–321; Hart and Ksir, *supra* note 10, at 339–340; Meyer and Quenzer, *supra* note 7, at 472–475; Grisel, *supra* note 25, quote at 54–55.

30 Hart and Ksir, *supra* note 10, at 342–343; Meyer and Quenzer, *supra* note 7, at 476.

31 Hancock and McKim, *supra* note 10, at 329.

32 Hart and Ksir, *supra* note 10, at 342–343.

33 Laura Dellazizzo et al., "Evidence on the Acute and Residual Neurocognitive Effects of Cannabis Use in Adolescents and Adults: A Systematic Meta-Review of Meta-Analyses," 117 *Addiction* (2021), 1, https://onlinelibrary.wiley.com/doi/epdf/10.1111/add.15764.

34 Emmet Power et al., "Intelligence Quotient Decline Following Frequent or Dependent Cannabis Use in Youth: A Systematic Review and Meta-Analysis of Longitudinal Studies," 51 *Psychol Med* (2021), 1, www.cambridge.org/core/journals/psychological-medicine/article/intelligence-quotient-decline-following-frequent-or-dependent-cannabis-use-in-youth-a-systematic-review-and-metaanalysis-of-longitudinal-studies/26BEC9CBD2A39010C26100278F8CA813; Nanna Weye et al., "Association of Specific Mental Disorders with Premature Mortality in the Danish Population Using Alternative Measurement Methods," 3 *JAMA Netw Open* (2020), data in table 3, https://jamanetwork.com/journals/jamanetworkopen/fullarticle/2766668.

35 Tom P. Freeman et al., "Changes in Delta-9-tetrahydrocannabinol (THC) and Cannabidiol (CBD) Concentrations in Cannabis over Time: Systematic Review and Meta-analysis," 116 *Addiction* (2021), 1000.

36 Power et al., *supra* note 34, Weye et al., *supra* note 34.

37 Hancock and McKim, *supra* note 10, at 245, 247; Meyer and Quenzer, *supra* note 7, at 352, 354.

38 Meyer and Quenzer, *supra* note 7, at 354, 356.

39 Ibid., at 255–257.

40 Ibid., at 259; Grisel, *supra* note 25, at 74.

41 Hart and Ksir, *supra* note 10, at 305; Hancock and McKim, *supra* note 10, at 259; Meyer and Quenzer, *supra* note 7, at 355.

42 Hart and Ksir, *supra* note 10, at 305.

43 Hancock and McKim, *supra* note 10, at 258; Grisel, *supra* note 25, at 64–65.

44 Hancock and McKim, *supra* note 10, at 263.

45 Grisel, *supra* note 25, at 64, 76–77.

46 Anna Lembke, Dopamine Nation: Finding Balance in the Age of Indulgence (Dutton, 2021), 67.

47 Ibid., at 1–2, 20–23.
48 Ibid., at 53–54.
49 Ibid., at 55–57.
50 Ibid., at 57–58.

9 THE IMPORTANCE OF FUEL

> Our brains are a reflection of what we put into our bodies, and one of the most important ways that we influence them is the quality of what we eat.
>
> —Austin Perlmutter[1]

> If it came from a plant, eat it; if it was made in a plant, don't.
>
> —Michael Pollan[2]

Food, a hot-button topic. We all have to eat, and what we eat has been established by numerous cultural forces. When we begin to view food as fuel for our brain, we may have to confront our dietary eating patterns in order to enhance brain health and mental strength.

Nutrition is defined as "the process of providing or obtaining the food necessary for health and growth," or "the science that links food to health and disease." The online *Merriam-Webster Dictionary* defines the term *diet* as (1) food and drink that is habitually consumed, or (2) a regimen of eating and drinking sparingly in order to reduce one's weight.[3]

This book, and all the nutrition research summarized here, uses the term diet to describe dietary eating patterns. This chapter is not about deprivation or weight loss. Nutrition research summarized here is largely devoted to lowering the risks of dementia and Alzheimer's disease, and it examines the impact of various diets on brain and mental health. The focus of this chapter is on the forms of nutrition or dietary practices that support optimal brain health and mental strength.

THE SUMMARY

> We both know food is the catalyst that unlocks our brains, binds our families, and determines our futures.
>
> —Bonnie Garmus[4]

The average American eats 156 pounds of sugar a year in candy, desserts, and soda and hidden in processed foods like yogurt, peanut butter, and energy drinks, which food manufacturers add to make their products intentionally addictive. Processed foods make up about 70 percent of the Western diet. They have a bliss point, which is the combination of sugar, fat, and salt, designed by food scientists to make food irresistible. Food companies process food products with a specific goal of creating insatiable overconsumption.[5]

The consumption of hyperpalatable foods, often ultra-processed foods (UPFs), can lead to self-medication with food and compromised brain health. Chapter 6 detailed the motivation and reward system in our brain that can lead to our habits, including the overconsumption of unhealthy food. Chapter 8 described self-medication with substances of abuse, and food can be one of those substances.

This chapter covers the critical neurodestructive conditions that are impacted by our diet; argues that UPFs and comfort foods with high concentrations of sugar and fat are bad for the brain, are highly addictive, and are targets for self-medication; and concludes with foods to avoid and foods to consume to optimize brain health and mental strength.

THE SCIENCE

NEURODESTRUCTIVE CONDITIONS

Aging

Aging is marked by increased frailty and risk of disease and death. Aging impacts our cells, organs, and bodily systems.[6] Over time, aging is caused by damage to our cells, genes, and DNA.[7]

Cognition integrates complex mental processes such as consciousness, attention, knowledge acquisition, memory, and intelligence. These processes depend on synaptic transmission between brain cells. Normal aging causes a decrease in the speed of synaptic signaling, which results in declines in learning and memory. Cognitive deficits are likely caused by age-related reduction in the volume of brain structures (prefrontal cortex, hippocampus, and cerebellum), decrease in the number of synapses between neurons, and compromised integrity of white matter.[8]

Mild Cognitive Impairment, Dementia, and Alzheimer's Disease

With aging comes the risk of cognitive problems ranging from mild cognitive impairment to dementia and finally Alzheimer's disease. A person with *mild cognitive impairment* experiences a small amount of cognitive loss, such as a slight decline in recall that does not interfere with daily activities, and an increased risk of dementia.

Dementia involves a marked and irreversible cognitive decline that is severe enough to undermine daily life, which includes weakened executive function, attention, concentration, and memory. Executive functions include information processing, decision-making, and initiating movement. They rely on a distributed network of brain regions in the thinking brain and the emotional brain, including the hippocampus and amygdala. Autobiographical memory decline is associated with hippocampal deterioration. Approximately 55 million people suffer from dementia worldwide, and the World Health Organization expects that number to increase to 78 million by 2030.

The most common cause of dementia, for nearly 70 percent of elderly patients, is *Alzheimer's disease.* Alzheimer's is known for two key features in the brain: increased amyloid plaque deposits and neurofibrillary tangles. These brain insults, associated with increased inflammation and oxidative stress, cause neurodegeneration. Cognitive decline can be experienced for over a decade prior to an Alzheimer's diagnosis, highlighting the long and slow progression of the disease. Imaging studies show a loss of brain cells in the basal forebrain and hippocampus of Alzheimer patients.[9]

Inflammation

Inflammation is the body's normal response to infection and injury. Our immune system rushes to fight the germs or heal the wound, frequently including swelling in the area. Inflammation often increases with age, and chronic inflammation, when the immune response is activated routinely, can fuel the aging process. Low-grade chronic inflammation is associated with heart disease, cancer, diabetes, autoimmune diseases, depression, and cognitive decline.[10]

Factors that contribute to inflammation include poor nutrition, lack of exercise, stress, sleep deprivation, vitamin D deficiency, smoking, and being overweight. Dietary stressors that increase inflammation include refined sugars, fructose, refined carbohydrates, gluten, polyunsaturated oils (canola, corn, peanut, safflower, sunflower, soybean, vegetable), and alcohol.[11]

Reducing inflammation has been correlated with memory improvements. Consider taking the following steps to reduce inflammation: manage stress; limit sugar and refined carbohydrates; eat a variety of vegetables and fruit, which are rich in antioxidants; consume omega-3 fatty acids; and exercise regularly.[12]

Oxidative Stress

Alzheimer's disease involves both inflammation and oxidation, but researchers do not know whether these conditions are a cause or an effect. One theory of brain aging is that the brain suffers from a progressive inability to prevent inflammation and oxidative stress.[13]

Oxidation is the process in which atoms and molecules lose electrons as they touch other's atoms and molecules. Car rust and the browning of cut fruit are examples of oxidation. Oxidation is beneficial when it facilitates absorbing energy from food, or transforming harmful substances into water-soluble waste that is eliminated during urination.[14]

Excess oxidation creates free radicals that hasten aging, stimulate cancer, and rupture plaques that can cause heart attack and stroke. Extensive metabolic activity and production of free radicals occur in the brain. The brain is highly susceptible to oxidative stress due to its high metabolic load and rate of oxygen consumption. When excess oxidation leads to more free radicals than there are antioxidants to neutralize them, this causes oxidative stress.[15]

The generation of free radicals is a normal part of human metabolism, but surplus free radicals lead to interference in neuron functioning, disruption of signaling, and brain cell death. A meta-analysis of research on the presence of oxidative stress in psychiatric disorders has concluded that most of those disorders are associated with increased levels of oxidation. Anxiety, depression, and dementia are associated with inflammation and oxidative stress.[16]

High-protein diets may promote free radical production. Plants produce free radicals during photosynthesis, but they also contain antioxidants, which bind to and neutralize free radicals. When we eat plants, they are protective against free radicals, while beneficial oxidation is left unaffected. Antioxidants help protect the brain cells from free radical damage. The following nutrients have been shown to reduce oxidative stress and improve cognitive performance: vitamin C, vitamin E, DHA, beta-carotene, and selenium. Animals that were fed antioxidants showed superior memory and learning capacity.[17]

Blood Sugar, Insulin Resistance, and Glycation

Glucose is found in table sugar, honey, maple syrup, agave, cane juice, corn syrup, fructose, sucrose, wheat, corn, rice, and potatoes.

All carbohydrates are broken down into glucose, which is the substance tested for blood sugar. Glucose is the energy source for brain cells, and insulin helps unlock the cells so glucose can enter. Insulin's purpose is to transport sugar out of the blood and into the fat and muscle cells.

An ideal meal allows blood sugar and insulin to rise and recede gradually. The consumption of simple sugars causes a spike in blood sugar and a flood of insulin. Excess insulin triggers the use of glucose for energy, rather than burning fat, which makes weight control very challenging. Eating simple sugars routinely creates a demand for more insulin to normalize blood sugar, and eventually the body becomes insulin-resistant, which can evolve into diabetes. Insulin ensures that the blood in a human body, about five liters, contains only a single teaspoon of sugar at a time.

Type-2 diabetes is often associated with cognitive impairment, and a study of 50 to 90-year-olds has found that both insulin-dependent and noninsulin-dependent diabetics scored lower on cognitive tests of intellectual ability and verbal memory compared to control participants. Early detection of diabetes risk and effective diabetes treatment may prevent or delay such cognitive decline.

The consumption of high-sugar snacks and meals results in short-term attention and memory problems in healthy adults and children. Rats exposed to long-term high-sugar diets exhibited learning and memory deficits. A consistent intake of high-sugar foods maintains high blood glucose levels and increases the risk of glycation.

Glycation is a normal progression where glucose bonds with protein to form glucose–protein molecules called advanced glycation end products (AGEs). Glycation in cooking, called the Maillard reaction, occurs when a crust develops on bread or when meat is seared.

AGEs are resistant to the body's restorative processes, and their formation is irreversible. They are toxins and are strongly associated with aging, inflammation, and oxidative stress. They are responsible for joint stiffness, kidney problems, cataracts, plaque buildup and hardening of arteries, and compromised brain cells and neuron connections. In Alzheimer patients, there are triple the number of AGEs than in normal brains, which are accumulated in amyloid plaques and neurofibrillary tangles.

Elevated blood sugar creates more AGEs, accelerating aging. Foods that create the largest spike in blood sugar (sugar, honey, maple syrup, agave, cane juice, corn syrup, fructose, sucrose, wheat, corn, rice, and potatoes) and processed foods (candy, desserts, soda, yogurt, peanut butter, and energy drinks) trigger the greatest AGE formation. Foods that contain the highest levels of *preformed* AGEs are meat and cheese; cured meats (e.g., bacon, sausage, pepperoni, and hot dogs) and meats cooked at high temperatures (frying or broiling) represent the highest risk.

Reducing AGE exposure can promote better health and longevity, especially since glycation is irreversible for currently glycated blood cells. The HbA1c (also known as A1c) test evaluates AGE formation by determining the glycation rate, the rate at which glucose bonded to red blood cells for the prior two to three months.

A person who limits the intake of carbs will have 4.0–4.8 percent of all hemoglobin glycated, expressed in the A1c test result in the range of 4.0–4.8. Normal A1c range is 5.0–6.4, and the diabetes threshold is 6.5, although some diabetics have 8–12 percent glycated hemoglobin.

About 70% of Americans have A1c levels between 5.0 and 6.9, and for every 1% A1c increase, there is a 28% increased risk of mortality. Because red blood cells have a lifespan of about three months, it is possible to lower your A1c levels by reducing your intake of sugar and refined carbs. To lower blood sugar, consider reducing the consumption of foods that spike blood sugar. Decreasing the consumption of high-glycemic-index carbs (containing sugars and high-fructose corn syrup [HFCS]) and preformed AGEs (cured meats, cheese, and meats cooked at high temperatures) will help stave off rising glycation A1c numbers.

While all carbs can raise blood sugar, wheat products skyrocket blood sugar to near diabetic levels. Wheat constitutes about 20 percent of all calories consumed worldwide and is second only to corn in planted farmland. Fifty years of genetic engineering has increased wheat crop yield and created new gluten proteins. Hybridization of wheat has produced a *supercarb* made up of 75 percent amylopectin A, the most digestible form of amylopectin, giving wheat bread the power to raise blood glucose more than table sugar. The startling consequence of modern engineered wheat is that wheat products can raise blood sugar higher than nearly every other carbohydrate. The consumption of wheat products triggers high insulin levels, greater fat deposits, inflammation, and a hunger cycle that features fatigue and mental fog when blood sugar drops.

Wheat products also raise blood sugar and increase the production of AGEs. Giving up wheat could be very challenging for some people because wheat polypeptides (also called exorphins) bind to opiate receptors in the brain. In research animals, naloxone, the drug that knocks opiates off their receptors and blocks their action (stopping an overdose of opioids), also prevented the effects of wheat-derived exorphins. In humans, naloxone reduces food craving, appetite, and calorie consumption. This is because wheat products are addictive.

Finally, added sugar, often in the form of HFCS, is guaranteed to spike blood sugar and increase AGE production. Fructose travels quickly from the blood to your liver and induces lipogenesis, which is fat creation. The stress on the liver creates inflammation, and once it is filled with fat, the excess fat enters the bloodstream as triglycerides.

While glucose provides immediate fuel, fructose is stored as fat and glycogen in the liver, which can be used as fuel in the future. Fructose activates a survival mechanism that prepares the body for a period of scarcity of food, which in turn causes thirst, hunger, craving, fat accumulation, and increased body weight, blood pressure, and insulin resistance. In animals, this process helps them survive hibernation and long-distance migration.

In humans, the fructose survival pathway is ignited when we consume HFCS-based foods (candy, soda, juice, baked goods, ice cream, condiments, and fast food) that are high sugar and salt, some umami foods (processed red meat, organ meats, shellfish, and beer), and alcohol. Stress also engages the fructose survival pathway when the fight-or-flight response causes glucose to be converted to fructose to provide the body with immediate energy to deal with a challenge. The engagement of the fructose survival pathway, either from stress or from eating unhealthy foods, causes a craving for foods that keep it activated.

Although the brain represents only 2% of our body mass, it consumes 20% of our energy that is consumed in calories. Of this 20% of calories, 70–80% is utilized by our brain cells.

Researchers theorize that the overactivation of the fructose survival pathway leads to the degradation and death of brain cells, which are features of Alzheimer's disease. Research has shown that foods high in sugar and salt, processed meats, and alcohol increase the risk of developing Alzheimer's, and people with Alzheimer's have higher levels of fructose in their brains.

Most foods in the Western diet could initiate our fructose survival pathway, and the chronic stress of our school and work environments also engages this system. When this pathway is activated, we experience hunger and craving. Routine engagement of the fructose survival pathway causes fat accumulation and increased body weight, blood pressure, and insulin resistance.

Consuming foods high in sugar and salt, processed meats, and alcohol creates a vicious cycle of craving for more of those foods.

Stress also increases our desire to consume these types of foods. These foods increase our risk of developing Alzheimer's disease.

When facing the task of reducing highly palatable foods, you may want to substitute them with vegetables and fruit. Whole fruit does not activate the fructose survival pathway because:

- it contains relatively low fructose content;
- it also contains neutralizing factors such as fiber, flavanols, potassium, and vitamin C; and
- the small intestine metabolizes some of this fructose before it reaches the liver and brain.

Besides minimizing stress, a diet rich in vegetables, whole fruit, and lean protein minimizes the risk of Alzheimer's. If you can muster the willpower to limit the foods that engage the fructose survival pathway, your cravings for these foods should subside over time.

Controlling AGE formation is also important because high levels of AGEs lead to greater inflammation and oxidative stress, aging, degradation of brain cells and synaptic connections, and Alzheimer's disease.[18]

Cardiovascular Disease

The two most serious brain diseases are Alzheimer's and stroke. Cardiovascular disease, including heart disease and stroke, is caused by inadequate blood supply to the heart and brain. When blood flow to the heart is disrupted, the result is often a heart attack. When blood flow to the brain is interrupted for a sufficient period of time, a stroke occurs, and part of the brain dies. It is normal for blood clots to form and break down in blood vessels, but a combination of normal clotting and plaque buildup in the arteries can cause obstructions that limit blood supply to the heart or brain.

Consequences of a major stroke can include paralysis, loss of speaking skills, and death. Silent strokes involving short-term blood clots can multiply and slowly reduce cognitive capacity until dementia develops.

High-fiber diets from whole plant-based foods reduce the risk of stroke by helping to control cholesterol, blood pressure, and blood sugar. Plant-based food enhances potassium and antioxidant intake.

Antioxidants are protective against stroke because they prevent the circulation of oxidized fat in the blood that can damage the small blood vessels in the brain. They also lower blood pressure, reduce inflammation, and prevent the formation of blood clots.[19]

Malfunctioning Gut Microbiome

The gut microbiome is the ecosystem of the GI tract. An adult body has approximately 100 trillion bacteria, and 95 percent of them reside in the gut. These bacterial cells outnumber our human cells by a ratio of 10 to 1, and they weigh 2–3 pounds.

The large intestine, or colon, is home to most of the bacteria in the microbiome. Its responsibilities include digestion of food; the production of critical neurotransmitters, vitamins, amino acids, and fatty acids; and support for a healthy immune system.

Information is carried between the digestive system and the brain via the vagus nerve. The microbiome is key to the development of the transmitters GABA and serotonin. A malfunctioning microbiome can cause cravings, sleep problems, stress dysregulation, and an increased risk of anxiety, depression, and dementia. Longevity may also be impacted. Research has demonstrated that people who consume a diet high in fiber and low in animal fat, over their lifespan, have the healthiest microbiomes, while those who consume diets low in fiber and high in animal fat have weakened microbiomes.

Fiber supports brain health by assisting the microbiome in the production of short-chain fatty acids. The most frequently studied is butyrate. Eat more fiber to create more butyrate, which reduces inflammation and increases the production of BDNF, the antiaging fertilizer for brain cells in the hippocampus. One study has followed 1,600 adults for a decade, and those who consumed the most fiber were 80 percent more likely to be free of depression, diabetes, dementia, and disability than those who consumed the least fiber. Fiber consumption has established healthy aging more than any other variable studied, including the intake of sugar.

A healthy microbiome requires both prebiotic and probiotic foods. Prebiotic foods contain a carbohydrate called oligosaccharide, which, since it cannot be digested by the small intestine, travels to the large intestine where it feeds the bacteria. Prebiotics include artichokes, arugula, asparagus, avocado, bananas, bell peppers, berries, broccoli, garlic, leafy greens, leeks, jicama, kale, onions, spinach, and sprouts. Probiotic foods contain live bacteria that help replenish the healthy bacteria in the microbiome. Probiotics are found in fermented foods such as yogurt, kefir, kimchi, and kombucha, and in brine-pickled vegetables such as sauerkraut, cabbage, and beets.[20]

FOODS THAT IMPAIR BRAIN HEALTH

Foods that are bad for the brain tend to be calorie-dense and nutrient-deficient. The main foods to avoid are processed foods, simple sugars and carbs, and unhealthy oils.

Processed Food

Much of the packaged food at the grocery store is UPFs. Research has demonstrated that the greater the consumption of UPFs, the higher the rates of anxiety and depression. High UPF consumption is also associated with cognitive decline and the reduction of memory, reasoning, and problem-solving.[21]

The NOVA classification system was developed by Brazilian researchers to describe the degree to which food has been processed, altering it from its natural form.

Group 1 is unprocessed foods (unaltered food obtained directly from plants or animals) or minimally processed foods (submitted to processes such as cleaning, removal of inedible parts, drying, cooling, freezing, fermentation, or pasteurization, but no salt, sugar, oil, fat, or other substances are added). Examples include:

- whole fruit and vegetables;
- chilled or frozen fruit and vegetables;
- dried fruit;
- fruit or vegetable juice with no added sugar or substances;
- fresh and dried mushrooms, herbs, and spices;
- nuts and seeds without salt or sugar;
- beans and lentils;

- grains: oats, rice, wheatberry;
- grits, flakes, and flour from corn, wheat, or oats;
- pasta, couscous, and polenta;
- eggs;
- fresh, chilled, or frozen meat, poultry, fish, and seafood in steak or fillet form;
- fresh or pasteurized milk or yogurt without added sugar; and
- coffee, tea, and spring or mineral water.

Group 2 is oils, fats, salt, and sugar. Examples include:

- oils from seeds, nuts, and fruits, such as olive, corn, soybean, or sunflower;
- sugar, molasses, honey, and maple syrup;
- butter, lard, or coconut fat;
- starches from corn or other plants; and
- salt.

Group 3 is processed foods, which contain added salt, sugar, oils, or other substances. Examples include:

- canned or bottled fruit, vegetables, and beans;
- salted or sugared nuts and seeds;
- canned, dried, or smoked meat and fish;
- freshly made bread and cheese; and
- fermented alcoholic beverages, such as beer and wine.

Group 4 is UPFs, which incorporate ingredients that are rarely used in home cooking, such as HFCS, sweeteners, hydrogenated oils, artificial flavors, and preservatives, and rely on only a small portion of group 1 foods. Examples include:

- chocolate, candy, ice cream, cookies, pastries, and cakes;
- salty snack foods;
- breakfast cereals and bars;
- carbonated soft drinks, energy and sport drinks;
- flavored yogurt and milk;
- sweetened juice;
- margarine and spreads;
- packaged bread and buns;

- packaged meat, fish, burgers, hot dogs, nuggets, pizza, and pasta; and
- distilled alcoholic beverages, such as gin, rum, vodka, and whiskey.[22]

A diet high in processed foods impairs cognitive function, likely by increasing inflammation. Processed food also contributes to weight gain and the development of chronic diseases. It contains high levels of refined carbohydrates, saturated fats, and minimal fiber. Research has shown that processed foods can harm the brains and impair the cognitive function of rodents, primates, and humans.

Researchers fed groups of young and aging rats a processed food diet for twenty-eight days. The older rats suffered from memory problems and increased inflammation gene expression in the memory-processing hippocampus and the panic button amygdala. The younger rats did not suffer from these problems. A third group of rats was fed the processed food diet along with an omega-3 DHA supplement. The supplement prevented memory deficits and improved inflammatory gene expression in older rats.

To protect brain health, strive to eat more whole fruits and vegetables and minimize processed foods. An omega-3 DHA supplement could improve memory and inflammation harm that processed food can cause.[23]

Sugar

There are simple and refined carbs that provide quick energy and spike blood sugar, and there are complex carbs that require more time in digestion for their nutrients to be absorbed and that provide slow-released energy.

Our bodies rely on both sugar and fat for energy, but our brains use glucose to function twenty-four hours a day. Simple sugars, such as honey or maple syrup, and refined carbs, such as pasta, soda, candy, and bake goods, are not healthy sources of glucose for our brain. In his book *Genius Foods*, Max Lugavere provides a list of foods he describes as "uniquely designed to screw up your brain," including bagels, biscuits, cake, cereal and granola, chips, milk and white chocolate, cookies, crackers, doughnuts, energy and granola bars, fries, ice cream and frozen yogurt, jams and jellies, pancakes, pasta, pastries, pie, pretzels, pizza, and white bread.

The brain works best when supplied with complex carbs that contain sufficient fiber, which break down slower and don't spike blood sugar. These include vegetables such as carrots, squash, and sweet potatoes with skin; cruciferous vegetables such as Brussels sprouts and cabbage; fruit such as berries and citrus; dark leafy greens; beans; and whole grains.[24]

In recent research, scientists were interested in the impact of dietary sugar intake on the hippocampus, a brain structure involved in emotion response and memory. Prior research has shown that people under stress often consume high-sugar and high-fat foods as a coping strategy.

Much neuroscience research has been conducted on rodents because their brains are so anatomically similar to the human brain. Recent research has examined the impact at the gene level in the hippocampus of rats that were stressed and fed a high-sugar diet. Exposure to early-life stress reduces the expression of hippocampal genes that are important for stress regulation and decreases the birth of new brain cells. This study showed that a high-sugar diet produced a similar deficit in gene expression, leading researchers to believe that high-sugar diets may produce mental health issues in humans of similar magnitude as those that emerge as a result of early-life adversity. Another rat study showed that the consumption of a high-sugar diet early in life had a negative impact on memory tasks.

Finally, a human study where participants consumed either a high-sugar/high-fat yogurt snack or a low-sugar/low-fat yogurt snack, in addition to their normal diet for eight weeks, has demonstrated that processed food that is high in fat and sugar rewires the brain in the same way that drugs of abuse do. This rewiring process inspires repeat behavior – the increased consumption of highly palatable, energy-dense food.

To summarize, the consumption of foods that are high in sugar:

- rewires the brain to prefer and consume high-sugar food;
- has a negative impact on hippocampus functioning, and a healthy hippocampus is important for memory and learning; and
- may also contribute to mental health challenges.[25]

Fat

Saturated fats are in solid form at room temperature and found mostly in meat, cheese, and butter. Chemically they are made up of a chain of carbons that is fully covered, or saturated, with hydrogen. Polyunsaturated fats are not fully covered with hydrogen and are mostly derived from plant oil, including canola, corn, grapeseed, peanut, safflower, soybean, sunflower, and vegetable oils. Monounsaturated fats are even less covered with hydrogen and found in olive oil, avocados, nuts, and seeds. Finally, trans-fats are created in an industrial process called hydrogenation, where hydrogen is added to vegetable oil, making them saturated. When you see "partially hydrogenated" on a food label, that is a trans-fat. Trans-fats are mostly found in processed foods.

Saturated fats can cause inflammation and reduce oxygen flow to the brain. Consuming large amounts of saturated fat can increase the risk of heart disease, type-2 diabetes, and dementia. Limiting meat and dairy consumption will limit the amount of saturated fat in your diet.

Consuming trans-fat is associated with an increased risk of brain shrinkage, dementia, and cognitive problems. Trans-fats are commonly found in processed foods such as cakes, cookies, crackers, coffee creamers, doughnuts, frozen pizzas, margarines, and nut butters.

Polyunsaturated fats are vulnerable to oxidation, which creates free radicals in the body, especially the brain. Excess oxidation creates inflammation and increases the risk of memory loss and Alzheimer's disease. These fats are hidden in all types of processed foods and make up 8–10 percent of the typical Western diet.

Digging a little deeper into fats, the body requires omega-3 and omega-6 fatty acids for immune function. Omega-6s are necessary to launch an inflammatory response to protect us from injuries and disease. Omega-3s work to quiet this response when no longer necessary. The problem with the Western diet is that our intake of omega-6s and omega-3s is out of balance. We ingest too many omega-6s and too few omega-3s.

Sources of omega-6s include meat and polyunsaturated oils such as corn, sunflower, sesame, and peanut oil. Sources of omega-3s include wild cold-water fish such as salmon and sardines, walnuts, and flaxseed. Omega-3s support brain health by increasing BDNF, which helps in the generation of new brain cells and protection of existing hippocampal cells. Adequate BDNF enhances mood, memory, and executive functions, and lowers the risk of Alzheimer's disease.

The bottom line on fat is that sources of brain-healthy fats include olive oil, avocado, salmon, sardines, herring, caviar, walnuts, hemp seeds, flax seeds, and chia seeds. Fat sources to limit include vegetable oils, meat, dairy, and processed foods. Processed foods are particularly unhealthy because they combine sugar, refine carbs, and fat, all low in nutrients and high in hyperpalatable appeal and designed to promote overconsumption.[26]

FOODS THAT OPTIMIZE BRAIN HEALTH

The topic of nutrition, what is brain-healthy and what is not, may be supercharged for most people. We consume food for our entire lives, in patterns established by our families, social gatherings, economic conditions, residential locations, and preferences.

This chapter makes the argument that making nutritional changes to optimize brain health and mental strength is a research-backed investment in reducing inflammation, oxidative stress, glycation, and harm to the gut microbiome, which in turn will decrease the risk of cognitive decline, dementia, and Alzheimer's disease. It can slow down aging and increase longevity as well.

Nutrient scarcity causes inflammation, and research links inflammation to accelerated brain aging and impaired cognitive function. Nutrient-deficient foods include sugar, refined carbs, unhealthy oils (canola, corn, peanut, safflower, sunflower, soybean, vegetable), trans-fat (hydrogenated oils), and processed foods that combine these industrially refined ingredients.[27]

Nutrient-rich, high-fiber fuel is the goal to support optimal brain health. Specific traditional diets that have been shown to result in longevity, good general health, and durable brain health in their populations include:

- **the Mediterranean diet** (**MedDiet**): vegetables, fruits, beans, nuts, whole grains, wild fish, and olive oil;

- **the Okinawan diet**: vegetables (including purple sweet potato and seaweed), fresh fish, fruit, soy (tofu and natto), brown rice, green tea, shitake mushrooms, ginger, and garlic; and
- **the antioxidant diet** focuses on the inclusion of the most powerful antioxidants (vitamins C and E and beta-carotene) found in asparagus, berries, Brazil nuts, citrus, dark-colored beans, extra-virgin olive oil, peppers, spinach, and walnuts; and the phytonutrients carotenoids (carrots, sweet potatoes), anthocyanins (cherries), and the master antioxidant glutathione (asparagus, avocado, broccoli, cabbage, cauliflower, garlic, onions, and spinach).[28]

To create a better balance between omega-3s and omega-6s, reduce meat and choose brain-healthy fats including olive oil, avocado, salmon, sardines, herring, caviar, walnuts, hemp seeds, flax seeds, and chia seeds.

To minimize the risks of inflammation, oxidative stress, glycation, gut microbiome malfunction, cognitive decline, dementia, and Alzheimer's disease, reduce processed foods and increase the intake of a diverse selection of vegetables and fruits.

FOODS THAT REDUCE ANXIETY AND DEPRESSION

Anxiety

Research has shown a link between malfunctioning gut microbiome and anxiety. There is also a connection between the microbiome and the amygdala panic button that launches the fight-or-flight response system as well as an exaggerated HPA axis stress response. People with anxiety disorder have fewer and less diverse gut bacteria than people without.

A typical Western diet can exacerbate anxiety. Research indicates that people with anxiety should avoid or limit high-fat and high-carb foods, gluten, artificial sweeteners, caffeine, and alcohol.

Foods that can calm anxiety include those that improve the microbiome (almonds, apples, apple cider vinegar, artichokes, bananas, beans, berries, broccoli, brown rice, Brussels sprouts, carrots, kombucha, miso, pears, pickled vegetables, tempeh, walnuts, and yogurt), foods rich in omega-3s (fatty fish, such as herring, mackerel, tuna, salmon, and sardines, and walnuts), foods with tryptophan (turkey, chickpeas), and vitamins D, B1, B6, A, C, and E.[29]

Depression

It will come as no surprise that depression is also linked to a weakened gut microbiome. Research shows that people suffering from depression experience a reduction in beneficial bacteria and an elevation in harmful bacteria causing inflammation. In a study of fifty-five healthy adults, those who took a daily probiotic supplement reported less depression and had lower levels of the stress hormone cortisol in their urine compared to participants who received a placebo.

Multiple studies have revealed that the more sugar you consume, the more likely you are to have depression. Processed foods, loaded with sugar and refined carbs, lead to inflammation in the brain and a reduction in BDNF, the protein that builds and protects neurons. Fried foods, unhealthy oils, and nitrates are also linked to depression. Foods to avoid include baked goods, candy, soda, white bread, white rice, pasta, potatoes, French fries, fried chicken, fried seafood, trans-fat, unhealthy oils, bacon, salami, and other cured meats.

To reset the microbiome, add both probiotics (yogurt with active cultures and fermented food such as miso, tempeh, natto, sauerkraut, kefir, kimchi, kombucha, or a supplement) and prebiotics (asparagus, bananas, beans, berries, leeks, garlic, and onions).

Other foods that relieve depression include foods rich in omega-3s (fatty fish, such as herring, mackerel, tuna, salmon, and sardines, and walnuts); healthy fats (olive oil, avocados, nuts, and nut butters); and vitamins B, A, and C.[30]

FOOD AND LONGEVITY

Understanding the health potential of food can enable people to increase their life expectancy. One diet that has been subjected to the most research is the MedDiet.

Researchers have examined data from the UK Biobank, an ongoing prospective cohort study with health data from over half a million adults, aged 40–60, between 2006 and 2010. They limited the data to 60,298 participants who were over the age of sixty and who identified as white British or Irish citizens.

A diet questionnaire that collects information on 206 types of food and thirty-two types of drinks was completed five times per participant between April 2009 and June 2012. Researchers scored the MedDiet using two different scoring instruments and assessed dementia risk using hospital records and death registries.

Participants with the highest MedDiet adherence had a 23 percent lower risk of developing dementia compared to those with the lowest MedDiet adherence.

Another study has examined data from 581 participants, average age of eighty-four years at the time of assessment, who agreed to donate their brains upon death to a study of Alzheimer's disease risk. Researchers assessed the number of amyloid plaques and tau tangles, which are known to be increased in patients with Alzheimer's.

Researchers compared the MedDiet to the MIND diet. For the MedDiet, they analyzed the consumption of fruit, vegetables, whole grains, beans, olive oil, fish, and potatoes. Participants lost points if they consumed red meat, poultry, or full-fat dairy. For the MIND Diet, researchers analyzed the consumption of green leafy vegetables, other vegetables, nuts, berries, beans, whole grains, fish, poultry, olive oil, and wine. Participants lost points if they consumed red meat, butter and margarine, cheese, sweets and pastries, fried foods, and fast foods.

Researchers divided the participants into three groups and compared the highest one-third and lowest one-third adherence to either the MedDiet or the MIND diet, eliminating the middle third. After adjusting for age at death, gender, education, calorie intake, and Alzheimer's disease gene risk, they found:

- People in the top one-third of consumption of the MedDiet had average brain plaque and tangle amounts, similar to being eighteen years younger than the one-third who had the lowest adherence to the MedDiet.
- People in the top one-third of consumption of the MIND diet had average brain plaque and tangle amounts, similar to being twelve years younger than the one-third who had the lowest adherence to the MIND Diet.

- People who ate the most green leafy vegetables, seven or more servings a week, had brain plaque amounts similar to being nineteen years younger than those who ate the fewest leafy green vegetables.[31]

Researchers have reviewed data from the 2019 Global Burden of Disease study to compare the typical Western diet to an optimal diet. The optimal diet had substantially higher intake than a typical Western diet, of fruit, vegetables, fish, beans, whole grains, and nuts while reducing red and processed meats, sugar-sweetened beverages, and refined grains.

Researchers have found that a sustained change away from the Western diet to adopt the optimal diet would increase life expectancy:

- for twenty-year-olds, by 10.7 years for women and 13 years for men;
- for sixty-year-olds, by 8 years for women and 8.8 years for men;
- for eighty-year-olds, by 3.4 years.[32]

SIMPLE WAYS TO START MAKING BRAIN-HEALTHY NUTRITION CHANGES

Foods that are likely to lower your risk of dementia and Alzheimer's disease include green leafy vegetables, other vegetables, fruit, beans, whole grains (except wheat), fish, olive oil, nuts, and seeds. Foods that are likely to increase the risk of dementia and Alzheimer's disease are sugar, refined carbs, red and processed meats, unhealthy oils (canola, corn, peanut, safflower, sunflower, soybean, vegetable), trans-fat (hydrogenated oils), and processed foods that combine sugar and fat.

Here are some simple ways to start improving your brain fuel:

1. To improve your gut microbiome:
   a. Eat a big salad every day. Use a base of dark leafy greens (chard, kale, Romaine lettuce, or spinach). Include a variety of different colored vegetables and fruits (red cabbage, beets, red or yellow peppers, cucumbers, onions, tomatoes, carrots). Include healthy fats (avocado, salmon, tuna). Dress with olive oil and vinegar.
   b. Add both probiotics (yogurt with active cultures and fermented food such as miso, tempeh, natto, sauerkraut, kefir, kimchi,

kombucha, or a supplement) and prebiotics (asparagus, bananas, beans, berries, leeks, garlic, and onions) daily.

2. To improve your omega-6 and omega-3 balance, periodically replace meat with:
   a. fatty fish, such as herring, mackerel, tuna, salmon, and sardines, and walnuts; or
   b. plant protein, such as beans and rice, vegetables and nuts, or quinoa.
3. To increase antioxidant intake, snack on raw vegetables, fruit, and nuts. Drink coffee and tea, including decaffeinated products. Sweeten with stevia.
4. To reduce cravings, slash sugar and bad fat consumption. Reduce processed foods in favor of fresh fruit, vegetables, and nuts.
5. To minimize oxidative stress,
   a. replace unhealthy oils (canola, corn, peanut, safflower, sunflower, soybean, vegetable) with healthy fats (olive oil, avocados, nuts, and nut butters); and
   b. eliminate trans-fat.

NOTES

1 Kells McPhillips, "The 'Big 3' Nutrients Known to Boost Your Mood, According to an Internal Medicine Physician," *Well and Good*, September 1, 2022, www.wellandgood.com/mood-boosting-nutrients.

2 Jane E. Brody, "Rules Worth Following, for Everyone's Sake," *New York Times*, February 1, 2010, www.nytimes.com/2010/02/02/health/02brod.html.

3 "Nutrition," *Oxford English Dictionary* (2nd ed., Oxford University Press, 1989); Anne M. Smith and Angela L. Collene, WARDLAW'S CONTEMPORARY NUTRITION (10th ed., McGraw Hill, 2016), 8; "Diet," *Merriam-Webster Dictionary*, www.merriam-webster.com/dictionary/diet#:~:text=%3A%20food%20and%20drink%20regularly%20provided,%3A%20habitual%20nourishment.

4 Bonnie Garmus, LESSONS IN CHEMISTRY (Doubleday, 2022) chapter 2; Stephy George, "31 Lessons in Chemistry Quotes: Inspiring & Motivating," *The Creative Muggle*, May 8, 2023, www.thecreativemuggle.com/lessons-in-chemistry-quotes.

5 John Casey, "Diet Sabotage: How Much Sugar Are You Eating?" *Medicine Net*, www.medicinenet.com/script/main/art.asp?articlekey=56589; Deane

Alban, "How to Stop Sugar Cravings (+8-Step Plan to Stop Eating Sugar)," *Be Brain Fit*, December 16, 2003, https://bebrainfit.com/sugar-cravings; Max Lugavere, GENIUS FOODS (Harper, 2018), 14.

6 Andrew Steele, AGELESS: THE NEW SCIENCE OF GETTING OLDER WITHOUT GETTING OLD (Doubleday, 2020), 2–3.

7 David A. Sinclair, LIFESPAN: WHY WE AGE – AND WHY WE DON'T HAVE TO (Atria Books, 2019), 17–19.

8 Valentina A. Andreeva and Emmanuelle Kesse-Guyot, "Nutrition and Cognition in the Context of Ageing: Role of Dietary Patterns," and Edwin D. Lephart, "Polyphenols and Cognitive Function," in NUTRITION FOR BRAIN HEALTH AND COGNITIVE PERFORMANCE (Tabitha Best and Louise Dye, eds.; CRC Press, 2015), 14, 145.

9 Tabitha Best and Louise Dye, "Good News Story: Nutrition for Brain Health," in NUTRITION FOR BRAIN HEALTH AND COGNITIVE PERFORMANCE (Tabitha Best and Louise Dye, eds.; CRC Press, 2015); Dale Purves et al., PRINCIPLES OF COGNITIVE NEUROSCIENCE (2nd ed., Oxford University Press, 2012), 326; Andrea C. Gore, "Neuroendocrine Systems," in FUNDAMENTAL NEUROSCIENCE (Larry Squires et al., eds., 4th ed.; Academic Press, 2013), 429, 431, 434–435; Edwin D. Lephart, "Polyphenols and Cognitive Function," in NUTRITION FOR BRAIN HEALTH AND COGNITIVE PERFORMANCE (Tabitha Best and Louise Dye, eds.; CRC Press, 2015), 144–145; Andreeva and Kesse-Guyot, *supra* note 8, at 14–15; World Health Organization, "A Blueprint for Dementia Research," October 4, 2022, www.who.int/publications/i/item/9789240058248.

10 Steele, *supra* note 6, at 92–93; Andreeva and Kesse-Guyot, *supra* note 8, at 26.

11 Leslie Korn, NUTRITION ESSENTIALS FOR MENTAL HEALTH: A COMPLETE GUIDE TO THE FOOD-MOOD CONNECTION (W.W. Norton, 2016), 3; Lugavere, *supra* note 5, at 36–37, 78, 108–109, 195.

12 Andreeva and Kesse-Guyot, *supra* note 8, at 26; Korn, *supra* note 11, at 3–4; Adrian L. Lopresti, "Contribution of Diet and Exercise in the Pathogenesis of Major Depression," in DIET AND EXERCISE IN COGNITIVE FUNCTION AND NEUROLOGICAL DISEASES (Akhlaq A. Farooqui and Tahira Farooqui, eds., Wiley-Blackwell, 2015), 96–97, 99.

13 Ruth Leyse-Wallace, NUTRITION AND MENTAL HEALTH (CRC Press, 2013), 89; Andreeva and Kesse-Guyot, *supra* note 8, at 30.

14 T. Colin Campbell and Thomas M. Campbell II, THE CHINA STUDY: THE MOST COMPREHENSIVE STUDY OF NUTRITION EVER CONDUCTED AND THE STARTLING IMPLICATIONS FOR DIET, WEIGHT LOSS AND LONG-TERM HEALTH (BenBella Books, 2004), 9 (hereinafter The China Study).

15 Ibid., at 9; Leyse-Wallace, *supra* note 1, at 89; Andreeva and Kesse-Guyot, *supra* note 8, at 27; Korn, *supra* note 11, at 217.

16 Leyse-Wallace, *supra* note 13, at 89, 190–191; Korn, *supra* note 11, at 217.

17 The China Study, *supra* note 14, at 9–10; Leyse-Wallace, *supra* note 13, at 89; Andreeva and Kesse-Guyot, *supra* note 285, at 27.

18 Tasneem Bhatia, What Doctors Eat: Tips, Recipes, and the Ultimate Eating Plan for Lasting Weight Loss and Perfect Health (Rodale Books, 2013), 18–19; Leyse-Wallace, *supra* note 13, at 87; Steele, *supra* note 6, at 82–83; William Davis, Wheat Belly: Lose the Wheat, Lose the Weight, and Find Your Path Back to Health (Rodale Books, 2011), 13–14, 18, 25, 31–36, 48–51, 133–142; Brant Cortright, The Neurogenesis Diet and Lifestyle: Upgrade Your Brain, Upgrade Your Life (Psyche Media, 2015), 87, 89; Akhlaq A. Farooqui and Tahira Farooqui, "Neurochemical Effects of Western Diet Consumption on Human Brain," in Diet and Exercise in Cognitive Function and Neurological Diseases (Farooqui and Farooqui, eds.; Wiley-Blackwell, 2015), 20; Lugavere, *supra* note 5, at 66–78; Richard J. Johnson et al., "Could Alzheimer's Disease Be a Maladaptation of an Evolutionary Survival Pathway Mediated by Intracerebral Fructose and Uric Acid Metabolism?" 117 *Am J Clin Nutr* (2023), 455; Jillian Kubala, "12 Common Foods with High Fructose Corn Syrup," *Healthline*, August 30, 2021, www.healthline.com/nutrition/foods-with-high-fructose-corn-syrup; Cleveland Clinic, "A1C: What It Is, Test, Levels & Chart," November 22, 2022, https://my.clevelandclinic.org/health/diagnostics/9731-a1c.

19 Michael Greger, How Not To Die (Flatiron Books, 2015), 42–50; Smith and Collene, *supra* note 3, 189–190.

20 Lisa Mosconi, Brain Food: How to Eat Smart and Sharpen Your Mind (Penguin, 2018), 117–124, 202; Korn, *supra* note 11, at 29, 48, 51–52; Lugavere, *supra* note 5, at 185.

21 Sally Wadyka, "The Link between Highly Processed Foods and Brain Health," *New York Times*, May 4, 2023, www.nytimes.com/2023/05/04/well/eat/ultraprocessed-food-mental-health.html.

22 Center for Epidemiological Studies in Health and Nutrition, "The NOVA Food Classification System," *ECU Physicians*, https://ecuphysicians.ecu.edu/wp-content/pv-uploads/sites/78/2021/07/NOVA-Classification-Reference-Sheet.pdf.

23 Michael J. Butler et al., "Dietary DHA Prevents Cognitive Impairment and Inflammatory Gene Expression in Aged Male Rats Fed a Diet Enriched with Refined Carbohydrates," 98 *Brain Behav Immun* (2021), 198, www.sciencedirect.com/science/article/abs/pii/S0889159121005043?via%3Dihub.

24 Lugavere, *supra* note 5, at 33–51; Mosconi, *supra* note 20, at 81–87, 92.

25 A. Maniam et al., "Sugar Consumption Produces Effects Similar to Early Life Stress Exposure on Hippocampal Markers of Neurogenesis and Stress Response," *Front Mol Neurosci* (2016), https://doi.org/10.3389/fnmol.2015

.00086; E. Noble et al., "Gut Microbial Taxa Elevated by Dietary Sugar Disrupt Memory Function," 11 *Transl Psychiatry* (2021), 94; Sharmili Edwin Thanarahah et al., "Habitual Daily Intake of a Sweet and Fatty Snack Modulates Reward Processing in Humans," 35 *Cell Metab* (2023), 584.

26 Lugavere, *supra* note 5, at 76; Mosconi, *supra* note 20, at 50–65.

27 Lugavere, *supra* note 5, at 65.

28 Mosconi, *supra* note 20, at 133, 135, 141–142.

29 Uma Naidoo, THIS IS YOUR BRAIN ON FOOD (Little, Brown Spark, 2020), 57–80.

30 Ibid., at 29–56.

31 Oliver M. Shannon et al., "Mediterranean Diet Adherence Is Associated with Lower Dementia Risk, Independent of Genetic Disposition: Findings from the UK Biobank Prospective Cohort Study," 21 *BMC Med* (2023), 81; Natalie Conrad, "MIND and Mediterranean Diets Associated with Fewer Alzheimer's Plaques and Tangles," *Science Daily*, March 8, 2023, www.sciencedaily.com/releases/2023/03/230308201051.htm#:~:text=People%20who%20eat%20diets%20rich,according%20to%20a%20new%20study.

32 Lars T. Fadness et al., "Estimating Impact of Food Choices on Life Expectancy: A Modeling Study," 19 *PLOS Med* (2022), e1003962, https://journals.plos.org/plosmedicine/article?id=10.1371/journal.pmed.1003889.

10 OPTIMIZING BRAIN HEALTH

> How we spend our days is of course how we spend our lives. What we do with this hour and that one is what we are doing.
>
> —Anne Dillard[1]

> A year from now you may wish you had started today.
>
> —Karen Lamb[2]

Well-being is a journey, not a quick fix. Research indicates that undertaking a plan to upgrade brain health can optimize cognitive capacity and improve resilience to impairment caused by stress and aging. The core activities for brain health upgrade are exercise, adequate sleep, and suitable and sufficient respite.[3]

THE SUMMARY

> Your brain is the most modifiable part of your whole body, and you can rewire your brain by how you use it every single day.
>
> —Sandra Bond Chapman[4]

Innovative organizations promote wellness to provide vibrant workplaces and support thriving employees. Research shows that perks such as onsite gyms and health-focused food, work–life balance and stress management programs, and mindfulness training improve the bottom line.

The aim of the ancient Greek achievement culture was to assist every male citizen in achieving the human ideal, and Greek society fostered this environment with robust public education, mentoring, and an emphasis on the journey rather than the outcome. This environment also featured a deep undercurrent of respect, concern, and admiration for all participants.

Neuroscience and psychology research supports the creation of neuro-intelligent cultures. Neuro-intelligent cultures provide brain-boosting benefits, acknowledge humanity and dignity in each individual, and promote environments for cognitive enrichment. Leaders in neuro-intelligent cultures make cognitive well-being a priority, reaping benefit at both individual and institutional levels.

Embracing the neuroscience of cognitive wellness is critical to protecting brain function and enhancing cognitive performance. We need not wait for institutional change to empower a neuro-intelligent culture and alleviate the impact a stressful environment has on an individual's cognitive capacity.

You can make cognitive fitness a priority by engaging in the practices recommended in this chapter. This will require subordinating other activities in favor of exercise, more sleep, and time spent recharging from the demands of work or school. Substituting beneficial brain habits for less healthy activities, such as cocktail hour or watching television, could provide the time needed to optimize cognitive performance. Neuroplasticity, the most promising of human features, allows every brain to become what is demanded of it.[5]

THE SCIENCE

EXERCISE

> We are what we repeatedly do. Excellence, then, is not an act, but a habit.
>
> —Will Durant[6]

Building Brain Health

Overworked lawyers make sacrifices to meet billable hour requirements, client needs, and court deadlines. Law students are no different. They may prefer to exercise daily but abandon their commitment under the strain of considerable reading and writing assignments, especially during their first year of law school. It is wrong to eliminate exercise if one wants optimal brain health.

Research has shown that exercise provides cognitive restoration in people of all ages, from children to the elderly. Getting at least thirty minutes of aerobic exercise two or three times per week, plus some strength training, provides cognitive benefits. In rodent studies, scientists have found that neurogenesis results in 5,000–10,000 new neurons in rat hippocampi every day. Rats that spent time on a running wheel generated twice as many new brain cells as those that were sedentary.

A school district in a suburb of Chicago has been testing the academic benefits of aerobic exercise since the early 1990s. Naperville District 203 has turned 19,000 students into some of the fittest and smartest in the United States with a fitness-oriented physical education (PE) program where students are assessed based on time spent with an increased heart rate.

The most compelling data is from the 1999 Trends in International Mathematics and Science Study (TIMSS), designed to compare the science and math knowledge of students from different countries. Typically, about half the students from Asian countries, but only 7 percent of American students, scored in the top tier. However, approximately 97 percent of the Naperville eighth graders took the test. On science they scored first, just ahead of Singapore. On math, they scored sixth, behind Singapore, Korea, Taiwan, Hong Kong, and Japan. All US students combined ranked eighteenth in science and nineteenth in math.

The Naperville program has influenced others through PE4life, an organization that trains PE educators about the link between fitness and academic performance. Since 2000, the standardized test scores of Titusville, PA, students have improved from below state average to 17% above the average in reading and 18% above the average in math. In 2001, the California Department of Education found that "fit kids scored twice as well on academic tests as their unfit peers." In 2004, a multidisciplinary panel of researchers reviewing over 850 studies on the impact of physical activity on schoolchildren confirmed the academic benefits demonstrated by the California study and showed that exercise has a positive influence on memory and concentration.[7]

Exercise benefits the brain in three ways: it enhances blood and oxygen flow, elevates the levels of key neurotransmitters, and stimulates the production of brain cell building blocks, especially brain-derived neurotropic factor (BDNF).

Exercise prompts blood vessels to produce nitric oxide, which in turn improves blood flow deeper into body tissues. The more exercise, the greater the benefits provided by the bloodstream, which include the distribution of nutrients and elimination of waste. The entire body will benefit from the improved functioning rendered by increased blood flow. Exercise increases blood volume in the dentate gyrus, a layer of the hippocampus. Increased blood flow also helps to maintain the health and functioning of the memory-processing hippocampus.

Three powerful neurotransmitters are increased and rebalanced by exercise: dopamine, serotonin, and norepinephrine. In addition, exercise stimulates endorphins.

Dopamine increases reward and satisfaction and influences learning. It inspires motivation and repeat behaviors that help us reproduce and survive, including having sex, eating food, and maintaining fitness. Less active people do not garner the same benefits from dopamine as regular exercisers because dopamine levels increase only while we are active and dopamine receptors are less vigorous in sedentary people.

Serotonin influences mood, sleep, impulsivity, and anger. While elevated levels of serotonin are associated with well-being and controlling impulsiveness, low levels of serotonin are associated with anxiety, depression, and impulsivity. Low serotonin levels in sedentary people make it harder for them to get motivated to exercise.

Norepinephrine amplifies the brain signals that activate attention, motivation, and perception. Endorphins are the body's natural opioids that increase pleasure and reduce pain. They help the body tolerate the exertion of physical activity. Although the effects of endorphins can last for hours, it takes about twenty minutes of vigorous exercise before they are produced, making them available only to people who can work out longer than that.

Exercise not only elevates these important neurotransmitters but also restores their delicate balance in the brain. Another brain benefit of exercise is its unique capacity to increase the production of BDNF.[8]

Exercise creates new brain cells and stimulates the production of BDNF. Aging occurs when the brain loses more brain cells than it can create. BDNF is a protein that acts like a fertilizer for hippocampal brain cells. It helps create new neurons, protect existing neurons, and encourage synapse formation, which is the connection between neurons that is vital for thinking and learning. The gene that turns on BDNF production is activated by exercise, intellectual stimulation, curcumin, and the omega-3 fatty acid docosahexaenoic acid (DHA). DHA is responsible for aiding synaptic connection, regulating inflammation, and enhancing gene expression of BDNF.

Lab rats that voluntarily choose to spend time on a running wheel produce significantly more BDNF than sedentary rats. Researchers have shown a direct relationship between elevated levels of BDNF in exercising rats and their improved ability to learn more effectively compared to sedentary rats.

An examination of the impact of exercise on human cognition showed results similar to rodent studies. In a study, elderly individuals who exercised twenty minutes per day for twenty-four weeks showed an 1,800 percent improvement in attention, language ability, and memory compared to the control group. In a larger study, elderly women who exercised lowered their risk of cognitive impairment by about 20 percent.

BDNF stimulates neurogenesis and neuroplasticity and hence protects neurons from trauma and environmental toxins. Learning requires the affinity between neurons to be strengthened through repeated activation. The presence of BDNF at the synapse enhances long-term potentiation, the process that consolidates memories and builds expertise. In 2007, German researchers discovered that people learned new vocabulary 20 percent faster after exercise than before and that the rate of learning correlated directly with their BDNF levels.

Three other hormones work closely with BDNF to build and maintain brain cell circuitry: IGF-1 (insulin-like growth factor), VEGF (vascular endothelial growth factor), and FGF-2 (fibroblast growth factor). Exercise helps BDNF to increase its uptake of IGF-1, which in turn activates the production of glutamate and stimulates the growth of new BDNF receptors, which support long-term memory formation. VEGF develops capillaries in the body and brain, and FGF-2 aids tissue growth and long-term potentiation.

Aging, stress, and depression cause a drop in the three growth factors and BDNF, but exercising increases them and enhances neurogenesis at the same time. Regular exercise will encourage the production of BDNF and other important growth factors, increase the generation of new neurons, and provide a powerful brain boost.[9]

Protecting the Brain against Aging

Exercise has shown a protective effect against cognitive decline, dementia, and Alzheimer's disease. A recent study has demonstrated that active older adults have bigger brains than inactive folks, helping to explain how being active defends against cognitive deterioration.

Researchers divided 1,557 multiethnic participants, whose average age was seventy-five, into three groups and collected information on leisure time physical activity along with MRI scan findings. When comparing the brain volume of the most active third to that of the least active third, the active group had larger brains. The active participants also had brains that were three to four years younger, based on their size. Active participants enjoyed walking, gardening, swimming, and dancing.

A 2011 meta-analysis of 1,603 articles on the relationship between cognition and exercise has found that exercise prevented cognitive decline and healed cognitive impairment. Exercisers had larger hippocampus volumes, the structure where memories are processed and stored, and greater synaptic connections, the links between brain cells that are vital for thinking and memory.

A mice study suggests that aerobic exercise, in the form of voluntary wheel running, caused older muscle cells to operate like younger cells and recover faster from injury. Exercise had a rejuvenating impact on old cells. The effects lasted a week after the mice stopped running, indicating that regular exercise provides antiaging benefits. In addition to preventing age-related diseases, exercise can also improve tissue function in humans.

Telomeres are nucleoprotein caps at the ends of chromosomes. Aging causes a gradual degradation and shortening of telomeres.

Chronic stress can prematurely shorten our telomeres. When telomeres get too short, cells can no longer divide, leaving us vulnerable to disease. Telomere length is also regarded as a marker of biological age.

Researchers have examined the relationship between physical activity and telomere length. DNA data from 5,823 American adult participants of the National Health and Nutrition Examination Survey were compared across four groups: high activity, moderate activity, low activity, and sedentary. The longer telomeres discovered in active adults revealed reduced cell aging. The high activity group had a biological aging advantage, showing their cells were:

- 9 years younger than the sedentary group;
- 8.8 years younger than the low activity group; and
- 7.1 years younger than the moderate activity group.[10]

Improving Mental Health

Mental health disorders have a substantial impact on individuals, society, and global health burdens. The pandemic significantly increased the incidence of mental health issues among the population.

Exercise improves physical and mental health by:

- providing distraction and a different focus for the mind;
- reducing muscle tension;
- building brain resources by increasing BDNF, growth factors, serotonin, norepinephrine, and GABA;
- improving resilience through self-mastery by preventing anxiety, panic attacks, and depression; and
- rerouting the fight-or-flight neural circuitry by teaching the brain to associate increased heart rate and breathing – physical sensations common during anxiety and exercise – with something positive.

To synthesize evidence on the impact of exercise on anxiety, depression, and psychological distress in adults, researchers have reviewed ninety-seven studies involving 128,119 participants experiencing good health, chronic diseases, and mental health conditions.

The review confirms that physical activity improved symptoms of anxiety, depression, and distress in all populations. The greatest benefits were seen in healthy people; people with depression, kidney disease, and HIV; and pregnant and postpartum people. All forms of physical activity, including aerobic exercise, resistance training, mixed aerobic and resistance exercise, and yoga, were beneficial. Higher-intensity exercise was associated with greater improvements in disease symptoms.

To better understand *how* exercise improves depression symptoms, a different review examined the impacts of exercise on depression. Studies involved moderate to vigorous aerobic exercise, such as running or cycling, for 30–60 minutes one to three times per week and reported impacts on:

- Neuroplasticity: Depression is associated with reductions in brain volume, especially the cerebrum (thinking brain) and the hippocampus (associated with memory, emotion processing, and stress regulation); decreases in blood flow throughout the brain; and low levels of BDNF. However, exercise can increase cerebrum and hippocampus volumes, improve blood flow throughout the brain, and increase BDNF levels.
- Stress hormones: Prolonged exposure to stress hormones can reduce the generation of new brain cells, decrease BDNF circulation, and increase hippocampal cell death. Exercise can reduce the stress hormone cortisol and increase BDNF levels, which are beneficial for brain health.
- Inflammation: Depression is associated with chronic increased low-level inflammation. Exercise can reduce numerous inflammatory factors, creating a lasting anti-inflammatory environment.
- Oxidative stress: Oxidative stress can cause damage to DNA, proteins, lipids, and eventually cell death. Our brain is particularly vulnerable to oxidative stress because it has a high metabolic rate and low antioxidant levels. Exercise can reduce oxidative stress and increase the availability of antioxidants.
- Psychological factors: Exercise can improve self-esteem, enhance socialization and social support, and increase self-efficacy.[11]

You may be wondering how intense a workout must be to benefit mental health. Researchers assigned fifty-five university students (71 percent female) to three groups: high-intensity interval training, moderate continuous training, and no exercise for six weeks during the academic term. The interval and continuous training consisted of cycling for twenty-seven minutes three times per week. College students are at a higher risk of perceived stress due to continuous exposure to high-stakes assessments across an academic term. The study measured changes in perceived stress, depression, and inflammation.

The no-exercise group reported higher levels of perceived stress and depression symptoms than the exercise groups at the end of six weeks. Their inflammation markers were elevated. These results show evidence of rapid declines in mental and physical health for stressed university students.

The moderate-intensity continuous cycling training group had lower inflammation markers and fewer depression symptoms than the no-exercise group. The high-intensity interval training group had fewer depression symptoms than the no-exercise group, but had higher perceived stress and inflammation markers than the moderate training group. Researchers hypothesized that high-intensity training may exacerbate response to psychological stressors, which increases stress and anxiety because both stress and exercise activate the fight-or-flight stress response, increasing heart and respiration rates and cognitive vigilance.

This research indicates the optimal exercise intensity for people under persistent stress is moderate continuous intensity. Moderate-intensity exercise promotes both mental health by decreasing depression symptoms and physical health by reducing inflammation markers in the body.[12]

Exercise improves resilience from trauma. Traumatic experiences keep the brain on high alert. Chronic activation of the fight-or-flight response creates pathways of brain cells that promote hypervigilance. Unresolved trauma can keep stress arousal stuck in high gear.

Exercise can help rewire the trauma-induced neural pathways. Neurochemicals, such as BDNF and irisin, decrease with aging and exposure to stress. However, exercise helps to maintain higher BDNF and irisin levels, protecting the neurons from damage caused by stress and trauma. In addition, it helps to:

- increase brain volume in areas associated with learning, memory, and cognitive function, via the growth of new brain cells (neurogenesis);

- improve the health and functioning of brain cells, including the capacity for forming neural networks, which likely explains why exercise improves cognitive function;
- raise antioxidant levels in the brain, thus preventing oxidative stress; and
- restore stress arousal to a resilient level and improve mood and brain function, thus better preparing the brain for processing traumatic events and healing its neural networks.[13]

Physical activity improves mood, stress resilience, and brain health by:

- reducing symptoms of anxiety, depression, and stress;
- increasing neurotropic factors, including BDNF;
- regulating the fight-or-flight response;
- reducing inflammation and oxidative stress; and
- improving self-esteem, self-efficacy, and social support.

Becoming Enamored with Exercise

Despite its numerous brain and mental health benefits, it can be challenging to commit to a regular exercise plan. It is even more difficult for sedentary people to start exercising and keep it going until the benefits become apparent.

Exercise changes your brain to make it more susceptible to social connection and more capable of experiencing joy. Exercise increases the number of endocannabinoid receptors in our brain's reward system, and so we become more receptive to all pleasurable experiences. With more endocannabinoids comes greater enjoyment in life.

With every passing decade, we lose about 13 percent of our dopamine receptors in our reward system. This contributes to lesser enjoyment of everyday pleasures. However, exercise can prevent this decline. Compared to inactive older adults, active folks have reward systems more akin to those of much younger people.

In her book *The Joy of Movement*, Kelly McGonigal explains how exercise leverages the brain's reward system. "Regular exposure to exercise will over time teach the brain to like, want, and need it." During exercise, the brain releases many of the same neurotransmitters and other neurochemicals as when we take drugs of abuse such as dopamine, endorphins, and endocannabinoids. However, getting hooked on exercise takes at least six weeks. While drugs of abuse hijack the reward system, exercise gradually trains the reward system to enjoy physical activity. This may explain why exercise is strongly linked to happiness and a reduced risk of depression.[14]

Exercise is the most powerful activity lawyers can undertake to enhance and protect their brain function. The investment in getting hooked on exercise will optimize your brain, empower cognitive fitness, help you enjoy life more, and make it easier to sleep.

SLEEP

Sleep supports recovery and the lawyer brain needs sufficient time to recover. Sleep is a highly active metabolic process in which cells and tissues are repaired and regenerated, energy levels are restored, and brain structure is optimized. Learning, memory, creativity, and problem-solving are all processes that improve with adequate sleep, which averages between 7.5–8 hours each night. Lawyers who shortchange their sleep are at greater risk of obesity and developing diseases that involve chronic inflammation, such as asthma, arthritis, cancer, cardiovascular disease, type-2 diabetes, and depression.

Scientists have discovered that sleep deprivation can cause or speed up dementia and Alzheimer's disease because it is during sleep that the brain washes away the waste – amyloid beta – in patients who suffer from these neurodegenerative diseases.

It is during sleep that the brain develops new neurons and the connections between neurons, which allows for the most effective learning and memory consolidation. Sleep deprivation makes it harder to think, learn, and remember because it impairs attention, perception, vigilance, memory, and executive function.

Shortchanging our sleep is a form of sleep deprivation. Lawyers may sleep fewer hours when facing deadlines and feeling they cannot get their work done without giving up something. When they give up sleep, sleep debt will result.

The idea that a lawyer can recover over a weekend, after experiencing a few nights of little sleep, has been examined in a review of research studies. Shortchanging sleep interferes with our capacity to judge how sleep debt affects us. Sleep loss causes impairments in vigilance, episodic memory, and reading comprehension, and they are not resolved after several nights of recovery sleep. This is true even if the lawyer feels less tired after recovery sleep. These results suggest that trying to catch up on sleep over a weekend is insufficient to recover fully from cognitive problems arising out of sleep deprivation.

Studies of chronic sleep deprivation in rodents have shown that the hippocampus, critical to memory formation, suffers neuronal connectivity problems and a reduction in the development of new brain cells. Inflammation of the brain rises as well. This review also suggests that chronic sleep deprivation increases the risk of neurodegenerative disorders such as Alzheimer's disease and Parkinson's disease.

A study on the sleep quality and brain atrophy of 147 middle-aged adults found that poor sleep quality was correlated with reduced brain volume in the frontal, temporal, and parietal regions. However, the study did not reveal whether poor sleep quality was a cause or consequence of reduced brain volume. The affected areas of the brain are responsible for reasoning, planning, and language processing (frontal); hearing and memory (temporal); and movement, taste, and touch (parietal). These areas of the thinking brain process information and conduct higher-order reasoning.

There are many reasons for lawyers to get less than eight hours of sleep per night. Because sleep deprivation results in cognitive decline, increasing the amount of sleep is an important goal. Napping can provide a solution.

Researchers have compared the impacts of forty-five-minute naps and two-hour naps during a four-week study on twenty-two healthy adults over the age of fifty. Both short and long nappers experienced significant increases in their twenty-four-hour sleep totals, and neither nap length had a negative impact on nighttime sleep. Nappers experienced less daytime sleepiness and improved memory, logical reasoning, and math processing performance. Cognitive performance continued to improve over the course of the four-week study, suggesting that a regular nap practice might yield a greater cognitive boost.

If you get less sleep than you need, you might try a caffeine-nap (caff-nap). A caff-nap is having a power nap after a cup of coffee. This practice yields the cognitive benefits of the nap without the grogginess afterward. A study with six participants has shown improvement in performance and alertness after a caff-nap.[15]

Getting adequate sleep supports recovery for an overworked lawyer brain. It strengthens learning and memory and clears waste from the brain, lowering the risk of dementia and Alzheimer's disease. Sleep is not the only way that lawyers need to rest. They need time away from work to participate in other activities, or to do nothing.

RESPITE

> Efficiency is highly overrated; Goofing off is highly underrated. Regularly scheduled sabbaths, sabbaticals, vacations, breaks, aimless walks and time off are essential for top performance of any kind. The best work ethic requires a good rest ethic.
>
> —Kevin Kelly, founding editor of *Wired Magazine*[16]

In his book *Rest: Why You Get More Done When You Work Less*, Alex Soojung-Kim Pang argues that although the Western work culture has evolved to treat stress, sleep deprivation, and overwork as badges of honor, those toxic aspects of work make us less creative or productive than we could be. Pang provides scores of stories about prominent scientists, authors, politicians, and business leaders who, as they matured, established sustainable routines incorporating exercise, hobbies, naps, and vacations away from work. Like premier athletes, they experimented and tweaked their schedules, searching for just the right combination of work and respite that fueled their creativity and empowered their productivity.

Pang advances the idea that burned-out workaholics, and the employers who create strained cultures featuring performatively extensive hours in the office or online, are doing it wrong. If we want to promote innovation, creativity, and optimized achievement, we must recognize that a customized schedule that combines work with rest activates productivity.

Neuroscience supports Pang's argument that a powerful sequence of work and rest will yield the best results. Researchers have discovered that when we turn away from our work on external tasks, our brain automatically switches to its default mode network (DMN). Our brain transitions from outward-focused to inward-focused cognition when it utilizes the DMN, but in this resting state, it is still pondering problems and generating ideas.

Like how the right physical training protocol helps elite athletes to improve, exposure to the right kind of rest can train our brain to be healthier and more productive. Research has shown that the DMNs of creative people have stronger connections between the brain areas responsible for memory and verbal and visual skills. This is likely to empower their DMNs to problem-solve during this resting state.

Pang discusses the theory of insight outlined by Graham Wallas in his 1926 book *The Art of Thought.* Wallas proposed a four-step model consisting of preparation, incubation, illumination, and verification. Getting organized to start work on a project, in the preparation stage, fine-tunes the brain to focus on it. In the incubation stage, often taken if you hit the mental wall, the brain works on the problem offline via the DMN. Insights reveal themselves during the illumination phase. Verification occurs when a person incorporates their contribution to a larger project, or when a writer edits a draft. This can only happen when you give your brain sufficient time for DMN processing, and rest is one strategy for gaining insight.

Crafting a personal program designed around intentional rest is a skill. Pang discusses studies of two accomplished populations – violin students and scientists – that provide guidance. The study of violin students at a conservatory in Berlin demonstrated that the outstanding students committed to a schedule of three deliberate practice sessions of approximately 80–90 minutes, with thirty-minute breaks in between. Deliberate practice is highly structured, intensive, and focused on improvement. The students also had classes and homework to attend to, but they were equally committed to a rest schedule.

The best violin students also took naps. They were masterful at developing a schedule that made the most of their deliberate practice, but also provided the rest they needed to recover. We have seen how important sleep is to memory consolidation, cleaning our brains of waste, cell repair, and recovery. Naps can decrease fatigue, increase concentration, and upgrade energy. Some of the most famous nappers were US Presidents John F. Kennedy and Lyndon Johnson and British

Prime Minister Winston Churchill. Research has shown that establishing a regular habit of napping can also improve memory consolidation.

The study involving scientists examined the differences between highly accomplished experts and their colleagues who achieved less. UCLA sociologist Bernice Eiduson followed a group of early- and mid-career scientists in California for over twenty years. She discovered that the best scientists experimented with exercise and chose sports that could be enjoyed throughout a lifetime.

Many creative thinkers such as Thomas Jefferson, Charles Dickens, and Steve Jobs were committed to taking regular walks. In addition to raising the heart rate and all the other benefits of exercise, walking provides time for the incubation and illumination stages of the Wallas model of insight. This explains why we benefit from sudden insights about our work or other problems while we exercise or while the DMN is engaged during automated activities such as showering or brushing our teeth. One study demonstrated that walking through nature or a park produces less arousal and a calmer brain than walking on a busy city street. Insights might be more attainable, especially for introverts, while walking through a quieter environment.

Finally, Pang examined the benefits of detaching from work via weekends, vacations, or deep play. Detachment – putting work totally out of your mind and doing other activities – is a source of deep recovery. Many American workers do not take all their vacation days and stay connected to work during nonwork hours via technology. This leads to errors, burnout, low productivity, and unhappy workers.

Rest can be active. Travel, music, art, and sports are deep-play activities that are engaging, rewarding, and meaningful. Deep play requires skills and is often connected to a childhood interest. It enhances our physical and psychological reserves. Research shows that people who take time off from work have better attitudes, can focus more intently on work, and are more productive.

Incorporating respite into our busy schedules is a strategy for recovery and an investment in creativity, innovation, productivity, and achievement. Crafting your most effective sequence of work and rest requires experimentation to discover the right activities and the operative balance. The result will be a sustainable plan for optimized brain health, increased life satisfaction, and more productive work.[17]

NOTES

1 Cited in Laura Schadler, "Is How We Spend Our Days How We Spend Our Lives?" *KQED*, July 3, 2013, www.kqed.org/pop/6380/what-do-you-plan-to-do-with-your-one-wild-and-precious-life.

2 *Quotes*, August 20, 2022, www.quotes.net/quote/14998.

3 Shawn Achor, The Happiness Advantage: The Seven Principles of Positive Psychology That Fuel Success and Performance at Work (Currency, 2010), 22–23, 28–31.

4 Sandra Bond Chapman, Make Your Brain Smarter: Increase Your Brain's Creativity, Energy, and Focus (Simon & Schuster, 2013), 4.

5 Edward M. Hallowell, Shine: Using Brain Science to Get the Best from Your People (Harvard Business Review Press, 2011), 31; Chade-Meng Tan, Search Inside Yourself: The Unexpected Path to Achieving Success, Happiness (and World Peace) (HarperOne, 2012), 3; David Shenk, The Genius in All of Us: Why Everything You've Been Told about Genetics, Talent, and IQ Is Wrong (Anchor, 2010), 118–119.

6 *Brainy Quote*, www.brainyquote.com/authors/will-durant-quotes.

7 John J. Ratey, Spark: The Revolutionary New Science of Exercise and the Brain (Little, Brown Spark, 2008), 9–15, 21–22, 31–32, 49–50; John Medina, Brain Rules: 12 Principles for Surviving and Thriving at Work, Home and School (Pear Press, 2009), 13–18; David Perlmutter and Alberto Villoldo, Power Up Your Brain: The Neuroscience of Enlightenment (Hay House, 2011), 148; Judith Horstman, The Scientific American: Brave New Brain (Jossey-Bass, 2010), 15.

8 Daniel G. Amen, Change Your Brain Change Your Body: Use Your Brain to Get and Keep the Body You Have Always Wanted (Harmony, 2010), 110; Horstman, *supra* note 7, at 29; Medina, *supra* note 7, at 21–22; Perlmutter and Villoldo, *supra* note 7, at 87–97; Ratey, *supra* note 7, at 37–38; Rita Carter, The Human Brain Book (DK, 2019), 65; Eric Kandell, James Schwartz, Thomas Jessell, Steven Siegelbaum, and A. J. Hudspeth, eds., Principles of Neural Science, 5th ed. (McGraw Hill, 2015), 349; Daniel E. Lieberman, Exercised: While Something We Never Evolved to Do Is Healthy and Rewarding (Pantheon, 2020), 268–269.

9 Deepak Chopra and Rudolph E. Tanzi, Super Brain: Unleashing the Explosive Power of Your Mind to Maximize Health, Happiness, and Spiritual Well-Being (Harmony, 2012), 35; Kandell, *supra* note 8, at 1202–1203; Perlmutter and Villoldo, *supra* note 7, at 87–97; Amen, *supra* note 8, at 110; Medina, *supra* note 7, at 22; Ratey, *supra* note 7, at 39, 44–45, 51–53.

10 Yian Gu et al., "Leisure Time Physical Activity and MRI-Based Brain Measures in a Multi-ethnic Elderly Cohort," American Academy of Neurology's 72nd Annual Meeting in Toronto, April 25–May 1, 2020, https://aanfiles.blob.core.windows.net/aanfiles/71556e42-2d07-4ea5-b147-a1698a4c4593/EMBARGOED%202020%20AAN%20AM%20Abstract%20-%20Leisure%20Time%20Physical%20Activity%20and%20MRI-based%20Brain%20Measures%20in%20a%20Multi-ethnic%20Elderly%20Cohort%20-%20Gu%20titled.pdf; J. O. Brett et al. "Exercise Rejuvenates Quiescent Skeletal Muscle Stem Cells in Old Mice through Restoration of Cyclin D1," 2 *Nat Metab* (2020), 307, https://doi.org/10.1038/s42255-020-0190-0; Ali Pattillo, "One Type of Exercise Reverses Aging's Effect on Stem Cells," *Inverse*, April 13, 2020, www.inverse.com/mind-body/exercise-can-rejuvenate-stem-cells; Larry A. Tucker, "Physical Activity and Telomere Length in U.S. Men and Women: An NHANES Investigation," 100 *Prev Med* (2017), 145, www.sciencedirect.com/science/article/abs/pii/S0091743517301470?via%3Dihub; University of California San Francisco, "The Mysteries of the Super-Ager Revealed," *Neuroscience News*, January 4, 2019, https://neurosciencenews.com/super-ager-mystery-10428.

11 Ratey, *supra* note 7, at 106–108; Ben Singh et al., "Effectiveness of Physical Activity Interventions for Improving Depression, Anxiety, and Distress: An Overview of Systematic Reviews," 57 *Br J Sports Med* (2023), 1203; Aaron Kandola et al., "Physical Activity and Depression: Towards Understanding the Antidepressant Mechanisms of Physical Activity," 107 *Neurosci Biobehav Rev* (2019), 525.

12 Emily M. Paolucci et al., "Exercise Reduces Depression and Inflammation but Intensity Matters," 133 *Biol Psychol* (2018), 79.

13 G. R. Schiraldi, "Adverse Childhood Experiences, Exercise, and the Brain," *Psychology Today*, January 12, 2022, www.psychologytoday.com/us/blog/hidden-wounds/202201/adverse-childhood-experiences-exercise-and-the-brain. Schiraldi is the author of The Adverse Childhood Experiences Recovery Workbook (New Harbinger, 2021).

14 Kelly McGonigal, The Joy of Movement (Avery, 2019), 5, 34–35, 37–42, 53–54.

15 Greg Wells, The Ripple Effect: Sleep Better, Eat Better, Move Better, Think Better (Collins, 2018), chapter 2; Zachary Zamore and Sigrid C. Veasey, "Neural Consequences of Chronic Sleep Disruption, 45 *Trends Neurosci* (2022), 678; Claire E. Sexton et al., "Poor Sleep Quality Is Associated with Increased Cortical Atrophy in Community-Dwelling Adults," 83 *Neurology* (2014), 967, https://www.ncbi.nlm.nih.gov/pmc/articles/PMC4162301/#!po=2.08333; S. S. Campbell, M. D. Stanchina, J. R. Schlang, and P. J. Murphy, "Effects of a Month-Long Napping Regimen in Older Individuals," 59 *J Am Geriatr Soc* (2011), 224, www.ncbi.nlm.nih.gov/pmc/articles/PMC3074345; Stephanie Centofanti et al., "A Pilot Study

Investigating the Impact of a Caffeine-Nap on Alertness during a Simulated Night Shift," 37 *Chronobiol Int* (2020), 1469, www.tandfonline.com/doi/citedby/10.1080/07420528.2020.1804922?scroll=top&needAccess=true; University of South Australia, "A Coffee and a Cat Nap Keep You Sharp on the Night Shift, Study Suggests," *Science Daily*, August 28, 2020, https://neurosciencenews.com/neuroscience-newsletters.

16 Kevin Kelly, "103 Bits of Advice I Wish I Had Known," *The Technium*, April 28, 2022, https://kk.org/thetechnium/103-bits-of-advice-i-wish-i-had-known.

17 Alex Soojung-Kim Pang, Rest: Why You Get More Done When You Work Less (Basic Books, 2018), 7–8, 11–12, 14, 35–38, 43–44, 47–49, 68–73, 93–100, 110–116, 160–166, 176–178, 200–202.

11 ENHANCING MENTAL STRENGTH

> Mindfulness gives you time. Time gives you choices. Choices, skillfully made, lead to freedom. You don't have to be swept away by your feeling. You can respond with wisdom and kindness rather than habit and reactivity.
>
> —Bhante Henepola Gunaratana[1]

There are a series of research-based practices with which you can improve your relationship to stress, self-regulation, and self-improvement. "A practice is the skills, attitudes, knowledge, and habits of mind of the practitioner. Just about any activity you can think of can be broken down into the component parts of a practice: writer, musician, painter, lawyer, doctor, parent, groundskeeper, mechanic, etc."[2]

Not every tool or practice works for every person. It will take some experimentation to learn which techniques effectively calm your fight-or-flight response and engage your rest-and-digest recovery system. Those who are willing to try might just gain a competitive edge.

THE SUMMARY

You can experiment, like the scientists described in Chapter 10, with practices that help you gradually build resilience. Identify what works and create a routine. Plug your practices into your daily schedule. This is skill-building and the development of habits of mind.

Mentally strong people are willing to learn new modes of self-development. They are able to adapt to our constantly changing world, take responsibility for their improvements and periodic failures, and assume control of their lives. They do not let negative environments or distractions deter them from their goals, and they are willing to experiment. This is a growth mindset. This answers Brene Brown's anti-perfectionism question: *How can I improve?*

The practices suggested below fall into one of two categories: exercises that address specific obstacles to mental strength, and pro-active strategies that empower your rest-and-digest system. They all contribute by enhancing your mental strength. Select the ones that appeal to you and build a mental strength protocol.[3]

THE SCIENCE

Lawyers may wonder why this book includes a chapter on mental strength. Research has shown that the state of your mental health will have an impact on your physical health. Scientists have examined data from 2.3 million New Zealanders – aged 10–60 years and 49.3 percent female – from three decades. They had information on mental and physical conditions, hospital stays, and healthcare costs. The research revealed that individuals with mental health disorders developed subsequent chronic health problems, and even experienced death, at younger ages than those without mental health conditions. The implications of this research are that ameliorating mental health problems might improve physical health, extend lifespan, and reduce healthcare costs.[4]

Chapter 2 distinguished between mental wellness and languishing. The WHO describes mental health as "a state of well-being in which the individual realizes his or her own abilities, can cope with the normal stresses of life, can work productively and fruitfully, and is able to make a contribution to his or her community."[5] Languishing is the inability to experience joy or inspiration or function at full capacity. It may increase your risk of mental illnesses, including anxiety, depression, or substance use disorder.[6]

The PERMA well-being framework, developed by Professor Martin Seligman, maintains that in order to flourish, a person must experience:

- Positive Emotion – happiness and life satisfaction;
- Engagement – deep involvement in life activities;
- Rewarding Relationships – strong connections to other people;

- Meaning – participation in and service to an endeavor that is larger than oneself; and
- Accomplishment – mastery or proficiency that is pursued for its own sake.[7]

Lawyers who have languished or suffered from a mental condition may wonder whether it is possible for them to flourish. This chapter covers interventions that individuals can try to improve and maintain mental strength. People with mental strength do not simply practice healthy habits; they also refuse to indulge in counterproductive, unhealthy behaviors.[8] These aspects of our inner game can help us deal with the obstacles that keep us stuck in a state of languishing.

STRATEGIES TO IMPROVE OBSTACLES TO MENTAL STRENGTH

> Life is not about waiting for the storms to pass. It's about learning how to dance in the rain.
>
> —Vivian Greene[9]

The obstacles to mental strength, covered in Chapter 2, include lack of self-awareness, perfectionism, imposter syndrome, social comparisons, trained pessimism, emotion regulation, identifying whether one is an extrovert or an introvert, and discovering the nature of one's neurosignature.

The interventions discussed here are practices, not perfects. They are habits you can experiment with to calm your fight-or-flight system and empower your rest-and-digest system. Much like the scientists and creatives who seek a routine that provides a sustainable amount of energy to optimize their work, lawyers can try these research-based interventions to address obstacles to their mental strength.

Lack of Self-Awareness

Becoming more self-aware requires an objective self-assessment in service to continuing self-improvement. Self-improvement is a focus of the ABA's *Path to Lawyer Well-Being* report. In the report, well-being is defined as the continuous endeavor to thrive in all domains of life: physical, emotional, intellectual, occupational, social, and spiritual.

Lawyers might consider therapy or working with a professional at their local Lawyer Assistance Program as part of improving self-awareness.[10]

In her book *Lawyering from the Inside Out*, professor and author Nathalie Martin discusses several exercises to promote self-awareness: a character strengths assessment and the identification of your peak experiences.

The VIA Institute on Character has developed a research-based assessment, which can be found online at www.viacharacter.org. This survey will help you identify your specific constellation of strengths.

To help you determine your values, Professor Martin recommends you answer the prompt: *I feel most alive when …*

Professor Martin states, "Knowing about yourself and how you operate will help you succeed in your career and do so using less of your personal time and while having more positive experiences."[11]

Perfectionism

> Kindness in words creates confidence. Kindness in thinking creates profoundness. Kindness in giving creates love.
>
> —Lao Tzu[12]

Perfectionists might suffer from a fixed mindset where they believe they have a limited amount of talent or intelligence. People with a fixed mindset seek to prove themselves to appear smart, gain acceptance, and affirm their core aptitudes and sense of status. They tend to overestimate their abilities, limit exposure to challenging endeavors to avoid possible failure, and respond to constructive feedback as an attack on the key features of their identity. According to mindset researcher Carol Dweck, "The fixed mindset limits achievement. It fills people's minds with interfering thoughts, it makes effort disagreeable, and it leads to inferior learning strategies. What's more is it makes other people into judges instead of allies."[13]

People with a growth mindset believe they can improve their strengths, weaknesses, and character with practice and experience. They take on challenges and focus on personal development. They identify goals, create plans, develop strategies, work hard, and persist through obstacles. They view feedback as a tool that helps them to learn and grow. Dweck says, "People who accomplish the most are more likely to take risks, learn from their mistakes, and accept that failure is part of the process."[14]

Brene Brown reminds us that perfectionism is about trying to earn approval. Perfectionism is other-focused. Perfectionists acquire "a dangerous and debilitating belief system: *I am what I accomplish and how well I accomplish it. Please. Perform. Perfect. Prove.*" Brown argues that rather than perfectionism, the beneficial approach is healthy striving, which is self-focused and centered on the question "How can I improve?"[15]

To manage perfectionism, practice self-compassion and embrace imperfections. Flaws make us both unique and human. Practicing self-kindness requires minimizing negative self-talk, accepting that mistakes are part of the journey, forgiving yourself, and understanding that you can recover from a failure. The principle of neuroplasticity supports a growth mindset because as we learn, our brain grows its network of brain cells with every thought, action, and experience. We enhance our expertise when we learn from both our successes and our mistakes.[16]

One practice that enhances self-compassion, as well as empathy for others, is lovingkindness meditation (LKM). LKM is a reflection designed to extend happiness and peace to yourself and others. There are several ways to practice LKM, but most apply the mantra to oneself, then to loved ones, and finally to all people or beings. Here are two examples:

Jack Kornfield's LKM is:

May I be filled with lovingkindess.
May I be safe from inner and outer dangers.
May I be well in body and mind.
May I be at ease and happy.

Followed by:

May you be filled with lovingkindess.
May you be safe from inner and outer dangers.
May you be well in body and mind.
May you be at ease and happy.[17]

Another version goes:

May I be happy.
May I be safe.
May I be healthy, peaceful, and strong.
May I give and receive appreciation today.

Followed by:

May you be happy.
May you be safe.
May you be healthy, peaceful, and strong.
May you give and receive appreciation today.[18]

Imposter Syndrome

Self-doubt can paralyze people and devolve into a self-fulfilling prophecy of mistakes and failures. To counter imposter syndrome, mindful awareness of your emotions can produce a more realistic assessment of a challenging time or situation. There are three interventions that can help us alleviate imposter syndrome: identifying the emotions that trigger imposter syndrome, objectively evaluating the facts, and examining the worst-case scenario.

Naming your emotions might help clarify that anxiety has caused you to underestimate your abilities and overestimate how difficult an experience will be. Make an online search for Plutchik's Wheel of Emotions to find examples of the subtleties of the six key emotions: sadness, fear, anger, disgust, surprise, and joy. For example, surprise might be experienced as amazement on one end of the spectrum and distraction on the other, while anger might range from rage to annoyance.

Assessing the facts about a stressful experience is another strategy for minimizing self-doubt. Make two columns and record the evidence for both positive and negative potential outcomes. This exercise outlines evidence that you might fail but also that you can succeed, which could encourage you to change the way you think or behave.

Another tactic for tackling self-doubt is to list out everything that flows from a worst-case scenario. Once you realize that you can handle rejection, embarrassment, or failure, you may find that the emotional turmoil caused by self-doubt is more painful than the worst-case scenario you have been afraid of.[19]

Social Comparisons

Rachel Hollis supplies a great deal of wisdom in *Girl, Wash Your Face: Stop Believing the Lies about Who You Are So You Can Become Who You*

Were Meant to Be. Perhaps the best nugget for lawyers is to stop comparing yourself with others because "comparison is the death of joy, and the only person you need to be better than is the one you were yesterday."[20]

The most impactful aspect of developing a professional identity as a lawyer is the law school's assessment practice of grading on a curve. The grade curve inspires a culture of comparison and competition because every grade is determined by how an individual's performance compares to that of their colleagues'. This harmful aspect of legal education creates the greatest risk to a law student's mental strength.

The competition that begins in law school carries over into legal practice. Law firms engage a steep social hierarchy with associates at the bottom, and partners at the top. The billable hour competition fuels overwork and burnout for lawyers.

To limit social comparisons:

- reduce your consumption of social media – it portrays a very small snapshot into someone else's life and may make you feel bad about yourself;
- resist being judgmental and avoid sorting people into categories – judgmental language promotes describing others with words that end in "-er," such as happier, smarter, or thinner;
- appreciate that what people display to the world is likely to be different than what they feel on the inside – basketball player Kevin Love stated that "everyone is going through something you can't see" in an article about his panic attack during a game and his process of improving his mental health; social comparison involves exaggerated thinking, so reframe your thoughts about the realistic experiences of others;
- acknowledge that there will always be someone who appears smarter than you or has more than you, which may cause you discomfort; accepting your jealousy or grief will help you move past it so you can focus on your own goals;
- consider people you admire as role models rather than competitors; think about what you can learn from others and how you can develop your own expertise.[21]

Overcoming Trained Pessimism

Lawyers are trained to be pessimistic from the first day of law school, via a practice known as issue spotting. This is important because lawyers need to evaluate all the problems that could impact a client. Constantly scanning your environment for the negative comes with costs. Hypervigilance can increase your stress levels while decreasing your motivation and capacity to accomplish your goals.

To counteract the pessimism that legal education trains for, lawyers must intentionally cultivate optimism. Deciding to use more of your time for uplifting activities, as well as spending more of your time doing things that make you happy, are practices that can increase your optimism.[22]

Gratitude to Enhance Optimism

> The struggle ends when gratitude begins.
>
> —Neale Donald Walsch[23]

> At times our own light goes out and is rekindled by a spark from another person. Each of us has cause to think with deep gratitude of those who have lighted the flame within us.
>
> —Albert Schweitzer[24]

Another way to improve optimism is to internalize the positive. Cultivating a sense of appreciation enhances the impact of pleasant experiences. When lawyers practice mindful awareness of positive events, they train their neural networks to savor them. Noticing the rewarding aspects of any environment and expressing gratitude can rewire the brain toward a positive bias. Focusing on the reward also increases the release of dopamine.

Research shows that optimism is linked to strong work performance. Optimists develop more work objectives and set more challenging goals compared to pessimists. They exert more effort, cope with stressors more effectively, and persist in the face of obstacles. One way to enhance optimism is with gratitude practice.

Practicing gratitude develops mindful awareness of what is going well in your life. One strategy is to keep a gratitude journal in which you can note things you are thankful for, good things that happened during the day, or the people who have been helpful to you. This practice teaches your brain to be alert to the positive aspects of your life and career.

In more than a hundred studies, researchers have found that people who maintain a daily gratitude practice:

- sleep better,
- have lower blood pressure,
- experience more positive emotions,
- feel more alert, enthusiastic, and energetic,
- accomplish more personal goals, and
- live an average of seven to nine years longer than people who don't practice gratitude.

If you are short on time, here are some two-minute practices you can simply reflect on. You don't have to write anything; only *think* about what you are grateful for. Gratitude reflections work to improve optimism because your brain cannot tell the difference between visualizing and having an actual positive experience. Two practices reflect on the past, and two are priming exercises to help you more effectively notice positive aspects of your life. Ritualize a gratitude practice by putting a Post-it note somewhere, like the bathroom mirror or where you keep the dog's leash, to remind yourself to do your gratitude reflection while brushing your teeth or walking the dog.

Gratitude is a longevity practice. Take two minutes and

- reflect on three things you are grateful for or three things that went well,
- think about one positive experience from your day,
- visualize small things that delight you in your daily life, or
- ask yourself: how can I enjoy my day.[25]

Regulating Negative Thoughts and Feelings

> Everyone is going through something that we can't see.
>
> —Kevin Love[26]

Negative emotions serve to narrow our thoughts and actions, limiting our creative problem-solving. On the other hand, positive emotions broaden our scope of cognition, making us more thoughtful, creative, and innovative. The practices in this chapter are meant to empower a shift toward a more positive outlook. However, negative emotions can provide a window into our values and character.

In his powerful book *Feeling Great: The Revolutionary New Treatment for Depression and Anxiety*, Dr. David D. Burns advises that "negative thoughts and feelings can be really helpful and appropriate because they always reflect your core values as a human being." He details the potential cognitive distortions that our brains create that culminate in our negative feelings and then proposes that our feelings of depression and anxiety demonstrate that there is something *right* with us rather than something *wrong*.

Dr. Burns offers a reframing exercise, with two steps, designed to help you identify your core values:

1. Reflect and record all the negative thoughts and feelings you are experiencing.
2. Then reflect and record what you care about that is causing these thoughts and feelings. This should help illuminate your core values using your negative emotions as a guide.

In *Feeling Great*, Dr. Burns provides detailed explanations and robust tools to promote a shift in thinking that eases the suffering of anxiety and depression.

Recent research indicates that people who view their adverse emotions negatively also suffer from worse psychological health. Researchers investigated the habitual emotion judgments of 1,647 college students. Those who routinely reacted to emotions such as fear, sadness, or anger as inappropriate or bad had more anxiety and depression symptoms, as well as lower life satisfaction, than those who judged negative emotions as positive or neutral. The research demonstrated that *it is the reaction to, or judgment of, negative emotions that causes the suffering, not the emotion itself.*

Starting in law school, lawyers may be taught to ignore or suppress emotions related to their work. One study examined the capacity of 219 undergraduate students to tolerate the pain and stress of having their hands immersed in ice water. The participants were divided into three groups: acceptance, suppression, and spontaneous coping. The study found that the group instructed to suppress their reactions to the ice water bath had the shortest tolerance time, as well as the highest perception of pain and distress. The acceptance group had the longest tolerance time. The researchers discovered that the acceptance strategy is the most effective for pain management.[27]

Lawyers may need to work to recognize and accept negative emotions as a normal part of life. The reframing exercise proposed by Dr. Burns can help lawyers better understand their negative emotions and how they connect to what is important to them.

Regulating Anxiety

Dr. Kelly McGonigal says that anxiety occurs when our "heart is in it." We feel anxious when we care deeply about something, and our body is signaling that we value the event or outcome we are facing. She argues that when we feel our heart pounding, we can *reframe our reaction to our anxiety by telling ourselves our heart is in it.*

McGonigal compares our anxiety to the neurotransmitter cocktail we seek when we try something daring: a combination of adrenaline, dopamine, and endorphins. She says this feeling is the "energy of anxiety" and that if we learn to reinterpret it as our body's response to help us perform, we can develop a healthier relationship with anxiety.[28]

Professor Tracy Dennis-Tiwary says that when dopamine is released, we are motivated to take action to create a future that we want. She argues that anxiety is not the problem; it is our relationship with anxiety that is broken. Because the physical symptoms of anxiety can feel uncomfortable, we assume that it is bad for us. A common reaction is to try to suppress or avoid anxiety. "We've lost the acceptance that mental health does not equal the absence of emotional suffering or discomfort, that actually mental health is the engagement with emotional suffering and working through rather than around."[29]

In her book *Future Tense: Why Anxiety Is Good for You (Even Though It Feels Bad)*, Professor Dennis-Tiwary defines anxiety as the "nervous apprehension about the uncertain future." Anxiety grabs our attention and prepares us for that uncertain future. When you reframe anxiety as information you need to pay attention to, you can utilize the energy to craft positive outcomes. We can use anxiety to be productive.[30]

Professor Maurice Schweitzer has developed two methods for reducing anxiety and improving performance. The first is to reframe our anxiety as excitement. Instead of focusing on all the things that could go wrong with a performance, list all the potential positive outcomes if things go well.

The second strategy is to develop a go-to ritual before a task is likely to induce anxiety. Athletes use rituals routinely: adjusting their cap or batting gloves, wearing lucky gear, or placing important equipment in a precise location. Calming rituals could include visualization of a positive performance, donning our favorite clothing or jewelry, short meditations, positive affirmations, or taking a few minutes in the restroom to strike a power pose or shake out our limbs.[31]

Antifragility, a term coined by Nassim Nicholas Taleb, is the idea that we can learn, grow, and change by being challenged or by experiencing some failures. Just like challenging our muscles or the immune system helps us grow stronger, a strain on our emotions can help us develop coping skills. Reframing our relationship with anxiety can help us build resilience and become antifragile. Learning to use anxiety as a tool for navigating outcomes we care about can become a source of mental strength.[32]

Reevaluating Stressful Events

Two emotion regulation strategies are objective evaluation and cognitive reappraisal. For objective evaluation, reflect on what you would think about and advise your best friend if they were facing a similar stressful situation. For cognitive reappraisal, try to look at the stressful event from a different perspective. Try to replace negative thoughts with a different view of the problem. Both strategies require shifting your thinking, which enhances your capacity to adapt to change.[33]

Reshaping Negative Emotions

Because lawyers tend to be action-oriented, they might benefit from a set of practices suggested by author Chris Guillebeau in his blog *The Art of Non-conformity*. When he experiences negative emotions, he starts by asking: *How am I feeling?* followed by *What do I want?* This is emotion literacy.

Guillebeau proposes having a list of go-to activities when you are feeling negative emotions but want to respond by doing something positive. He suggests some future-oriented and some reflection-oriented practices to turn to when you are feeling down.

If you are feeling future-oriented:

- set intentions in order to shape experiences;
- leverage curiosity and plan a new experience or learn something new;
- plan to get out into nature; or
- devote some time for deep work on a meaningful project.

If you are feeling reflection-oriented:

- consider whether and how your day mattered, or
- reflect on your eulogy virtues – those qualities for which you hope to be remembered, which moves your thinking away from your achievements and toward your character strengths.[34]

STRATEGIES FOR INTROVERTS

Introverts can use some strategies to help them thrive as authentic law students and lawyers. Recall the strategy suggested in Chapter 2. After logging your activities for a few days, reflect: What activities energize or invigorate me? What activities deplete or drain me?

Introverts need to schedule periods of strategic solitude. Solitude provides time to process information and make decisions, but it also provides space to recalibrate our brain and the nervous system. Strategic solitude should appear on the calendar as time for rest, exercise, meditation, recreation, creative work, and solitary professional development. Scheduling strategic solitude is restorative. It decreases the risk of anxiety, depression, and burnout; empowers authenticity and creativity; and improves productivity and the capacity to reach long-term goals.[35]

Scheduling strategic solitude is critical after a depleting experience. Another strategy for recovery is to schedule activities that bring you joy. Introverts love spending time with pets because they are nonjudgmental and nonverbal. They also recharge by spending time with their special friends and family members, who understand their need for deep connection. They benefit from time disconnected from technology and time spent in an engaging book or movie.[36]

If a trial was a depleting experience, schedule a few days off after it is over. If a professional conference was draining, take the following weekend off to do activities that energize you. Even if you are excellent at trials or great at conference networking, if you are an introvert, you are performing out of character in the service of a core personal project, and you need to schedule some recovery time.

Counteract negative thinking with reflection. Because introverts utilize a long processing path through their brains, they draw from long-term memory and notice more detail, making them sensitive to mistakes. Introverts can be prone to worry and self-criticism. Taking time to reflect honors the longer processing required by your brain, and it makes space for developing insights and problem-solving.

Introverts will likely benefit from reflecting about their work: What was effective, and what could be improved? You might want to keep a project journal. Gratitude reflections can shift the brain from pessimism to optimism by focusing on the good things in life. What is going well? What am I proud of? What am I grateful for? What delights me? How can I enjoy this day?[37]

Network with a designated extrovert. Happy hours and conferences are energy-depleting for introverts. Socializing with an extroverted friend makes introductions and conversations less stressful and more productive. Outgoing extroverts are also likely to benefit at these events from the excellent observation and listening skills of their designated introvert.[38]

To craft the most effective work environment, introverts need solitary spaces, time when they can work uninterrupted, and the capacity to communicate in writing and after reflection. Introverts need to find ways to guard productive time and produce their most excellent work. This might mean working with a mentor to create a hybrid schedule or being stationed in a low-traffic office.[39]

Contributing to a culture that encourages people to show up as authentic and capitalize on their strengths is protective against languishing because this type of environment supports the capacity for positive functioning and optimized contribution and therefore creates greater satisfaction with life.

INCREASE YOUR NEUROSIGNATURE AWARENESS

Lawyers are invigorated or depleted by different experiences depending on their introverted or extroverted temperaments. The four neurosignatures based on the action of dopamine, serotonin, estrogen, and testosterone in the lawyer's brain impact their personality. The various aspects of lawyer temperament mean they bring a diverse array of strengths to legal practice.

Friederike Fabritius explains in *The Brain-Friendly Workplace* that although everyone has all four brain systems, our unique combination of high activation of either dopamine or serotonin, combined with high estrogen or testosterone, influences our behavior. To help one identify their neurosignature, here is a review.

People with a high-dopamine neurosignature thrive with autonomy, creative freedom, and engaging projects. They are:

- curious, creative, optimistic, and future-oriented;
- adaptable and tolerant of change;
- explorers who enjoy travel;
- funny and inspiring; and
- sometimes impulsive and easily bored.

People with a high-serotonin neurosignature thrive with security, regular routines, and a dependable system of responsibilities and promotions. They are:

- reliable, loyal, detail-oriented, and careful;
- respectful of authority and rules;
- comfortable in stable, orderly, and consistent environments; and
- sometimes overwhelmed with worry and anxiety over what others think of them.

People high in estrogen are:

- empathetic, intuitive, inclusive, and cooperative;
- diplomatic, insightful with strong verbal and writing skills;
- focused on making connections and building community;
- less driven by money and status, and more motivated by creating an impact with their work and maintaining a healthy work–life balance;

- adept at lateral thinking, so they consider problems from multiple perspectives, make innovative connections, and evaluate long-term consequences of decisions;
- sometimes anxious, indecisive, or overwhelmed when under stress;
- concentrated on the big picture and might lose focus on important details; and
- about 72% who identify as female and 28% who identify as male.

People high in testosterone are:

- independent, outspoken, and direct;
- self-directed and prefer autonomy in their work;
- into competition, debate, taking risks, and exercising power;
- driven by achievement and external rewards such as money and status;
- skilled at linear systems thinking, so they use logic and analytical reasoning to proceed step by step using the system's rules to solve problems;
- sometimes oblivious to the feelings of others and responsible for creating competitive and stressful work environments;
- sometimes impatient, impulsive, or aggressive or prone to bullying, power trips, or angry outbursts when under stress; and
- sometimes postmenopausal women, who often become more confident and assertive when estrogen declines and testosterone becomes more influential.

Lawyers can dig deeper into their neurosignature awareness with the online Fisher Temperament Inventory.[40]

HEALTHY PRACTICES THAT BUILD MENTAL STRENGTH

Some proactive practices can be used to downregulate the fight-or-flight response and develop equanimity – the "mental calmness, composure, and evenness of temper, especially in a difficult situation."[41]

Growth Mindset and Motivation

Research has shown that people with a growth mindset outperform those with a fixed mindset. If you have a growth mindset, you understand that abilities are malleable and can be enhanced with practice and experience. The growth mindset proposition is supported by neuroscience because the brain changes with every thought, action, and experience via the superpower of neuroplasticity.

Lawyers with a growth mindset love challenges and understand that feedback helps them improve their performance. They persevere during setbacks and believe their effort upgrades their work. Leaders who inculcate a growth mindset in their followers cultivate an environment where experimentation and failure are stimulating and the only thing to fear is missed opportunity.[42]

A key to understanding motivation is determining what people value, which are autonomy, mastery, and purpose. People with a growth mindset also value human improvement and focus on skill development and enhancing deficiencies. They scrutinize mistakes, deploy feedback, and strategize to improve. Growth mindset leaders are driven by a commitment to human potential and inspire others to participate with open communication, humility, inclusivity, and teamwork.[43]

Reshaping Your Reaction to Short-Term Stress

Dr. Kelly McGonigal outlines a strategy for reframing the stress one experiences before beginning a challenge or event. She distinguishes a survival-based fight-or-flight threat response from a challenge response. She argues that by developing the understanding that our body's response system is designed to help us succeed by providing an energy boost to enhance our performance, we can leverage the biological reaction. We can reframe our stress for a challenge response.

The three-step process for reframing our mindset about a stressful challenge involves (1) noticing the challenge response and how it feels in our body, (2) welcoming the stress response as a signal that we care about the challenge, and (3) making use of the energy boost to motivate us rather than using the energy to try to manage the stress. McGonigal says that peak performers, such as musicians, artists, and athletes, understand how to use the challenge response to increase confidence, enhance concentration, and achieve a flow state.[44]

Our perceptions of stress, and our responses to stress, have ramifications for how well we function. Researchers were interested in whether reevaluation of stress-induced arousal as a challenge response, in a mind-over-matter experiment, could improve cardiovascular and cognitive performance.

According to the Biopsychosocial Model of Challenge and Threat, when stressed, there are two types of responses. When people believe they have enough resources to deal with the challenge, they can mount a *challenge response*. But when they believe that stressful demands exceed their coping resources, they experience a *threat response*.

When under stress, the first signal our body shows is increased heart rate, which feels like our heart is racing. We often interpret this signal as anxiety or fear. This negative interpretation can lead to a threat response and the perception that stressful demands exceed our resources to deal with them.

A challenge response is characterized by increased blood flow and cardiac efficiency, stimulating a cognitive approach orientation to the challenge. An approach orientation to a challenge is a helpful adaptive response. It is the belief that our body is preparing to deal with a challenge that is important to us.

A threat response is characterized by reduced cardiovascular efficiency and vasoconstriction, which increases blood pressure. This instigates a cognitive avoidance orientation and the preparation of the body for defeat and damage. A threat response also increases our attention to threat-related information, such as negative words or body language. A bias for threat-related information, experienced as a state of high alert, is associated with anxiety, social anxiety, panic disorder, and PTSD.

One form of emotion regulation is reappraisal, or the capacity to rethink about stress arousal as the body's ability to marshal resources to meet a challenge – a challenge response. To examine the reappraisal strategy, forty-nine participants (25 percent female, average age twenty-two years) were randomly assigned to one of three groups during a stressful public-speaking task:

- The Reappraisal Group was told that arousal is adaptive and helpful to performance.
- The Attention Reorientation Group was told the best way to reduce nervousness and improve performance was to ignore the stress.

- The Control Group was given no instructions.

The participants' cardiovascular and attentional bias responses were recorded. Compared to the other two groups, participants in the Reappraisal Group experienced more adaptive cardiovascular stress responses (increased cardiac efficiency and lower vascular resistance) and decreased attentional bias.

Researchers have found that reappraising stress arousal can provide physiological and cognitive benefits. Reshaping how stress arousal is interpreted can result in a challenge response, where attention bias toward negative information is reduced, and the cardiovascular response is beneficial rather than harmful.[45]

Mindfulness

> Remember, remember, this is now, and now, and now. Live it, feel it, cling to it. I want to become acutely aware of all I've taken for granted.
>
> —Sylvia Plath[46]

Mindfulness and meditation are restorative practices designed to lower stress and increase calm. They should help minimize regret about the past and worry about the future.

Mindfulness has been defined as:

- "paying attention in a particular way, on purpose, in the present moment, nonjudgmentally,"[47]
- "being aware of the present moment without judgment or preference,"[48] and
- "the love of being present."[49]

For a lawyer, a mindfulness practice helps to calm the racing mind, develop poise, and cultivate flow. Flow is the experience where the challenge of a task merges with the appropriate skill level, time seems to fly, and the work is accomplished in a zone of optimal performance. Flow is the state of complete immersion in an activity.[50]

Research shows that mindfulness decreases distraction, improves information processing and decision-making, and increases gray matter and connections between brain areas. Secondary students who practiced mindfulness experienced a reduction of negative mood and an increase in calm and self-regulation.

The STOP mindfulness practice can calm automatic reactions. When you face a stressful trigger:

Stop and take a beat to suspend the reflex of an impulsive reaction;

Take a deep breath or two;

Observe to become aware of your thoughts or feelings; and

Proceed with intention.[51]

Mindfulness can enhance leadership capacity by increasing curiosity, and acceptance of the present as it is, and by augmenting metacognition, the capacity for self-reflection, and observation of one's thinking. Possessing all these meta-capacities will assist leaders with emotion regulation, empathy, perspective-taking, adaptability, cooperation, and leadership in complex cultures.[52]

One mindfulness practice that can keep lawyers grounded in the present, based on a Leo Tolstoy short story, is the Three Questions Practice:

- What is the most important time? It is the present because that is the only time you have control over.
- Who is the most important person? It is the person you are currently connecting with.
- What is the most important thing to do? The most important thing is to do your best to serve the person you are interacting with.[53]

Meditation is the most common practice to enhance mindfulness.[54]

Meditation

> Yesterday's the past, tomorrow is the future, but today is a gift. That's why its called the present.
>
> —Bil Keane[55]

Mindfulness meditation can lead to a capacity to create calm on demand, empowering the meditator to respond intentionally rather than react. Focusing on the breath is the core activity in meditation, which activates the rest-and-digest calming system. Meditation involves taking slow deep breaths and – when the mind wanders away from attention to the breath – noticing nonjudgmentally and returning the attention to the breath.[56]

In their book *The Anxious Lawyer*, authors and lawyers Jeena Cho and Karen Gifford state:

> Self-care is something we can only do for ourselves. No one else can consume healthy, nutritious meals for us. No one else can spend five minutes walking around the block during lunch. No one else can meditate for us. By zealously guarding our well-being, we will better be able to prepare for any challenges that will arise in our life. By being more mindful, we can tune into our own needs and desires. The more sensitized we become to this, the more we are able to attend to our inner world.[57]

The Anxious Lawyer offers an eight-week guide to establishing mindfulness and meditation practices. There are meditations and exercises, invitations to set intentions, and logs to track your progress, all designed for a busy lawyer.

Meditation induces both physiological and psychological calm. The rest-and-digest system is initiated with slow deep breathing, which can reduce stress, decrease heart rate, and lower blood pressure. One psychological benefit of focused attention on the breath is that it makes it difficult to regret the past or worry about the future.

Meditation reduces stress and illness. Research has found that meditation enhances attention, mood, compassion, and empathy; improves immune function, cardiovascular disease, type II diabetes, asthma, chronic pain, insomnia, and anxiety; decreases the stress hormone cortisol; and increases gray matter in the thinking brain and hippocampus in the emotional brain.[58]

In *Lawyering from the Inside Out*, Professor Nathalie Martin states that lawyers use their minds continuously, rarely pausing to let them rest. She discusses a study where lawyers meditated for six minutes per day for a total of twenty-one days. The six-minute timeframe was chosen because many lawyers are used to billing their time in six-minute increments. At the end of the study, the lawyers reported increases in both well-being and productivity.[59]

Mindful singletasking is the practice of working on one thing at a time without interruption. While we may believe multitasking makes us more productive, research indicates that this is not the case. To prepare for singletasking, create and prioritize a to-do list. Organize everything you need to work on the first task. Remove all obstacles by closing all the active windows on your computer and silencing your phone. If working from an office, close all doors. Focus deeply on one task for 15–30 minutes. Calendar singletasking into your schedule for strategic efficiency.[60]

Nature Therapy

Nature therapy – time spent enjoying therapeutic landscapes – is meant to reverse the effects of nature-deficit disorder for those who spend most of the time indoors.

Richard Louv coined the phrase *nature-deficit disorder* to describe "the human costs of alienation from nature" in his 2005 book *Last Child in the Woods*. Research indicates that nature-deficit disorder contributes to inactivity, obesity, inattention, decreased use of the senses, and increased mental and physical health problems. Disconnection from nature impairs ecological literacy and weakens our stewardship of nature.

A slow and mindful walk through a forest, appreciating the experience with all your senses, can reduce stress, anxiety, and depression while also improving sleep, the immune system, and cardiovascular health. Such health benefits may come from the higher oxygen concentration and the presence of phytoncides – natural oils that defend plants from insects, bacteria, and fungi – in the forest. Evergreens are the greatest generators of phytoncides.

Exposure to therapeutic landscapes – green spaces in parks or the wilderness, and blue spaces near bodies of water – can improve both physical and mental health.

Metadata research synthesizing 143 studies of over 290 million people reveals that nature therapy lowers the stress hormone cortisol, heart rate, and blood pressure, as well as reduces the risk of type-2 diabetes, cardiovascular disease, and premature death. Participants lived in twenty countries, including the United States, the United

Kingdom, Australia, France, Germany, Spain, and Japan where forest bathing is popular. Greenspace includes both undeveloped land with natural vegetation and urban parks.

In an effort to determine the effective dose of nature therapy, researchers reviewed 155 studies and analyzed 14 of them. Participants were aged 15–30 from Japan, the United States, and Sweden, and time spent in natural settings was compared to time spent in urban settings. The review revealed that 10–30 minutes of sitting or walking in nature decreased cortisol, heart rate, blood pressure, and anxiety while improving mood and boosting the rest-and-digest recovery system.[61]

A recent study examined why people value time spent in natural settings. To experience leisure, we require perceived freedom and intrinsic motivation, according to social psychologists. In that study, data was collected from 795 adult participants who had visited a wilderness area in the southern Appalachian region.

Researchers discovered that we form attachments to natural landscapes because they support our psychological needs for autonomy, competence, and relatedness. Being in the wilderness allows us to choose to engage in challenging mental and physical activities with significant others. Satisfaction of these needs promotes mental and physical wellness.[62]

In addition to the restorative power of green spaces, research also shows that exposure to blue spaces – bodies of water such as rivers, lakes, and oceans – can improve mental health and physical activity. A seventeen-year study on the regeneration of canals in North Glasgow, Scotland, has shown a decrease in mortality over the duration of the study, with the most positive longevity results for the population closest to the improved canal system.[63]

Researchers evaluated how our relationship with nature influenced psychological well-being during the COVID-19 pandemic. They explored two worldviews: harmony with nature (connectedness) and mastery over nature (the right to control and exploit nature). Four hundred and nine American participants completed surveys on the personal impact of the pandemic, worldviews on nature, and mental health. Those with a harmony-with-nature worldview reported better mental health than those with a mastery-over-nature worldview. This finding supports the biophilia hypothesis that humans have an innate tendency to seek connections with nature and animals.[64]

Schedule doses of 10–30 minutes in therapeutic landscapes to improve both physical and mental health. Go outside.

Restorative Contributions of Dogs

The benefits of interactions of humans with animals have captured the interest of researchers for years. Animal-assisted interventions involve the use of animals to help people in settings such as schools, libraries, hospitals, assisted living facilities, courts, prisons, offices, and trauma scenes.

Interacting with dogs can reduce stress. Research shows that therapy dogs can help reduce stress hormones, lower heart rate and blood pressure, and cause the release of the bonding neurotransmitter oxytocin, assisting in the downregulation of the fight-or-flight response system.

When college students took the Trier Social Stress test in the presence of a dog, they showed reduced heart rate and stress hormone levels. The company of a pet has more effectively reduced the stress response during mental math testing than the presence of a spouse or friend.

Supporting the mental health of college students is important for their academic success and intellectual and personal development. Stress can erode resilience, and therapy dog visits are a low-cost stress reduction intervention.

Interacting with dogs can improve mood and enhance happiness. Although therapy dogs have been coming to college campuses for many years as a way to support students' mental health, researchers have explored the impact on student well-being of being able to touch a therapy dog versus only seeing a therapy dog with no contact.

Researchers randomly assigned 284 self-selected Canadian undergraduate students (77% female, 22% male, 2% nonbinary) to one of three groups: (1) a touch therapy dog intervention, (2) a no touch therapy dog intervention, or (3) a handler only with no therapy dog. Data was collected on participants' perception of well-being (happiness, life satisfaction, and positive affect) and ill-being (stress, loneliness, and negative affect).

Participants in all three groups experienced an improvement on some well-being measures, but only those who experienced direct contact with therapy dogs reported significant improvements on all well-being measures. The greatest benefits of direct contact with a therapy dog were improvements in happiness, stress, loneliness, and negative emotions.

Interacting with dogs can enhance cognitive capacity. A study examined the impact of interacting with therapy dogs on the executive skills of 309 college students. Executive function (EF) describes three brain functions: working memory, mental flexibility, and inhibitory control. EF empowers cognitive skills that are necessary for success in school and work, including motivation, concentration, planning, prioritizing, emotion regulation, and the capacity to understand different points of view.

Students were randomly assigned to the therapy dog interaction group or the stress management instruction group. The results showed that at-risk students who interacted with therapy dogs demonstrated greater EF and metacognitive skills (understanding their own thinking) than stress management instruction students, and that these dog interaction benefits were still present six weeks later.

The benefits of interacting with therapy dogs outperformed stress management instruction. One explanation for the strong and enduring impact on cognitive skills is due to the downregulation of the stress response in these students after therapy dog interactions.

Interacting with dogs can increase human brain activation. Researchers investigated the impact of different forms of interaction with dogs on the prefrontal cortex of healthy participants. The prefrontal cortex is involved in social cognitive processing and understanding yourself and others.

The study was conducted at the University of Basel in Switzerland. The researchers used functional near-infrared spectroscopy (fNIRS) to measure the brain activity of nineteen adults (nine women, average age thirty-two years) with no dog phobias or allergies during three interactions with a dog and three interactions with a plush lion stuffed with a hot water bottle. The therapy dogs, all of which worked in hospital settings and were with their handlers, included a female Jack Russell (six years), a female Golden Retriever (four years), and a female Goldendoodle (four years). The fNIRS technology uses two sensors placed on the participant's forehead, mimicking a clinic setting.

Researchers measured oxygen saturation in the prefrontal cortex of participants during five two-minute phases, with short breaks in between phases, while they sat on a couch and:

1. looked at a white wall and relaxed (neutral phase 1),
2. watched a dog or a plush from a distance (watching),
3. had a dog lying next to them or the plush placed on their thigh (feeling),
4. petted the dog or the plush (petting), and
5. looked at a white wall and relaxed (neutral phase 2).

Researchers analyzed data from fifty-three dog conditions and fifty-five plush animal conditions. The findings were:

- prefrontal activity of the brain increased with greater intensity of contact with both the dog and the plush;
- interaction with the dog resulted in significantly greater brain activation than interaction with the plush;
- each phase of interaction with the dog, which increasingly engaged more senses from watching to feeling to petting, led to an increase in brain activation;
- the petting condition resulted in the highest level of brain activation; and
- during neutral phase 2, after the interaction phases, the brain activation did not calm to the level of neutral phase 1.

The prefrontal cortex is involved in EFs such as attention, working memory, and problem-solving, as well as social and emotional processing. Prior research has shown that interacting with animals is highly emotionally relevant for a majority of people. Emotional salience, coupled with the gradual development of a relationship with the therapy dog, may help explain the greater brain activation with dog contact in this study. This research indicates that interacting with therapy dogs may promote social attention, motivation, and emotional arousal in people, which could improve performance on learning and therapeutic goals.

Interacting with dogs can:

- reduce stress hormones;
- lower heart rate and blood pressure;

- increase the bonding and attachment neurotransmitter oxytocin;
- improve happiness;
- reduce stress, loneliness, and negative emotions;
- enhance EF – responsible for motivation, concentration, planning, prioritizing, emotion regulation, and the capacity to understand different points of view;
- improve metacognition – the ability to understand one's own thinking; and
- increase brain activation in the prefrontal cortex, dedicated to EFs such as attention, working memory, and problem-solving, as well as social and emotional processing.[65]

If you are a dog owner, you might want to add your dog to the list of things you are grateful for. Go hug your dog and fire up your brain.

Creative Play

> Let yourself be silently drawn by the strange pull of what you really love. It will not lead you astray.[66]
>
> —Rumi

In his book *Rest,* Alex Soojung-Kim Pang argues that rest can be active. Creative play activities, such as music and art, can be engaging, rewarding, and meaningful. They can also provide a much-needed brain break. Deep play often involves a childhood interest, requires skills, and enhances our physical and psychological reserves.[67]

> When we age, we are more concerned with appearing foolish or incompetent, so we no longer try artistic activities for the sake of process or fun. As adults, if we don't feel competence in an activity, we stop doing it. We stick to what we are good at. But when we abandon creative play, we miss out on fun and joy. Creative expression reduces stress. It teaches non-judgment and non-attachment, and how to enjoy a process. When we embrace curiosity, we also access our courage.[68]

In their book *Your Brain on Art*, Susan Magsamen and Ivy Ross detail how acts of creating or enjoying art can empower our brain.

> An aesthetic mindset is simply the ways in which you are aware of the arts and aesthetics around you, and how you bring them into

> your life with purpose. Those who have an aesthetic mindset share four key attributes: (1) a high level of curiosity, (2) a love of playful, open-ended exploration, (3) keen sensory awareness, and (4) a drive to engage in creative activities as a maker and/or beholder.[69]

When we learn or make a memory, we are strengthening synaptic connections between our brain cells while they fire together. Neuroplasticity develops in our brain according to the intensity of the information that enters our senses. When that information is important to us, it is salient. The more powerful the experience, the stronger the synaptic connections. Saliency is intensified when the brain releases a potent cocktail of neurotransmitters, including norepinephrine and dopamine.

Enriched environments offer extensive salient stimuli. The neuroscientist Marian Diamond discovered that enriched environments stimulate brain development. She took three groups of mice and gave the impoverished group a plain cage, the second group a cage with a running wheel, and the third group an enriched environment full of toys and objects to play with. She euthanized the mice after several weeks and learned that the enriched environment group showed an increased thickness of their cerebral cortex while the impoverished group lost their brain mass.[70]

The type of creative play that will resonate with you is very individualized because it is seated in the default mode network (DMN), believed to be the neurological basis of the self. When we stop concentrating on an outward-focused task, such as a work project, the DMN is engaged and we utilize inward-focused cognition. Our DMN determines what art we make, or what art we enjoy and find beautiful, meaningful, and memorable.[71]

Here are some important research findings:

- Making art is calming. Spending forty-five minutes on making art lowers the stress hormone cortisol, no matter your skill level, experience, or performance.
- Making art at least once a week, or attending a cultural event one to two times per year, increases satisfaction with life.
- Coloring for twenty minutes reduces stress and anxiety and increases focus and calm.

- Coloring, doodling, and free drawing all activate the thinking brain.
- Rhythmic, repetitive movements with the hands, such as sculpting, can release serotonin, oxytocin, and dopamine, improving mood.
- Expressive writing can reduce stress hormones and blood pressure and improve depression, immune function, and self-awareness.
- Dancing releases serotonin, improving mood and depression, as well as increasing brain cell connections and communication between the two hemispheres of the brain.
- Music training accelerates brain growth in areas responsible for reading, language development, executive function, and decision-making.
- Students who participate in arts education enjoy improved cognitive, social, and behavioral outcomes; are five times less likely to drop out of school; and are four times more likely to be recognized for high achievement.
- People who patronize the arts every few months, such as a museum or theater, enjoy a 31 percent lower risk of dying early compared to those who don't. The arts contribute to longevity.

Neuroscientists now recognize that creativity is the result of interaction between the brain's DMN and the memory and executive function networks. To empower creative thinking, you must devote time to active rest, daydreaming, and mind wandering. Your external outward cognition is offline and your DMN engaged. Creative play can improve your work.[72]

NOTES

1 *Goodreads*, www.goodreads.com/quotes/603699-mindfulness-gives-you-time-time-gives-you-choices-choices-skillfully#:~:text=Time%20gives%20you%20choices.,rather%20than%20habit%20and%20reactivity.

2 John Warner, "Building a Creative Practice," *The Biblioracle Recommends*, July 9, 2023, https://biblioracle.substack.com/p/building-a-creative-practice.

3 Casey Imafidon, "8 Daily Habits to Build Your Mental Strength," *Success*, February 17, 2017, www.success.com/8-daily-habits-to-build-your-mental-strength.

4 Leah S. Richmond-Rakerd et al., "Longitudinal Associations of Mental Disorders with Physical Diseases and Mortality among 2.3 Million New Zealand Citizens," 4 *JAMA Netw Open* (2021), e2033448, https://jamanetwork.com/journals/jamanetworkopen/fullarticle/2774902.

5 World Health Organization, "Strengthening Mental Health Promotion," www.who.int/europe/health-topics/health-services/strengthening-mental-health-promotion-programmes.
6 A. Grant, "There's a Name for the Blah You're Feeling, It's Called Languishing," *New York Times*, April 19, 2021, www.ncbi.nlm.nih.gov/search/research-news/13309.
7 Martin E. P. Seligman, FLOURISH: A VISIONARY NEW UNDERSTANDING OF HAPPINESS AND WELL-BEING (Atria, 2012), 14–20.
8 Amy Morin, 13 THINGS MENTALLY STRONG WOMEN DON'T DO (William Morrow Paperbacks, 2020), 3.
9 *Goodreads*, www.goodreads.com/author/quotes/769264.Vivian_Greene.
10 Morin, *supra* note 8, at 8–9.
11 Nathalie Martin, LAWYERING FROM THE INSIDE OUT: LEARNING PROFESSIONAL DEVELOPMENT THROUGH MINDFULNESS AND EMOTIONAL INTELLIGENCE (Cambridge University Press, 2018), 12–19; VIA Institute on Character, "VIA Character Strengths Survey & Character Reports," www.viacharacter.org.
12 *Goodreads*, www.goodreads.com/quotes/46874-kindness-in-words-creates-confidence-kindness-in-thinking-creates-profoundness.
13 Carol S. Dweck, MINDSET: THE NEW PSYCHOLOGY OF SUCCESS (Ballantine, 2007), 6, 11, 16, 57–58, 61, 67, 76.
14 Ibid., at 7, 61, 76–77, 80–81; Morin, *supra* note 8, at 42.
15 Brene Brown, DARE TO LEAD: BRAVE WORK. TOUGH CONVERSATIONS. WHOLE HEARTS (Random House, 2019), 79.
16 Morin *supra* note 8, 45–47, 51–52.
17 Jack Kornfield, "Meditation on Lovingkindness," November 2, 2016, https://jackkornfield.com/meditation-on-lovingkindness/#:~:text=May%20I%20be%20safe%20from,in%20a%20heart%20of%20lovingkindness.
18 Elizabeth Scott, "How to Practice Loving Kindness Meditation," *Very Well Mind*, February 11, 2020, www.verywellmind.com/how-to-practice-loving-kindness-meditation-3144786.
19 "Plutchik's Wheel of Emotions: Exploring the Emotion Wheel," *Six Seconds*, www.6seconds.org/2022/03/13/plutchik-wheel-emotions; Morin *supra* note 8, at 87–90.
20 Rachel Hollis, GIRL, WASH YOUR FACE: STOP BELIEVING THE LIES ABOUT WHO YOU ARE SO YOU CAN BECOME WHO YOU WERE MEANT TO BE (Thomas Nelson, 2019), chapter 1.
21 Morin *supra* note 8, at 17–20, 22–24, 29; Kevin Love, "Everyone Is Going through Something," *Player's Tribune*, March 6, 2018, www.theplayerstribune.com/articles/kevin-love-everyone-is-going-through-something.
22 Shawn Achor, THE HAPPINESS ADVANTAGE: THE SEVEN PRINCIPLES OF POSITIVE PSYCHOLOGY THAT FUEL SUCCESS AND PERFORMANCE AT WORK (Currency, 2010), at 91–93.

23 Neale Donald Walsch, *Facebook*, June 23, 2014, www.facebook.com/NealeDonaldWalsch/photos/a.400017592343.181782.40638047343/10152145478042344/?type=3.

24 *Brainy Quote*, www.brainyquote.com/authors/albert-schweitzer-quotes#:~:text=One%20who%20gains%20strength%20by,strength%20which%20can%20overcome%20adversity.&text=The%20true%20worth%20of%20a,that%20come%20alive%20in%20others.&text=Constant%20kindness%20can%20accomplish%20much.

25 Rick Hanson, BUDDHA'S BRAIN: THE PRACTICAL NEUROSCIENCE OF HAPPINESS, LOVE, & WISDOM (Brilliance, 2009), 68–70, 80–84; Linda Graham, BOUNCING BACK: REWIRING YOUR BRAIN FOR MAXIMUM RESILIENCE AND WELL-BEING (New World Library, 2013), 274; Achor, *supra* note 22, at 98, 100–101; Mary Pipher, WOMEN ROWING NORTH (Bloomsbury, 2020), 202; Shawn Achor, "These Two Minute Daily Habits Will Make You Happier Immediately," *Independent*, July 3, 2015, www.independent.co.uk/life-style/health-and-families/healthy-living/these-two-minute-daily-habits-will-make-you-happier-immediately-researchers-say-10364823.html.

26 Love, *supra* note 21.

27 Dr. David D. Burns, *Feeling Great: The Revolutionary New Treatment for Depression and Anxiety* (PESI, 2022), 16–28; Ana I. Masedo and M. Rosa Esteve, "Effects of Suppression, Acceptance, and Spontaneous Coping on Pain Tolerance, Pain Intensity, and Distress," 45 *Behav Res Ther* (2007), 199; Emily C. Willroth et al., "Judging Emotions as Good or Bad: Individual Differences and Associations with Psychological Health," 23 *Emotion* (2023), 1876; Achor, *supra* note 22, at 43–44.

28 Matt Abrahams and Kelly M. McGonigal, "Feeling Nervous? How Anxiety Can Fuel Better Communication," *Insights by Stanford Business*, October 11, 2022, www.gsb.stanford.edu/insights/feeling-nervous-how-anxiety-can-fuel-better-communication.

29 Dacher Keltner and Kira M. Newman, "How We Misunderstand Anxiety and Miss Out on Its Benefits," *Greater Good Magazine*, September 7, 2022, https://greatergood.berkeley.edu/article/item/how_we_misunderstand_anxiety_and_miss_out_on_its_benefits.

30 Ibid.

31 Knowledge at Wharton, "Taming Anxiety: Techniques That Work," March 1, 2021, https://knowledge.wharton.upenn.edu/article/taming-anxiety-techniques-work/#:~:text=Reframe%20anxiety%20as%20excitement.,their%20heart%20rate%20remained%20elevated.

32 Ibid.

33 Madhuleena Roy Chowdhury, "Emotion Regulation: 6 Key Skills to Regulate Emotions," *Positive Psychology*, August 13, 2019, https://positivepsychology.com/emotion-regulation.

34 Chris Guillebeau, "9 Simple Ways to Improve Your Life Right Now," *The Art of Non-Conformity*, https://chrisguillebeau.com/9-simple-ways.
35 Holley Gerth, The Powerful Purpose of Introverts (Revell, 2020), 49–56.
36 Jenna Taylor, "10 Things That Fill Introverts with Joy," *Introvert, Dear*, September 4, 2023, https://introvertdear.com/news/10-things-that-fill-introverts-with-joy.
37 Gerth, *supra* note 35, at 118–128.
38 Ibid., at 64–66.
39 Hana Ayoub, "Introverted or Extraverted? How to Leverage Your Energy Style," *Shine*, September 7, 2016, https://advice.theshineapp.com/articles/introverted-or-extraverted-how-to-leverage-your-energy-style.
40 Friederike Fabritius, The Brain-Friendly Workplace: Why Talented People Quit and How to Get Them to Stay (Rowman & Littlefield, 2022), 9–11, 13–14, 28–29, 32–39; Open-Source Psychometrics Project, "Fisher Temperament Inventory," https://openpsychometrics.org/#:~:text=Fisher%20Temperament%20Inventory%3A%20The%20FTI,associated%20with%20specific%20neuro%2Dchemicals.
41 *Oxford Lexico Online Dictionary*, www.lexico.com/en/definition/equanimity.
42 Carol S. Dweck, Mindset: The New Psychology of Success (Ballantine, 2007), 7, 11–12, 15, 61; John Medina, Brain Rules: 12 Principles for Surviving and Thriving at Work, Home and School (Pear Press, 2009), 86–87.
43 Dweck, *supra* note 13, at 100–111, 125–129; Amy Brann, Neuroscience for Coaches: How to Use the Latest Insights for the Benefit of your Clients (2nd ed.; Kogan, 2017), 180.
44 Kelly McGonigal, The Upside of Stress: Why Stress Is Good for You (and How to Get Good at It) (Avery, 2016), 29–30, 50–51.
45 Jeremy P. Jamieson et al., "Mind over Matter: Reappraising Arousal Improves Cardiovascular and Cognitive Responses to Stress," 141 *J Exp Psychol Gen* (2012), 417.
46 Sylvia Plath, "The Journals of Sylvia Plath 1952–1960 at 20," *The Guardian: First Chapters Books*, May 19, 2000, www.theguardian.com/books/2000/may/19/firstchapters.reviews1.
47 George Mumford, The Mindful Athlete: Secrets to Pure Performance (Parallax Press, 2016), 65 (quoting Jon Kabat-Zinn).
48 Jeena Cho and Karen Gifford, The Anxious Lawyer: An 8-Week Guide to a Joyful and Satisfying Law Practice through Mindfulness and Meditation (American Bar Association, 2016), 62.
49 Mumford, *supra* note 47, at 202.
50 Ibid., at 67–69, 136–137; Lindsay G. Oades, Paula Robinson, Suzy Green, and Gordon B. Spence, "Towards a Positive University," 6 *J Positive Psych* (2011), 436, at 432.

51 Rhonda Magee, "The S.T.O.P. Practice: Creating Space around Automatic Reactions," *Mindful*, March 23, 2020, www.mindful.org/the-s-t-o-p-practice-creating-space-around-automatic-reactions/?utm_medium=email&utm_source=newsletter&utm_campaign=weekly_wakeup&mc_cid=707323c2f3&mc_eid=57aaf1254a.

52 Srinivasan S. Pillay, Your Brain and Business: The Neuroscience of Great Leaders (Pearson, 2011), 50; Scott L. Rogers and Jan L. Jacobowitz, Mindfulness and Professional Responsibility: A Guidebook for Integrating Mindfulness into the Law School Curriculum (Mindful Living Press, 2012), 22–23; Peter H. Huang, "Can Practicing Mindfulness Improve Lawyer Decision-Making, Ethics, and Leadership?" 55 *Hous L Rev* (2017), 63, at 69–71, 74; Oades et al., *supra* note 50, at 435.

53 Leo Tolstoy, "The Three Questions" (1885).

54 Cho and Gifford, *supra* note 48, at 7–8, 12.

55 Bil Keane, *The Family Circus* (WorthyKids, 2000).

56 Mumford, *supra* note 47, at 73–76, 92, 103–105, 209; Gayatri Devi, A Calm Brain: How to Relax into a Stress-Free, High-Powered Life (Plume, 2013), 61–65; Linda Graham, Bouncing Back: Rewiring Your Brain for Maximum Resilience and Well-Being (New World Library, 2013), 215; Scott L. Rogers and Jan L. Jacobowitz, Mindfulness and Professional Responsibility: A Guidebook for Integrating Mindfulness into the Law School Curriculum (Mindful Living Press, 2012), 17; Cho and Gifford, *supra* note 48, at 84–85.

57 Cho and Gifford, *supra* note 48, at 150.

58 Chade-Meng Tan, Joy on Demand: The Art of Discovering the Happiness Within (HarperOne, 2016), 67; Mumford, *supra* note 47, at 161; Daniel G. Amen, Change Your Brain Change Your Body: Use Your Brain to Get and Keep the Body You Have Always Wanted (Harmony, 2010), 167; Hanson, *supra* note 25, at 85–86.

59 Martin, *supra* note 11, at 108–109.

60 Sandra Bond Chapman, "Why Single-Tasking Makes You Smarter," *Forbes*, May 8, 2013, www.forbes.com/sites/nextavenue/2013/05/08/why-single-tasking-makes-you-smarter.

61 Richard Louv, "What Is Nature Deficit Disorder?" October 15, 2019, http://richardlouv.com/blog/what-is-nature-deficit-disorder; Caoimhe Twohig-Bennett and Andy Jones, "The Health Benefits of the Great Outdoors: A Systematic Review and Meta-Analysis of Greenspace Exposure and Health Outcomes," 166 *Environ Res* (2018), 628, www.ncbi.nlm.nih.gov/pubmed/29982151; Karin Evans, "Why Forest Bathing Is Good for Your Health," *Mindful*, September 10, 2018, www.mindful.org/why-forest-bathing-is-good-for-your-health/?mc_cid=845d550759&mc_eid=57aaf1254a; Genevive R. Meredith et al., "Minimum Time Dose in Nature to Positively Impact the Mental Health

of College-Aged Students, and How to Measure It: A Scoping Review," 10 *Front Psychol* (2020), 2942, www.frontiersin.org/articles/10.3389/fpsyg.2019.02942/full.

62 Adam C. Landon, Kyle M. Woosnam, Gerard T. Kyle, and Samuel J. Keith, "Psychological Needs Satisfaction and Attachment to Natural Landscapes," 53 *Environ Behav* (2020), https://doi.org/10.1177/0013916520916255.

63 Magdelena van den Berg et al., "Health Benefits of Green Spaces in the Living Environment: A Systematic Review of Epidemiological Studies," 4 *Urban For Urban Green* (2015), 806, www.sciencedirect.com/science/article/abs/pii/S1618866715001016; Mireia Gascon et al., "Outdoor Blue Spaces, Human Health and Well-Being: A Systematic Review of Quantitative Studies," 220 *Int J Hyg Environ Health* (2017), 1207, www.sciencedirect.com/science/article/abs/pii/S1438463917302699; Zoë Tieges et al., "The Impact of Regeneration and Climate Adaptations of Urban Green-Blue Assets on All-Cause Mortality: A 17-Year Longitudinal Study," 17 *Int J Environ Res Public Health* (2020), 4577, www.mdpi.com/1660-4601/17/12/4577; Alvin Powell, "Pandemic Pushes Mental Health to the Breaking Point," *Harvard Gazette*, January 27, 2021, https://news.harvard.edu/gazette/story/2021/01/pandemic-pushing-people-to-the-breaking-point-say-experts.

64 Brian Haas, Fumiko Hoeft, and Kazufumi Omura, "The Role of Culture on the Link between Worldviews on Nature and Psychological Health during the COVID-19 Pandemic," 170 *Pers Individ Differ* (2021), 110336, www.ncbi.nlm.nih.gov/pmc/articles/PMC7547372.

65 Changwon Son et al., "Effects of COVID-19 on College Students' Mental Health in the United States: Interview Survey Study," 22 *J Med Internet Res* (2020), e21279, www.ncbi.nlm.nih.gov/pmc/articles/PMC7473764; Nancy R. Gee, Aubrey H. Fine, and Peggy McCardle, How Animals Help Students Learn: Research and Practice for Educators and Mental-Health Professionals (Routledge, 2017), 48, 102, and 107; Patricia Pendry, Alexa M. Carr, Jaymie L. Vandagriff, and Nancy R. Gee, Incorporating Human–Animal Interaction into Academic Stress Management Programs: Effects on Typical and At-Risk College Students' Executive Function (American Educational Research Association, 2021), https://journals.sagepub.com/doi/10.1177/23328584211011612; J. T. Binfet, F. L. L. Green, and Z. A. Draper, "The Importance of Client-Canine Impact in Canine-Assisted Interventions: A Randomized Controlled Trial," 35 *Anthrozoös* (2021), 1, www.tandfonline.com/doi/abs/10.1080/08927936.2021.1944558?journalCode=rfan20; Changwon Son et al., "Effects of COVID-19 on College Students' Mental Health in the United States: Interview Survey Study," 22 *J Med Internet Res* (2020), e21279, www.ncbi.nlm.nih.gov/pmc/articles/PMC7473764; Nancy R. Gee, Aubrey H. Fine, and Peggy Mccardle, How Animals Help Students Learn: Research and Practice for Educators and Mental-

HEALTH PROFESSIONALS (Routledge, 2017), 48, 102, and 107; Rahel Marti et al., "Effects of Contact with a Dog on Prefrontal Brain Activity: A Controlled Trial," 17 *PLOS One* (2022), https://doi.org/10.1371/journal.pone.0274833.

66 *Goodreads*, www.goodreads.com/quotes/7360487-let-yourself-be-silently-drawn-by-the-stronger-pull-of#:~:text=Join%20Goodreads&text=Let%20yourself%20be%20silently%20drawn%20by%20the%20stronger%20pull%20of,will%20not%20lead%20you%20astray.

67 Alex Soojung-Kim Pang, REST: WHY YOU GET MORE DONE WHEN YOU WORK LESS (Basic Books, 2018), 200–202.

68 Tamara Levitt, "Daily Calm Meditation," May 5, 2022 (Tamara Levitt, https://tamaralevitt.com, produces daily meditations for the Calm app, and this quote came from her May 5, 2022 meditation, as the author was practicing meditation).

69 Susan Magsamen and Ivy Ross, YOUR BRAIN ON ART (Random House, 2023), xiii.

70 Ibid., at 11–144.

71 Ibid., at 19–20.

72 Ibid., at 28–29, 41–42, 62, 72, 76, 84, 109, 139–143, 188

12 DEVELOPING AN ACTION PLAN FOR THE NEURO-INTELLIGENT LAWYER

> Self-care has to become intentional. Simply put, you need a plan for looking after yourself.
>
> —Chris Guillebeau[1]

> Everyone can become the sculptor of their own brain.
>
> —Santiago Ramón y Cajal[2]

The Greeks have two words for time. *Chronos* means the time we measure with clocks. *Kairos* is the notion that some moments are more important than others. Kairos means significant, quality, or opportune time.[3]

This book argues that when a lawyer discovers the habits that protect brain health and empower mental strength, they will embark on a series of changes and move toward investing in their well-being. It's Kairos time.

Once you discover the practices that are most beneficial to you, you want to ritualize them by making them a regular part of your schedule. You will then deploy a system for tracking your progress to ensure durable change.

IT IS NEVER TOO LATE TO START

> A mind that is stretched by a new experience can never go back to its old dimensions.
>
> —Oliver Wendell Holmes, Jr.[4]

Famous pediatrician and author Dr. Benjamin Spock first published the influential *Baby and Childcare* in 1946. Its tenth edition was revised and updated by pediatrician Dr. Robert Needlman in 2018. Spock was very athletic as a young man, winning a gold medal on the Yale rowing crew at the 1924 Olympics.

In his eighties, Dr. Spock experienced numerous health problems: recurrent pneumonia, fluid around his heart and lungs due to exposure to tuberculosis, and chronic neuropathy that made walking difficult. His doctors told him his only recourse was to use a wheelchair, install an elevator in his home, and wait for the end. After getting the quote for a pricey elevator, Dr. Spock decided to try major dietary changes. He eliminated meat and cheese and shifted to a diet rich in vegetables and whole grains. His sleep improved within days; his strength and energy returned within three weeks; and he lost fifty pounds of fluid within six weeks. Dr. Spock became an advocate of a plant-based diet and lived until he was nearly ninety-five years old.

Olga Kotelko was a Canadian athlete who won hundreds of senior-division track-and-field events. Researchers found that her workout program had profound effects on her brain structure. She had greater white matter integrity – which increases capacity for planning and reasoning – and higher levels of fractional anisotropy – a measure of brain connectivity – than peers of her age group. She enjoyed a healthier brain and performed better on cognitive tests. Amazingly, she did not start working out and competing until she was seventy-seven years old, and she lived to be ninety-four.[5]

It is possible to heal your brain with healthy habits, no matter your age. A study on 160 sedentary adults over age fifty-five, who were at risk of cognitive decline, showed that aerobic exercise improved their executive functioning, and a combination of aerobic exercise and the heart-healthy DASH diet enhanced cognition even more. A combination of aerobic exercise, any activity that raises heart rate, and a diet rich in fruits and vegetables that also minimizes animal protein is an effective strategy for augmenting cognitive capacity.[6]

It takes only a few months of work to reap health and brain benefits. A recent clinical trial has demonstrated that an eight-week diet and lifestyle program can reverse biological aging in otherwise healthy adult males aged 50–72. The intervention included prescriptions for exercise, sleep, stress management, diet, and supplements.

The interaction of our genetic makeup with our environment can influence our health. Epigenetics is the study of how our environment impacts our gene regulation, which is how our genes are switched on or off. DNA methylation, a chemical process that adds a methyl group to DNA, typically leads to gene silencing and is implicated in advancing the aging process.

Scientists have developed a way to measure aging, called the Horvath DNAmAge clock. It predicts age by assessing fifty-one healthy tissues and cell types and estimating DNA methylation.

Participants in the intervention group scored 3.23 years younger than the control group, as measured by the Horvath DNAmAge clock. Over the course of the eight-week study, the control group participants aged by 1.27 years and the intervention group participants reversed their aging by 1.96 years, making 3.23 years the total difference between the groups.

The prescriptions of the intervention group included:

- exercise: at least thirty minutes a day for at least five days a week, at 60–80 percent of maximum exertion;
- sleep: on average seven hours per night;
- stress management: breathing exercises twice a day;
- eat: dark greens, cruciferous and colorful vegetables, beets, low-sugar fruit, pumpkin and sunflower seeds, 6 oz animal protein including eggs and liver;
- avoid: sugar, dairy, grains, and beans;
- supplements: PhytoGanix® and UltraFlora® Intensive Care, each twice a day.

More details of the intervention prescription can be found on page 9 (table 2) of the study.[7]

HEALTHY AGING AND MOTIVATION

Motivation science investigates how desires, dislikes, and fears are transformed into goals that are pursued or discarded over time. Researchers at the Gerontological Society of America have proposed a theoretical model that places motivation at the center of healthy aging.

The goals people pursue, which adapt and change over time, demonstrate what people value. We use the processes of setting, pursuing, and disengaging from goals throughout our lives. People must confront real and perceived constraints and opportunities when attempting to pursue their goals. This occurs within the person's culture or environment, such as family or work setting.

Goals provide direction and meaning in life, motivate action, and contribute to well-being. They can be extrinsic or intrinsic and oriented toward growth, maintenance, or avoidance of harm. Values represent beliefs about what is important in life. They are standards that help us determine our goals.

People commit to goals they believe are valuable and attainable, so this model proposes that finding the sweet spot where values and achievability intersect is the challenge for healthy aging and maintaining motivation.

To find your motivation sweet spot, make a list of short-term and long-term pros and cons of pursuing your goals. Consider recording behaviors that contribute to or undermine your goals, as well as what constraints might impede, and what opportunities might promote, your goals. Post the final plan so that you can see it daily to maintain your motivation.[8]

GRIT AND WELL-BEING

> If you are always trying to be normal, you will never know how amazing you can be.
>
> —Maya Angelou[9]

Researchers have synthesized eighty-three studies with 66,518 participants to discover that grit skills are related to well-being. Grit has been defined as the capacity to persevere in the face of adversity and to maintain a passion for long-term goals.

Well-being in this meta-analysis had two aspects: affect – the presence of positive emotions and the absence of depression – and life satisfaction. Perseverance was strongly related to well-being, and passion for long-term goals was weakly related to well-being.

One way to enhance perseverance skills is to recall a growth mindset and the neuroscience that supports it. People with a growth mindset believe they can improve learning and mastery with effort. They take charge of their motivation, identify goals, make plans, develop strategies, work hard, and power through obstacles. People with a growth mindset outperform those with a fixed mindset who believe they have limited ability or talent. Neuroscience research demonstrates that our network of brain cells grows and changes with every experience, action, and thought.

You are likely to improve your well-being if you embrace listing your goals, crafting strategies and an action plan to achieve each goal, and persisting through the inevitable challenges that arise.[10]

ACTION PLAN

Well-being is a journey, not a quick fix. When asked why he still practiced cello for four or five hours per day at age ninety, Pablo Casals responded, "because I think I am making some progress."[11]

Commitment to lifestyle changes can be difficult for some people. Research reveals two helpful strategies: *action planning*, to develop concrete steps for achieving a goal, and *coping planning*, to identify and overcome barriers to your goals. An action plan for exercise could include where, when, and with whom to exercise. A nutrition action plan could include grocery shopping and a cooking schedule. A nutrition coping plan could include avoiding the candy aisle at the store.[12]

Behavioral activation is a psychology theory, developed in the 1970s by psychologist Peter Lewinsohn, to help people who are languishing or suffering from depression. Behavioral activation is a strategic approach to increase adaptive activities related to experiencing pleasure or mastery, decreasing activities associated with risk of depression, and eliminating obstacles that reduce healthy rewards. Strategies include scheduling and structuring helpful activities.[13] The idea is that action can create motivation. Think of the Nike slogan: *Just Do It.*

Once you make a list of what matters to you, determine an action or two that you could take to get started with each plan. Taking these small steps can provide activation energy; the more steps you take, the easier it can become to reach your goal. Deploying activation energy strategically can give you the boost you need to get started and eventually empower motivation to continue working on your wellness plan.[14]

An action plan is an investment in optimizing brain health and mental strength. The brain's superpowers – neuroplasticity and neurogenesis – demonstrate that it is never too late to begin a brain-boosting action plan.

If *The Legal Brain* inspired you to make well-being changes, below are the most common areas that lawyers need to work on. Craft a customized action plan for the issues you want to address. Each area of concern will begin with a values reflection prompt, followed by listing your goals and the steps necessary to achieve them.

Stress Management

Values Reflection What did you learn that will impact your stress management goals? What changes do you want to make? What obstacles might make achieving your stress management goals more challenging? What is your coping plan for dealing with obstacles? What are the short-term and long-term pros and cons of pursuing your goals?

Stress Management Action Plan

Goal 1:

Action steps: Tasks to complete prior to launch

1.
2.
3.

Goal 2:

Action steps:

1.
2.
3.

Goal 3:

Action steps:

1.
2.
3.

Self-Medication

What did you learn that will impact your self-medication goals? What changes do you want to make? What obstacles might make achieving your self-medication goals more challenging? What is your coping plan for dealing with obstacles? What are the short-term and long-term pros and cons of pursuing your goals? Is stress a factor in your self-medication habits? What measures can you take to relieve the impact of stress?

Self-Medication Action Plan

Goal 1:

Action steps: Tasks to complete prior to launch

1.
2.
3.

Goal 2:

Action steps:

1.
2.
3.

Goal 3:

Action steps:

1.
2.
3.

Nutrition

What did you learn that will impact your nutrition goals? What changes do you want to make? What obstacles might make achieving your nutrition goals more challenging? What is your coping plan for dealing with obstacles? What are the short-term and long-term pros and cons of pursuing your goals? Is stress a factor in your eating habits? What measures can you take to relieve the impact of stress?

Nutrition Action Plan

Goal 1:

Action steps: Tasks to complete prior to launch

1.
2.
3.

Goal 2:

Action steps:

1.
2.
3.

Goal 3:

Action steps:

1.
2.
3.

Brain Health

For this part, a review of Chapter 10 might help. Common practices that enhance brain health are exercise, improvements in sleep habits, and incorporating respite breaks.

What did you learn that will impact your brain health goals? What changes do you want to make? What obstacles might make achieving your brain health goals more challenging? What is your coping plan for dealing with obstacles? What are the short-term and long-term pros and cons of pursuing your goals?

Brain Health Action Plan

Goal 1:

Action steps: Tasks to complete prior to launch

1.
2.
3.

Goal 2:
Action steps:
1.
2.
3.

Goal 3:
Action steps:
1.
2.
3.

Mental Strength

For this part, review Chapter 11 for identifying the obstacles to mental strength, as well as the practices that build mental strength.

What did you learn that will impact your mental strength goals? What changes do you want to make? What obstacles might make achieving your mental strength goals more challenging? What is your coping plan for dealing with obstacles? What are the short-term and long-term pros and cons of pursuing your goals?

Mental Health Action Plan

Goal 1:
Action steps: Tasks to complete prior to launch
1.
2.
3.

Goal 2:
Action steps:
1.
2.
3.

Goal 3:
Action steps:
1.
2.
3.

FROM ACTION PLAN TO DURABLE CHANGE

Research-based tips for creating lasting well-being changes include selecting meaningful start dates for practices, enacting habit stacking, and tracking progress.

Fresh Starts

In her book *How to Change*, Professor Katy Milkman coined the phrase *fresh start effect* based on research on the best time to start to make a change. She discovered that people are more likely to start something new when they feel they have a clean slate.

People are moved to start making a change on meaningful dates, such as their birthday, the new year, or a new month, week, semester, or season. People also tend to view their stages of life as episodes, and so they will be inspired to start a change when they begin a new life chapter such as college, a job change, becoming a parent, or retirement.[15]

Once you have identified the goals and action steps that are important to you, prioritize them. Determine a meaningful start date for each goal to leverage the fresh start effect.

Prioritized List of Goals and Timeline

Goal 1 and meaningful launch date:
Goal 2 and meaningful launch date:
Goal 3 and meaningful launch date:
Goal 4 and meaningful launch date:

Habit Stacking

Habit stacking is adding a new habit right before or after a fully integrated habit. For example:

- add a gratitude reflection or squats while brushing your teeth,
- do jumping jacks or push-ups right before your shower, or
- incorporate wall-sits while checking your phone.

Habit stacking works because networks of brain cells that "fire together, wire together." Those networks of neurons we use frequently get stronger, and those we neglect get weaker. Adopting a new behavior right before or after an ingrained behavior will leverage a strong network of brain cells.

To maximize your chances of integrating new practices, list new habits you want to deploy along with the current habit you plan to link it to. Use the formula for habit stacking: *After/before I (current habit), I will (new habit).*[16]

Tracking Habits

Research shows that tracking the progress on your goals improves your chances of changing your behavior. By logging your activities, you hold yourself accountable and minimize the likelihood you will forget your new practice. Tracking is a tool for engineering habits via regular repetition.

Benjamin Franklin utilized behavior tracking wherein he created a system of charts to monitor his daily performance on thirteen character virtues. He evaluated his success or failure every day on qualities such as moderation, industry, sincerity, humility, and tranquility.[17]

Develop a system for tracking your habits and consider a method to indicate success or failure in each. You can use a technology-based tracking system, a spreadsheet, a calendar, or a hand-drawn chart.

Maintaining Habits

Professor Katy Milkman notes that creating durable behavior change requires a series of customized interventions and tools that are to be used continuously, not habits that are simply learned and practiced for a short time. Working on well-being challenges is more like treating a chronic disease than healing a one-time injury.[18]

Your new practices and habits will become a consistent part of your life if you maintain a schedule and a tracking system. This is how you will take care of yourself so you can get the best value from yourself and live your best life. You will feel better, be better, and do better.

Well-being is a journey, not a quick fix.

NOTES

1 Chris Guillebeau, "Modern Self-Care," *The Art of Non-Conformity*, https://chrisguillebeau.com/modern-self-care.

2 Alvaro Fernandez, "Neuroplasticity as Seen by Neuroscience Pioneer Santiago Ramon y Cajal 100 Years Ago," *Huffington Post*, March 31, 2017, www.huffpost.com/entry/neuroplasticity-as-seen-by-neuroscience-pioneer-santiago_b_58de9125e4b03c2b30f6a5e2.

3 "The Ancient Greeks Had Two Words for Time: Chronos and Kairos – The Difference?" *Greek City Times*, August 14, 2022, https://greekcitytimes.com/2022/08/14/ancient-greeks-two-word-time/#google_vignette.

4 *Goodreads*, www.goodreads.com/author/quotes/432185.Oliver_Wendell_Holmes_Jr_#:~:text=A%20mind%20that%20is%20stretched,%2D%20BrainyQuote.

5 Neal D. Barnard, Power Foods for the Brain (1st ed., Grand Central Life & Style, 2013), 82–84; Benjamin Spock, Dr. Spock's 10th Edition of Baby and Child Care (Gallery Books, 2018); Alex Soojung-Kim Pang, Rest: Why You Get More Done When You Work Less (Basic Books, 2018), 193–194.

6 James A. Blumenthal et al., "Lifestyle and Neurocognition in Older Adults with Cognitive Impairments: A Randomized Trial," 92 *Neurology* (2018), e212, http://n.neurology.org/content/early/2018/12/19/WNL.0000000000006784

7 Epigenie, "DNA Methylation: Establishing the Methylome," https://epigenie.com/dna-methylation-establishing-the-methylome; Steve Horvath, "DNA Methylation Age and the Epigenetic Clock," https://horvath.genetics.ucla.edu/html/dnamage; Kara Fitzgerald et al., "Potential Reversal of Epigenetic Aging Using a Diet and Lifestyle Intervention: A Pilot Randomized Clinical Trial," 13 *Aging* (2021), 9419, www.aging-us.com/article/202913/pdf.

8 Alexandra M. Freund et al., "Motivation and Healthy Aging: A Heuristic Model," 76 *J Geront B Psychol* (2021), S97, https://academic.oup.com/psychsocgerontology/article/76/Supplement_2/S97/6316226?login=true.

9 *Goodreads*, www.goodreads.com/quotes/700564-if-you-are-always-trying-to-be-normal-you-will.

10 X. Hou et al., "Do Grittier People Have Greater Subjective Well-Being? A Meta-Analysis," 48 *Pers Soc Psychol Bull* (2021), 1701.

11 Unitarian Universalist Association, "Pablo Casals," www.uua.org/re/tapestry/adults/practice/workshop2/59194.shtml.

12 Ayse Yemiscigil and Ivo Vlaev, "The Bidirectional Relationship between Sense of Purpose in Life and Physical Activity: A Longitudinal Study," 44 *J Behav Med* (2021), 715.

13 Sona Dimidjian et al., "The Origins and Current Status of Behavioral Activation Treatments for Depression," 7 *Annu Rev Clin Psychol* (2011), 1, at 3–4, https://pubmed.ncbi.nlm.nih.gov/21275642.

14 Brad Stulberg, "You've Done Self-Care. You've Languished. Now Try This," *New York Times*, February 13, 2022, www.nytimes.com/2022/02/13/opinion/culture/pandemic-languishing-behavioral-activation.html.

15 Katy Milkman, How to Change (Portfolio, 2021), 18–26.

16 Dana Santas, "4 Ways to Stay Fit and Stress Less during the Holidays," *CNN*, December 9, 2020, www.cnn.com/2020/12/09/health/fitness-strategies-reduce-stress-holidays-wellness/index.html; James Clear, "How to Build New Habits by Taking Advantage of Old Ones," https://jamesclear.com/habit-stacking; Christian Keysers and Valeria Gazzola, "Hebbian Learning and Predictive Mirror Neurons for Actions, Sensations, and Emotions," 369 *Philos Trans R Soc B: Biol Sci* (2014), 20130175, www.ncbi.nlm.nih.gov/pmc/articles/PMC4006178.

17 Milkman, *supra* note 15, at 137–139.

18 Ibid., at 197–201.

13 THE NEURO-INTELLIGENT LEGAL ORGANIZATION

The purpose of information is to inform, to help us change our minds. Information has a point of view, it's useful. It turns data into actionable truth.

—Seth Godin[1]

It's incumbent upon both organizations and the individuals who work for them to play their own parts in maximizing workplace well-being. The responsibility cuts both ways.

—Gareth Craze[2]

Peace is not just the absence of conflict; peace is the creation of an environment where all can flourish.

—Nelson Mandela[3]

The rise of digital technology requires us, as a culture, to re-examine what it means for work to be humane.

—Tish Harrison Warren[4]

THE SUMMARY

Recall from Chapter 10 that innovative organizations foster high-performing cultures when they support constituent wellness with programs that encourage exercise, healthy eating, adequate sleep, sufficient work–life balance, and taking time off.

Ancient Greek achievement culture was designed to help people attain the human ideal. The Greeks curated a culture of deep respect, concern, and admiration for all male participants, and Greek society invested in robust public education, mentoring, and an emphasis on the quality of the journey rather than solely on the outcome.

This chapter provides an argument that lawyer leaders can transform cultures that feature chronic stress, overwork, and lawyer impairment into neuro-intelligent cultures that make cognitive well-being a priority, reaping benefit at both the individual and institutional levels. Neuro-intelligent cultures promote brain health and mental strength, and they develop environments rich with cognitive power.[5]

Neuroscience and psychology research reveals what a culture of concern and respect can mean to individual lawyers. It also supports moving away from grind culture and toward a healthier and more productive neuro-intelligent culture.

The American (ABA) and International (IBA) Bar Associations have called for action that improves the well-being of individual lawyers. They have also challenged legal organizations to make the legal profession more sustainable.

THE SCIENCE

LAWYER WELL-BEING RECOMMENDATIONS

The ABA's *Path to Lawyer Well-Being* report states that well-being is part of a lawyer's duty of professional competence; therefore, to promote lawyer well-being, members of the profession must reduce toxicity in the profession and take steps to change how law is practiced.[6] The report provides three reasons to address lawyer well-being: to enhance the effectiveness of legal organizations, to improve the professional and ethical behavior of lawyers, and to help individual lawyers flourish.[7] The report appeals to leaders in the field to transform the lawyering culture.[8]

Law schools are advised to survey students about their well-being, educate faculty and students on well-being issues, identify organizational practices that may contribute to well-being problems, and assess changes that can be made to improve student well-being.[9]

Legal employers are encouraged to provide professional development on lawyer well-being issues and to establish organizational policies, practices, and leadership incentives to promote lawyer well-being.[10]

The IBA, in its *Mental Wellbeing* report, states that lawyer impairment is a crisis. It recommends that leaders reform organizations with a focus on the structural and systemic aspects of the lawyering culture that are problematic for lawyers' mental well-being. Some of the impairing elements of the lawyering culture include the competitive environment and the expectation of overwork; sexism, racism, bullying, and harassment; lack of well-being support; and poor management training. To create work environments that optimize well-being, leaders should conduct well-being assessments; facilitate wellness conversations; discover and acknowledge the barriers to well-being, including the struggles and intersectionalities of minority lawyers and those who identify as female; develop supportive policies; engage well-being experts; deploy and disseminate best practices; and model healthy behaviors.[11]

ADDRESSING GRIND CULTURE AND OVERWORK

As we learned in Chapter 8, it is possible to become addicted to overwork, just like we might misuse substances. Grind culture is toxic to our mental and physical health. But we cannot just stop working, so we may need to detox from overwork. For an individual, this involves reimagining your relationship with work. For an organization, it requires developing an understanding of the impact grind culture has on productivity and embracing a modification of that culture.[12]

Grind culture comes from the idea that to have value as a person, you must be productive. It usually involves a competition for status and resources. Symptoms of grind culture include:

- the pattern of sacrificing sleep, exercise, or eating well to produce;
- the view that exhaustion or overwhelm demonstrates productivity;
- a sense of guilt when you rest or are not working;
- a tendency to compete with others who grind; and
- a feeling that you are never enough.

In any employment environment, there are deep work tasks and shallow work tasks. Deep work involves predicting, planning, thinking, and problem-solving. Shallow work can include tasks such as email, phone calls, and often meetings. With the attention span of about twenty minutes for adults, how deep and shallow work is organized will impact productivity. We are wired to be productive at deep work for up to three hours, but then we need a break. Recall the violin players from Chapter 10 who did deep deliberate practice for 80–90 minutes, followed by a thirty-minute break. They often took a nap to aid recovery as well.

Because of the emphasis on productivity, one metric used to assess it is the amount of time spent at the office. Research indicates that many employees spend considerable office time on nonwork activities during their long days. In a typical workday, people check news and social media for nearly two hours. They chat with coworkers, family, or friends for about seventy-two minutes, and they take eating or smoking breaks for about fifty-five minutes. They also spend roughly twenty-six minutes searching for a new job.[13] Although lawyers likely don't waste this much time at work, there are ways to structure their work to help them become more effective.

Outcome Cultures

Some organizations are restructuring their workdays around employee outcomes, rather than how much time people spend at work. Tower Paddle Boards cut the workday to five hours, challenging employees to be as productive as they had been during an eight-hour workday. The pilot was a success and the company experienced exponential growth and revenue increases. Microsoft Japan reduced its five-day workweek to a four-day workweek and increased sales by about 40 percent.

Successes for these work hour reduction initiatives are attributed in part to:

- the capacity for increased focus and concentration;
- the desire to limit distractions;
- the efforts to make meetings and conversations shorter and more constructive; and
- the appeal of having more time for other life activities.

Shifting to an outcomes culture improves employee engagement and satisfaction while reducing burnout, sick days, and attrition. Tips to help you shift to an outcomes culture include:

- start with a pilot program;
- measure relevant outcomes;

- develop ground rules for meetings, such as short timeframes, concise agendas, relevant participants, speaker limits, and use of emails in lieu of meetings, when possible;
- limit phone use, social media, and office small talk; and
- establish boundaries around email expectations and 24/7 availability. If client responses are necessary outside of work hours, create shifts so no one team member is constantly on call.[14]

Managing Deep and Shallow Work

For legal organizations, it may be helpful to train and support lawyers to manage deep and shallow work more effectively. Productivity is increased when:

- a lawyer identifies the specific conditions that support deep work;
- a lawyer can calendar deep work on a single task or case;
- a lawyer can eliminate distractions, interruptions, and shallow work (email, phone calls, colleague interactions, or meetings) during periods of deep work;
- a lawyer can schedule shallow work at specific times of the workday; and
- a lawyer can leverage brief, customized rest periods to improve concentration and longer reset activities to limit burnout.[15]

Reset Activities

A reset activity is something that provides a break from work. Reset activities can be built into our schedules as short rest periods after time on task, and they can be calendared after a demanding hearing or final exam.

Examples of reset activities include stretching, napping, walks, meditation, yoga, Tai Chi, exercise and sports, manicure, massage, acupuncture, therapy, time with family or pets, and time spent in nature or doing a creative hobby.

List your short reset activities. Where can you fit them in your daily schedule?

List your long-term thriving activities in the categories that have relevance to you: stress management, movement, creativity, social, and rest. Where do these activities fit into your weekly and monthly schedule?

Without sufficient rest, overwork can lead to burnout, a condition that can result in employee mistakes, absences, and attrition.

MINIMIZING BURNOUT

The WHO describes burnout as a situation specific to work or occupation, "resulting from chronic workplace stress that has not been successfully managed." The three dimensions of burnout are:

- feelings of energy depletion or exhaustion;
- increased mental distance from one's job, or feelings of negativism or cynicism related to one's job; and
- reduced professional efficacy.[16]

In her book *Beating Burnout at Work*, lawyer and author Paula Davis argues that the research supports a business case for addressing employee burnout. Burnout, a phenomenon specifically connected to work, is related to absenteeism, reduced productivity, employee mistakes, customer disapproval, and turnover.

Davis says that employees who experience burnout suffer from physical symptoms, including fatigue, headaches, digestive problems, and sleep issues; psychological symptoms, including anxiety, depression, panic attacks, irritability, pessimism, and hopelessness; and behavioral symptoms, such as isolation and job dissatisfaction.[17] These are also symptoms of chronic stress.

Burnout is described by Adam Grant, management professor at the Wharton School of the University of Pennsylvania, as "the persistent work-related stress that's exhausting and impairing." He explains that burnout can lead to disengagement and mistakes at work, as well as sleep issues, memory loss, depression, and a compromised immune system. He states that "burnout is not a problem in your head; it's a problem in your circumstances."

Grant proposes the Job Demand–Control–Support (JDCS) model for creating cultural change that reduces burnout for employees.[18] The JDCS model for examining workplace environments asserts that Job Demands, Job Control, and Social Support are elements associated with high employee stress and low employee well-being. Job Demands are the psychological stressors related to handling workload. Job

Control involves possessing the autonomy and skills to complete job tasks. Social Support is the degree of effective workplace social interaction among coworkers and supervisors.

Robert Karasek, researcher at the University of Copenhagen, and his colleagues developed the JDCS model and proposed that different combinations of Job Demands, Job Control, and Social Supports result in various employee job profiles, including:

- Participatory Leader (high job control and high social support),
- Obedient Comrade (low job control and high social support),
- Cowboy Hero (high job control and low social support), and
- Isolated Prisoner (low job control and low social support).

These scholars also developed the strain hypothesis about the interactions of JDCS elements, which contends that high job demands coupled with low control and social support, defined as *high isolation strain*, have negative impacts on well-being. Research has shown that high job strain is associated with burnout and poor physical and mental health.[19]

A recent study has examined whether workers in the JDCS profiles exhibited different levels of motivation or burnout and whether negative work relationships predict profile membership. Italian healthcare workers were surveyed from January 2016 to July 2017 and data from 1,671 participants, who were 68 percent female, was analyzed. Among the participants, 32.6% were 47–55 years old; 31.6% were aged over fifty-five years; 18.9% were 33–39 years old; and 14.7% were under thirty-two years old. The participants were physicians (30.6%), nurses (22.4%), and other health professionals, ranging from nurse aids to social workers to physical therapists (37.2%); and 47.8% of the participants had more than ten years of work experience.

The researchers described four profiles for Italian healthcare workers:

- 45.2% were Low Strain Profile (slightly below average job demands but slightly above average control with moderate social support);
- 37.2% were Moderate Strain Profile (slightly above average job demands but slightly below average control and support);
- 11.3% were Participatory Leader (low job demand but high control and support); and
- 6.3% were Isolated Prisoner Profile (high job demands but low control and support).

The study found support for the strain hypothesis because employees in the Moderate Strain and Isolated Prisoner Profiles reported the highest levels of exhaustion and cynicism, and that as the profile configuration deteriorated to the highest job demands, lowest control, and lowest support, levels of exhaustion and cynicism significantly increased.

Data indicated that employees in the profiles with the greatest job demands – the Moderate Strain and the Isolated Prisoner – also demonstrated the lowest level of intrinsic motivation for their work. The Participatory Leader, with the lowest job demands but highest control and support, showed the greatest work motivation.

Finally, the study found that negative work relationships and coworker incivility increased the likelihood of employees being categorized in the Moderate Strain or Isolated Prisoner Profile. This suggests that the degree of social support helps shape the worker profile.[20]

Grant suggests using the three-pronged Job Demand–Control–Support model for employers seeking to examine the impact of their employment cultures. Employers can assess each element and then facilitate modifications for employees.

1. The Demand Element: Ask the employee to identify the most depleting components of their job and collaborate to find strategies to lighten their workload.
2. The Control Element: Evaluate employee autonomy and skills and facilitate ways to provide the employee with greater autonomy and the skills they need to meet the demands of the workplace.
3. The Support Element: Promote a culture where social interaction among coworkers and supervisors is effective, struggle is normalized, and asking for and receiving support is commonplace.[21]

In *Beating Burnout at Work*, Paula Davis states that research supports investing in both individual and occupational strategies for the greatest success in relieving employee burnout. The most effective programs include structural changes that enhance job control and improve teamwork, as well as provide support for individual well-being. For organizations that want to assess burnout, Davis recommends the Maslach Burnout Inventory.[22]

DETOXING FROM OVERWORK

Employers can help employees address burnout and detox from grind culture. Training employees to recognize how they became part of the grind culture will support a healthier work environment. Employees can be asked:

- What were your family's values around work?
- How did your school performance influence your views on achievement?
- What are your current values on productivity?
- Do you sacrifice self-care practices because of work demands?[23]

A big part of helping individual lawyers flourish is for each lawyer – and for colleagues and leaders – to understand some of the differences that make individuals unique. Two major areas of individual difference are where each lawyer sits on the introvert–extrovert spectrum and what neurosignature each lawyer possesses.

Employees who can be more authentic will feel encouraged to innovate in and contribute to the enterprise, and there will be less self-doubt, burnout, and competition between employees.

LEVERAGING THE ENERGY OF INTROVERTED AND EXTROVERTED LAWYERS

Leaders must learn to understand the zones of energy stimulation and depletion for introverts and extroverts to curate a culture that supports their most effective work. People who can show up at work as their authentic selves are likely to be happier and more motivated. When leaders recognize the strengths of both introverts and extroverts, they can maximize their talents and optimize their contributions.

Professor Heidi K. Brown argues that legal practice is most supportive of extroverted lawyers. Aggressive, dominant, and vocal advocates who excel in showmanship and self-promotion capture many of the rewards in competitive law firms and law schools.[24] Therefore, introverted lawyers and law students will benefit from some support because their contributions add significant value to legal organizations.

Introverts may need professional development to gain clarity about their preferences and behaviors. Extroverts may need training on how people differ on the introvert–extrovert spectrum, so that they can understand why introverts need what they need, why they don't behave like extroverts, and why they should not be evaluated using the Extrovert Ideal standards.

The strengths of introverts parallel many lawyering tasks: "active listening, fact-gathering, researching, analyzing, creative problem-solving, legal writing, persuading, resolving conflicts, and impactfully communicating."[25] While many extroverts have some of these strengths, introverts can use thoughtfulness, planning, and patience to slow things down and lower the temperature during the process of representing clients through some of the most stressful moments of their lives.[26]

Professional development on the differences between introvert and extrovert temperaments, and how these differences contribute to the practice of law, will improve individual well-being, support the effective deep work of lawyers, expand social support, and enhance legal organization culture.

First, address lawyer energy by asking:

- What activities do you find energizing or invigorating?
- What activities do you find depleting or draining?
- Under what conditions do you do your most effective deep work?

Then explore the use and energy costs of lawyer free trait skills. When work requires you to act out of character, you are deploying free traits. After using free traits, a recovery period is necessary to recharge. A restorative niche is a place or experience that allows you to return to your true self. When people use their free trait skills without the benefit of recovery, they risk burnout and acquiring physical and mental health problems.

All lawyers can give extraordinary performances using free trait skills. Those who are introverts can conduct trials, and those who are extroverts can spend hours researching and writing complex court filings or transactional documents. Lawyers can deploy free trait skills for work that is especially meaningful and important to them, or for anything they highly value. Although we are born with a certain temperament, we can perform out of character in the service of core personal projects. Work that requires free trait skills will deplete more energy and require more recovery time.[27]

People can be asked:

- What free trait skills can you deploy?
- What restorative niches do you need after utilizing your free trait skills?[28]

Assist extroverts with:

- opportunities to interact with others;
- being able to converse in person or on a video call;
- cultivating a brainstorming partner or mentor;
- developing team collaborations; and
- energizing work environments that provide sufficient stimulation.

Assist introverts with:

- creating solitary and quiet work spaces;
- scheduling time to work uninterrupted, including working from home;
- solving problems alone before sharing their ideas;
- developing small or one-on-one teams;
- contributing ideas and feedback in writing and without public disclosure.[29]

One of the most important ways that leaders can support lawyer well-being is by recognizing that legal practice developed to encourage and reward extroverts, yet introverts can contribute some of the most impactful legal work. Therefore, introverted lawyers must be supported and evaluated on their strengths and not be expected to perform to the Extrovert Ideal.

Happiness as an aspect of well-being differs for extroverts and introverts. When asked to describe happiness, extroverts use words like excited, energetic, enthusiastic, and overjoyed. Introverts describe happiness using words like content, engaged, fulfilled, and satisfied. Because our brains are wired differently, extroverts need external stimulation to feel good, but introverts need to limit stimulation to feel their best. Happiness for extroverts is high arousal, whereas for introverts, it is calmness and contentment.[30]

Supporting well-being can be different for extroverts and introverts. Extroverts might enjoy forming walking brainstorming groups, while introverts might prefer a culture that supports taking individual walking breaks. Rewards should look different as well. An extrovert would appreciate being treated to a new group activity or an awards dinner, whereas an introvert would value a gift coupon to a spa or bookstore.

It is helpful to remember that introverts learn and work via deep processing, rather than spontaneous interaction.[31] At work, make room to capture the voices and contributions of introverts by facilitating written ideas or feedback. Consider a policy that no meetings should take place before lunch, giving introverts the morning to focus on their projects, and extroverts the assurance that they will have time for interaction later in the day. Establish communal spaces for coffee breaks and meals, but also provide quiet zones for uninterrupted work. Don't overload the day with meetings or allow the loudest people to dominate interactions. Encourage active listening. "Allow people to work the way they want to; extroverts should feel comfortable taking the time to socialize, while introverts should have license to work remotely or take breaks from the team." Don't expect introverts to attend purely social affairs, and don't evaluate them on the interest they fail to show in after work events.[32]

In law school, when class participation is assessed by how a student navigates a Socratic discussion, that evaluation privileges extroverted performance over introverted deep thinking. Faculty should provide opportunities for students to respond to a question in writing before facilitating a discussion to give introverts time to think about their answer. Encourage participation with the pair-share technique. Instead of a group discussion, the professor poses a question, and the answer is discussed by a team of two students. For group work, form small groups of only two or three students. Utilize online reflections to allow introverts to share their thinking in writing.

Because research demonstrates that introversion predicts successful university-level academic performance more effectively than cognitive capacity, learning activities that allow introverts to perform in an authentic way will leverage their strengths.[33]

Law schools and legal organizations that acknowledge and support introverted students and lawyers will be enriched by their contributions. Those that expect all constituents to perform to the Extrovert Ideal will exclude, diminish, and drive away some of the law's most thoughtful and capable contributors.

CULTIVATING NEUROSIGNATURE DIVERSITY

Lawyer neurosignatures will vary according to the actions of transmitters dopamine and serotonin, and hormones estrogen and testosterone. Developing a team of lawyers that possesses the various strengths of these neurosignatures will create a unique capacity for thinking and problem-solving.

Recall from Chapter 2, and in the discussion of *The Brain-Friendly Workplace* by Friederike Fabritius, that although we all possess the four brain systems, our personalities and behaviors reflect differing levels of these chemicals. Research indicates that leaders and executives are overrepresented in the high-dopamine/high-testosterone neurosignature, often resulting in grind culture workplaces featuring high stress. Leaders with a high-dopamine/high-testosterone neurosignature may thrive in this type of work environment, so they may be unaware of the impact on people with different neurosignatures. These leaders may also fail to develop neurosignature diversity in their workforce, and they can cause employee burnout and attrition when their work environment repels people with different neurosignatures who view this culture type as toxic.

While organizations and employers focus on increasing diversity in their workforce, research on 829 companies over three decades has demonstrated that diversity training has had little influence. This may be due to the leaders and executives with high-dopamine/high-testosterone neurosignatures who unknowingly recruit and retain employees with the same neurosignatures while rejecting or losing people with different neurosignatures. Because women and people of color who are direct, assertive, and self-advocates are viewed more negatively than white men who behave in the same way, they may be excluded from workplaces even if they have a high-dopamine/high-testosterone neurosignature.

Organizations that value and support people with all neurosignatures will be more diverse and enjoy the benefits that come with their range of strengths, cognitive resources, problem-solving capacities, and innovation potential. If they facilitate neurosignature education and high regard for diversity of thought, they should also decrease bias. They will leverage pools of talent that have been underrepresented, and they are likely to be more productive and profitable.[34]

Recall the strengths of people who have higher levels of either the neurotransmitter dopamine or serotonin, and either the hormone estrogen or testosterone. A neurosignature would combine high levels of one of the transmitters with one of the hormones. A lawyer could have a neurosignature combination with high dopamine/high estrogen, high dopamine/high testosterone (many leaders and executives have this), high serotonin/high estrogen, or high serotonin/high testosterone.

People high in dopamine are optimistic, curious, creative, future-oriented, adaptable, inspiring, humorous, and fun. They thrive with autonomy, creative freedom, and interesting projects.

People high in serotonin are reliable, loyal, careful, detail-oriented, and respectful. They thrive with regular routines, security, and a dependable system of steady increases in responsibilities and promotions.

People high in estrogen are empathetic, intuitive, inclusive, cooperative, diplomatic, insightful, and strong communicators. They excel in lateral thinking, which involves considering problems from multiple perspectives, making innovative connections, and assessing long-term consequences of decisions. They are motivated by intrinsic rewards and prioritize making connections and building community. Approximately 72% of people who identify as female and 28% of people who identify as male are high in estrogen.

People high in testosterone are independent, self-directed, assertive, competitive, and direct. They are linear systems thinkers, using logic to proceed step by step using a system's rules to solve problems. They value analytical reasoning, debate, and achievement. They are motivated by extrinsic rewards.[35]

> In a brain-friendly workplace, high-testosterone people will lead with decisiveness and energy. High-estrogen people will nurture

> team relationships and use lateral thinking to brainstorm surprising solutions to challenging problems. High-serotonin folks will stay on top of critical details such as regulations and compliance. High-dopamine people will bring creativity to problem solving and keep everyone feeling optimistic and goal-oriented.[36]

Workplaces and schools that understand, support, and leverage the strengths of introverts and extroverts, and folks with all neurosignatures, will be neuro-intelligent organizations. Like the Greek achievement culture, the neuro-intelligent organization fosters deep concern, respect, and admiration for all participants. This requires education, empathy, and an evaluation culture that rewards the varying strengths and contributions of individuals and does not penalize those who don't exhibit the Extrovert Ideal or the high-dopamine/high-testosterone neurosignature.

A neuro-intelligent organization is also a psychologically safe environment that encourages authenticity to promote robust contributions from all participants.

UNDERSTANDING PSYCHOLOGICAL SAFETY

Psychological safety is "the belief that you won't be punished or humiliated for speaking up with ideas, questions, concerns, or mistakes." Organizations benefit from a diversity of ideas, and teams are more innovative and productive when people enjoy psychological safety in the environment.[37]

According to Dr. Timothy Clark, author of *The 4 Stages of Psychological Safety: Defining the Path to Inclusion and Innovation*, employees must experience the following four phases of safety before they feel fully free to make valuable contributions.

- Stage 1, Inclusion Safety: *Can I be my authentic self at work?*
- Stage 2, Learner Safety: *Can I learn and grow by experimenting, asking questions, making mistakes, and getting feedback?*
- Stage 3, Contributor Safety: *Can I use my skills and abilities to add value?*
- Stage 4, Challenger Safety: *Can I speak up, challenging the status quo, to suggest changes or improvements?*

Stage 1 is a feeling of belonging. Without a sense of acceptance of your unique attributes and characteristics, it is impossible to attain the other three stages.[38]

The Importance of Belonging

Belonging is a critical human need. Individuals suffer and organizations deteriorate without a sense of belonging. But when a sense of belonging is cultivated, people and cultures thrive.

Belonging is about the degree of fit between a person and a setting.

> When one belongs, they feel emotionally connected, welcomed, included, and satisfied in their relationships. They know that they are valued for who they are as well as for their contributions, can bring their whole and authentic self to the table, and are comfortable expressing their thoughts and opinions regardless as to whether they diverge from dominant perspectives. In addition, they understand how things work within a given setting, feel treated equally, and perceive that they are able to influence decisions.[39]

Cultures that feature a sense of belonging improve the health of the constituents and the viability of the workplace. Social cohesion is enhanced, including more robust engagement, increased satisfaction, and greater sense of trust in the community.

Nonbelonging is a serious problem in the United States. Recent research has revealed that 64% of Americans reported nonbelonging in the workplace, 68% in the nation, and 74% in their local community.[40]

Greg Walton and Shannon Brady, in *The Many Questions of Belonging*, argue that individuals assess their capacity to belong in an environment using the following six questions:

- Does anyone here even notice me?
- Are there people here that I can connect with?
- Do people here value people like me?
- Do I want to belong here?
- Could I be more than a stereotype here?
- Are people like me compatible with this setting?

Belonging interventions can improve a culture. Leaders must be thoughtful and intentional when they create connections, organize teams, and design spaces. They construct cues in the environment that ensure constituents can answer the above six questions affirmatively.[41]

Examples of research-based belonging interventions include:

- small acts of social recognition (postcards from hospital staff to patients released after depression or suicidal ideation; use of name rather than generic Dear Student in welcome letter from school principals);
- small cues of similarity or connectedness (opportunities to discover shared aspects of identity, such as same birthday, dog lover, hiker; prospect of partnering on shared goal);
- shared stories of common challenges in the environment by senior members of a community with its new members; normalizing struggles that most people experience can minimize imposter syndrome and keep individuals from inferring that the challenges they face indicate that they don't belong;
- including a critical mass of diverse people in work and school environments to broaden representations of who belongs in a setting; statements that diversity is valued can increase trust;
- asking employees or students to review a list of values and select the ones that are important to them; ask them to write for 10–15 minutes about why the values they chose are meaningful to them.[42]

Psychological Safety Improves Organizations

In her book *The Fearless Organization*, Harvard Business School professor Amy C. Edmondson argues that organizations are driven by ideas, innovation, and ingenuity and that "no twenty-first century organization can afford to have a culture of fear."[43]

In her review of the research, Professor Edmondson demonstrates that organizations that foster psychological safety experience improved employee performance, engagement, and professional development, as well as a reduction in mistakes.

> Psychological safety is *essential* to unleashing talent and creating value. Hiring talent simply isn't enough anymore. People have to be in workplaces where they are able and willing to *use* their talent.

> In any organization that requires knowledge – and especially in one that requires integrating knowledge from diverse areas of expertise – psychological safety is a requirement for success.[44]

Numerous studies have demonstrated that teams with psychological safety outperform teams without. Without psychological safety, employees are unwilling to share knowledge or ideas for fear of rejection, embarrassment, or risk to their job. A psychologically safe environment allows employees to contribute their talents and pursue excellence. A study of highly accomplished Google employees revealed psychological safety to be the most important team success factor, followed by clear objectives, dependable colleagues, and meaningful and impactful work.

Engagement involves employee passion for work, commitment to the organization, and willingness to exert discretionary effort into the job. Employee disengagement is associated with mistakes, turnover, and increased safety risks. Research has demonstrated that psychological safety promotes employee engagement.

Psychological safety increases employee learning. In a study of nurses, when psychological safety was high, more nurses were willing to report mistakes to the head nurse, and fewer errors were made. But in hospitals where psychological safety was low, more errors were made. Psychological safety increases *learn-how* behaviors, such as brainstorming, proposing suggestions, and sharing knowledge. However, it does not improve *learn-what* activities, the kind of independent learning a person can do on their own, such as reading. Psychological safety reduces workarounds, the shortcuts that individuals take to resolve an immediate issue, but which do not address a long-term problem. Workarounds are often minimally helpful in the short term because they can create unintended consequences or prevent process improvement.[45]

> In a psychologically safe workplace, people are not hindered by *interpersonal* fear. They feel willing and able to take the inherent interpersonal risks of candor. They fear holding back their full participation *more* than they fear sharing a potentially sensitive, threatening, or wrong idea. The fearless organization is one in which interpersonal fear is minimized so that team and organizational performance can be maximized in a knowledge intensive world.[46]

Cultivating a Psychologically Safe Environment

Determined leaders can change a culture of fear. Through a process of continuous renewal, leaders can craft an organization where people bring their complete selves to work and are engaged and invested in an inspiring shared mission. To help people develop into their best selves with the talents and skills they possess, leadership must overcome the forces of fear in a work environment that motivate silence over contribution, and self-protection over self-expression.[47]

Professor Edmondson provides a framework of three skills that leaders must continuously deploy to create and support a culture of psychological safety. Leaders must frame the work, invite participation, and respond productively.

Today most work environments face volatility, uncertainty, complexity, and ambiguity (VUCA – an acronym coined by the US Army War College and adopted by the business community). To shift away from fear and toward psychological safety while contending with the challenging backdrop of VUCA, leaders must start by framing the work. Leaders set the direction and articulate the compelling purpose for work.

Frames are our assumptions or beliefs – how we think and feel – about our environment. Employees have probably experienced fear in most work environments and, in response, practiced a form of careful self-protection in order not to create a risk of losing their job. By framing the work, leaders can minimize bias and false assumptions in favor of a new fear-free reality they are trying to create. They create a shared understanding of why the work is important, the extent the work is VUCA, the way mistakes or failures will be viewed and handled in the future, and how interdependent the work of employees is.

Leaders must invite participation in the new culture. Thoughtful and customized invitations that explain the importance of individual involvement in new groups and processes are helpful. Leaders should demonstrate genuine curiosity, respect, vulnerability, and situational humility. They must admit they do not know everything and that they are committed to learning and improving the environment.

Next, leaders must create structures and processes for input and inquiry. They need to develop guidelines for discussion and conditions that welcome input from all voices and they must model curiosity, posing important questions, and listening intently.

Finally, a leader must respond productively. The goal is continuous learning, and when people are brave enough to speak up, a leader must demonstrate respect, appreciation, and interest. "Leaders who are approachable and accessible, acknowledge their fallibility, and pro-actively invite input from others can do much to establish and enhance psychological safety in their organizations."[48]

FACILITATING CHANGE

Seth Godin, author and visionary, states that you can change the culture by making people aware of new information and then creating tension that promotes change. When people experience change, they tend to tell others. He describes the cycle as awareness, tension, and change.[49]

The cultures of legal education and law practice are well established. Leaders must understand how failure to flourish harms individual lawyers, and how failure to thrive jeopardizes legal organizations. The profession must move to safeguard the light of individual lawyers and transform its culture to create sustainable lawyer well-being. "To have to pretend to be someone you're not in order to advance at your job sucks up cognitive resources. It can cause anxiety and depression."[50]

Neuro-intelligent organizations seek awareness and strive to change. Transformation of this kind will create tension by requiring action from individuals and organizations. This investment will improve individual well-being and enhance the organization's bottom line.

Better Employee Well-Being Improves the Bottom Line

The *Mental Health in America: A 2022 Workplace Report* states that "mental health is inextricably linked to economic vitality. Conversely, mental health issues lead to economic sickness."[51] In January 2022, the researchers used an online survey to collect data from 3,412 HR professionals working in American organizations that employ 10,000–25,000 employees.[52]

The survey showed that 88% of HR professionals believe that providing mental health resources can increase employee productivity, and 58% of them believe that a healthy work–life balance is more important than monetary compensation.[53] When HR professionals were asked why employees in their industries were suffering from more mental health issues than employees in other industries, the most common response was due to their "high pressure work environment."[54]

The report cites two incentives for employers to address the mental health issues of their employees, amounting to direct benefit to both:

1. Employees who receive mental health support are more likely to reduce their stress and exhaustion levels, burnout, and feelings of hopelessness.
2. Employers can help their employees improve productivity and the value they add to the company's bottom line.[55]

When legal organizations invest in lawyer well-being, they save money. Every dollar spent on lawyer wellness saves $3.27 in medical costs, and $2.73 by reducing absenteeism.[56] Improved lawyer well-being can reduce lawyer misconduct involving substance use and/or depression, both of which result in high percentages of disciplinary and malpractice claims.[57]

Individual and Organizational Action

Gareth Craze argues for well-thought-out, organization-led well-being initiatives as a treatment for employee burnout. He acknowledges that damage arising from excessively taxing workloads and negative work relationships cannot be undone with well-being programs alone. Scientifically backed initiatives that support employee capacity to regularly exercise, consume healthy meals, and take restorative breaks from work are likely to relieve burnout and support employee well-being.

Employees must avail themselves of these programs, so the responsibility falls to both the employer and employee to improve individual well-being. However, employees must also have the time, encouragement, and sufficient reserves to participate. "Wellness stipends and corporate wellness initiatives *can* become gimmicky bandages, but if well-intentioned, well-thought-through, and evidence-based, they could also become a vital, integral antidote to burnout – in concert with a focused, policy-level emphasis on minimizing overworking and ridding the workplace of toxic bosses."[58]

Professor Katy Milkman's research has revealed that supporting constituent changes requires the use of customized strategies rather than a one-size-fits-all program. To understand how to facilitate tailored well-being solutions and change, it is necessary to discover the needs of, and obstacles faced by, individual lawyers and law students.[59]

The ABA and the IBA have called for action and highlighted the need for training and surveying lawyers and law students about their needs and barriers. They also recommend addressing aspects of the culture that harm lawyer well-being and identifying changes that can be made.

The key aspects of facilitating lawyer well-being are:

- helping individuals develop well-being self-awareness, customized targeted strategies, and action plans;
- assisting individuals in identifying potential obstacles to success;
- creating a culture that normalizes lawyer well-being;
- addressing structural and systemic aspects of the lawyering culture that are problematic for lawyer well-being: competitive culture that promotes unsustainable workload and billable hour goals; sexism, racism, bullying, and harassment; lack of mental well-being support and poor management and professional development training;
- developing incentives, policies, practices, infrastructure, and leadership standards to create change;
- facilitating the communication necessary to support new well-being policies, foster systemic change, recognize and learn from mistakes, and create work environments that optimize well-being; and
- working with experts on well-being objectives.

Culture Change Is the Lawyer Well-Being Moonshot

Culture change is a formidable goal. In his book *Think Like a Rocket Scientist*, former law professor Ozan Varol states that "the ingredient behind every revolutionary innovation" is first principles thinking.[60]

Varol educates us about how reasoning from first principles can release us from the status quo and vault us into something new.

Varol discusses how difficult moving away from the status quo can be. We are taught to conform to conventions in the culture because fitting in ensures our acceptance and survival within our tribe. Our habits and patterns of behavior become reinforced within chains of neurons firing together, and research demonstrates that nonconformity fires up the amygdala, the first step in the fight-or-flight response. Our brain insists that it is safer to go along with the group than to challenge the culture.[61]

When Varol was a law professor, he taught law students to reason by analogy. When decided court cases are sufficiently similar to your client's issue, you can argue for a similar legal result. Scientists who seek to create something innovative often reason from first principles. Rather than reasoning by analogy, replicating other work with a slight deviation, reasoning by first principles requires identifying assumptions and recognizing invisible rules that support the status quo.

Varol teaches us that when we reason from first principles, we are creating new networks of brain cells that help us discover innovations. We must interrogate our deeply held assumptions about the problem. We must also reveal the invisible rules that bind the culture.[62]

Varol argues that transformational change also requires us to question our significance by acknowledging the story we tell ourselves about our identity, status, and behavior within our culture. In our tribe, we build an identity that makes us feel safe and significant. We resist change because we fear losing what we have worked for and how change might threaten our identity and alter our status. He advises, "When you risk your significance, you won't change who you are. You'll discover it."[63]

Varol challenges us to abandon the conformity of thinking analogously like a lawyer for the audacity of thinking like a rocket scientist who is trying to undertake something unreasonable – a moonshot. He describes a moonshot as a breakthrough "that brings a radical solution to an enormous problem."[64]

The first moonshot was President John F. Kennedy's 1962 challenge to send a human to the Moon and back.[65] Moonshots are formidable because years of acculturation in our environment encourage us to play it safe. We learn to "play not to lose instead of playing to win." We sell ourselves short because we don't believe we can do something incredible.[66]

> The story we choose to tell ourselves about our capabilities is just that: a choice. And like every other choice, we can change it. Until we push beyond our cognitive limits and stretch the boundaries of what we consider practical, we can't discover the invisible rules that are holding us back. There are tremendous benefits to taking moonshots even where – or particularly where – real-life conditions are out of sync with our imagination.[67]

Legal organizations may want to begin to address the lawyer well-being crisis by reasoning by analogy. This could involve:

- providing training and professional development on lawyer well-being issues and interventions, and
- surveying lawyers about the state of their well-being and/or their status as extroverts or introverts, their neurosignatures, and their preferences for getting deep work done.

Reasoning by analogy may improve resilience for those who have the resources to make some healthier changes. However, transforming the lawyering culture will require reasoning from first principles.

The moonshot in the transformation of the legal profession inquires: *What change in lawyering culture is required to improve lawyer well-being?* This will involve:

- considering the current evidence about the lawyer well-being crisis;
- questioning deeply held assumptions about the cultures of legal education and legal practice;
- identifying the habits and behaviors that have calcified into unwritten rules;
- acknowledging all the ways individual lawyers differ and the strengths they bring that add value to the work;
- discovering the ways to support deep work, shallow work, rest, and recovery of individual lawyers;
- displaying the courage to risk lawyer identity (and especially the leader's identity) under the old hierarchical paradigm for a healthier identity in a neuro-intelligent culture that values every lawyer; and

- communicating the new value proposition of the neuro-intelligent organization.

Legal organizations that take the lawyer well-being moonshot will differentiate themselves from their competitors. They will innovate the story of lawyering and empower humane lawyer leadership.

FLOURISHING INDIVIDUALS AND THRIVING ORGANIZATIONS

If you are considering the lawyer well-being moonshot, Seth Godin provides some guidance. In his book *The Song of Significance*, Godin argues that work, for many workers, is not working. "We need to decide what work is for. Whether we want to spend our days creating scarcity and harm, or if we want to commit to the regenerative work of building the best job any worker has ever had, and the best organization any customer has ever encountered."[68]

Godin's main argument is that organizations that want to create extraordinary value do so by creating change in the world. They focus on care, connection, innovation, and resilience. That requires leadership that synchronizes a culture of dignity and trust and deploys a vision concentrated on the potential of the possible.[69] Godin advises the aspirational "to engage in useful discussions about what *might* be."[70] It *might* be possible to practice law and educate law students in a way that appreciates and enhances humanity in each individual.

Godin explains that entities that are organized for the industrial age are dehumanizing. Because managers treat people as resources, they might overwork, bully, and harass them, which leads to employee dissatisfaction and burnout. "If humans are a resource, then we're here to squeeze them." These outdated systems are based on inequities, and employers with cultures featuring stagnant wages, long hours, deteriorating benefits, and layoff threats believe employees are expendable.[71]

Godin supplies many guiding questions and principles for organizations that want to reimagine themselves around the goal of creating transformational change in the world,[72] but some of the most helpful are:

- "What do these humans need?"[73]
- "How could this culture be different?"[74] and

- "How do we create the conditions for other people to do work that matters?" [75]

Godin advises that humans need to first feel safe so that leaders can build trust. Leaders can then invite participation, affiliation, and commitment to the endeavor. These steps are critical so that constituents in a moonshot transformation can engage with the tension that is necessary when striving to create extraordinary value by changing the world.[76]

LEGAL ORGANIZATION ACTION PLAN

Below are a series of questions that will guide entities striving to take the lawyer well-being moonshot and transform into a neuro-intelligent organization.

Neuro-intelligent Organization Guiding Questions

How can a legal organization do the regenerative work of building the best job any lawyer has ever had, and the best legal organization any client has ever encountered?
Or
How can a law school do the regenerative work of building the best legal education a law student has ever had?

- What do these individual lawyers or law students need?[77]
- How could the culture of this law practice or legal education be different?[78] and
- How do we create the optimal conditions for lawyers or law students to do work that changes the world?[79]

Reasoning from First Principles

Rather than maintaining the status quo and reasoning by analogy, transformation of the lawyering culture requires first principles thinking. Leaders can ask:

- What is the current evidence related to lawyer or law student well-being?
- What are the deeply held assumptions about the cultures of law practice or legal education?

   a. Why do we use this approach? Do we need this amount of fear and chronic stress to educate students or run legal organizations? What if the fear and chronic stress were greatly reduced?
   b. Can we create something better? Can we adapt from a high-dopamine/high-testosterone Extrovert Ideal-driven profession to one that also benefits from the contributions of folks who differ from this professional identity?
- What are the habits and behaviors that calcified into unwritten rules?
   a. What are the rules we follow when leading organizations?
   b. Are the rules supported by current, rather than outdated, evidence?
   c. Do we need the steep hierarchies in our legal organizations? Do our steep hierarchies still serve us?
   d. Does the power distance between lawyer leaders and their employees or students limit our understanding of and empathy for folks situated elsewhere in the hierarchy?
   e. Are we excluding or driving away individuals who could add unique value?
   f. Can we craft neuro-intelligent jobs for individual lawyers?
   g. Can we create a neuro-intelligent program of legal education?
- How can we challenge the status quo, risk our lawyer leader's identity under the old hierarchical paradigm, and create a neuro-intelligent culture that values every lawyer?
   a. Does leading based on hierarchy and exclusion still serve the organization?
   b. Does leading based on hierarchy and exclusion still serve the society?
   c. Can we discover an enlightened neuro-intelligent identity as the leader of a neuro-intelligent organization?
- How can we lead and communicate the new value proposition of the neuro-intelligent organization?

Neuro-intelligent Job Crafting

When lawyers nurture their brains, it is easier for them to reach flow state and empower peak performance. Managing stress, sleeping well, eating nutritiously, and exercising regularly support brain health. A healthier brain can think, learn, and develop expertise more effectively. Employers can support this process by nudging their employees to make good decisions about these important practices.

Helping employees in job crafting leverages their strengths to empower their contributions. Professional development programs will improve productivity and yield more time for employees to take care of themselves.[80] This addresses the Physical and Emotional Domains discussed below.

The Path to Lawyer Well-Being report acknowledges that legal organizations have a responsibility to help individual lawyers flourish by supporting their efforts in each of the following domains:

- Physical – enhancing exercise, nutrition, sleep, and recovery, and reducing self-medication
- Emotional – understanding and managing emotions to support mental health, achieve goals, and inform decision-making
- Intellectual – pursuing creative or intellectually challenging activities, fostering ongoing development, and monitoring cognitive wellness
- Spiritual – developing meaningfulness and purpose in all aspects of life
- Occupational – cultivating personal satisfaction, growth, and enrichment in work
- Social – developing a sense of connection, belonging, and a well-developed support network while contributing to organizations and communities.[81]

Neuro-intelligent job crafting requires a deeper understanding of lawyers as individuals. It acknowledges the humanity of each lawyer and is part of the Occupational and Social Domains. This approach involves a deep awareness of the temperament and neurosignature differences among lawyers.

- What are all the ways individual lawyers are different?
- What strengths do they bring that add value to the work?
- How can we support deep work, shallow work, rest, and recovery of individual lawyers?

Neuro-intelligent job crafting is an exercise in improving the fit between the employee and the job. Energy depletion and supporting deep work are important aspects of job crafting, which involve the Emotional Domain. Employees can be asked:

- Do you identify more as an introvert or an extrovert?
- What kinds of conditions support your deep work?

Customizing work around values, meaning, and purpose can improve productivity. This involves the Intellectual and Spiritual Domains. Employees can be asked:

- What kind of work would you like to focus on?
- What kind of work would you like to reduce or wish to stop doing?

If overwork causes employee burnout, neuro-intelligent job crafting will need to consider the demands of the job and the amount of autonomy and social support the employee has. Adam Grant suggests using the JDCS model for employers seeking to examine the impact of their employment cultures. This exercise supports the Emotional, Intellectual, Occupational, and Social Domains. Employers can assess each element and then facilitate suitable modifications.

1. The Demand Element: What are the most depleting components of your job? What adjustments would lighten your workload? What job components require free trait skills? How do you recover from deploying free trait skills?
2. The Control Element: Where do you feel you have adequate autonomy in your work? Where do you lack adequate autonomy? What additional skills do you need to meet the demands of the workplace?
3. The Support Element: Do all employees understand the goals of neuro-intelligent job crafting? Have they been made aware of employee differences? Have they embraced an individualized approach to neuro-intelligent job crafting? Is social interaction between coworkers and supervisors effective? How can we make it more effective? What are the obstacles to effective social interaction? Do you feel comfortable asking for support in your workplace? How can we make this process easier?[82]

Checklist for Neuro-intelligent Psychological Safety

For lawyer leaders to lead transformational change, they must establish psychological safety. Legal education and law practice have been organized around hierarchy, scarcity, stress, and fear. An ongoing initiative of culture change is required to lead a fear-free neuro-intelligent legal organization.

Leaders must frame the work. They can reflect: Have I articulated the compelling purpose for the work: creating the best job any lawyer has ever had, and the best legal organization any client has ever encountered? Have I created a shared understanding of why transformation is important? Have I communicated the extent the work involves volatility, uncertainty, complexity, and ambiguity (VUCA) involvement in work? Have I provided training on neuro-intelligent workplaces and workforces? Have I expressed the degree the work of employees is interdependent? Have I explained how mistakes or failures will be explored and handled in the future?

Leaders must invite participation. They can ask: Have I communicated that I cannot possibly know everything or have all the answers? Have I expressed that we all can always learn more? Have I shared the expectation that everyone needs to be humble, respectful, and curious while participating?

Leaders must create systems and processes of proactive inquiry. They can consider: Have I created systems and guidelines to facilitate dialogue, elicit ideas, and reveal concerns? Have I modeled curiosity? Are my questions both broad and deep?

Leaders must respond productively. They can ponder: Have I listened actively and thoughtfully? Have I expressed appreciation for a perspective? Have I emphasized learning and destigmatized mistakes or failures? Have I accepted bad news graciously and with gratitude? Have I responded with forward thinking and a focus on next steps?[83]

THE NEURO-INTELLIGENT LAWYER LEADER IS A MAVERICK

Lawyer leaders at the top of the hierarchy likely inhabit the Participatory Leader profile under the JDCS model. They enjoy high job control and high social support among their limited peers. But most people in organizations likely occupy high-isolation strain job profiles, high job demands coupled with low job control and social support.

These leaders may project the Extrovert Ideal and have a high-dopamine/high-testosterone neurosignature.

Seth Godin provides a way to think about an innovative neuro-intelligent lawyer leader. This leader will be willing to challenge the status quo, risk their leader identity under the old hierarchical paradigm, and create a neuro-intelligent culture that values every lawyer. This leader is a maverick. "The future isn't the same as the past. Technology develops, systems change and most of all, someone cares enough to make things better. The maverick isn't the selfish gunslinger of myth. In fact, she's focused on resilient, useful interactions that change what we expect, pushing back against the inertia of gobbledygook and bureaucracy."[84]

Maverick is defined as:

- a lone dissenter, such as an intellectual, an artist, or a politician, who takes an independent stand apart from their peers, or
- a person pursuing rebellious, even potentially disruptive, policies or ideas.[85]

Lawyer leaders who take the lawyer well-being moonshot can help their constituents enhance neuro-intelligence, dance with the tension that transformation entails, and create extraordinary value by generating pioneering change in the world.

NOTES

1 Seth Godin, "Insightful Data Is Called Information," December 29, 2022, https://seths.blog/2022/12/insightful-data-is-called-information.

2 Gareth Craze, "Why Adam Grant Is Only Half-Right about Burnout and Well-Being," *LinkedIn*, March 31, 2022, www.linkedin.com/pulse/why-adam-grant-only-half-right-burnout-well-being-craze-phd-bcc.

3 Nelson Mandela, "Message by Nelson Mandela to the Global Convention on Peace and Non-violence, New Delhi, India," January 31, 2004, www.mandela.gov.za/mandela_speeches/2004/040131_peace.htm.

4 Tish Warren Harrison, "How to Fight Back against the Inhumanity of Modern Work," *New York Times*, October 16, 2022, www.nytimes.com/2022/10/16/opinion/work-rest-sabbath.html.

5 David Shenk, The Genius in All of Us: Why Everything You've Been Told about Genetics, Talent, and IQ Is Wrong (Anchor, 2010), 118–119; Edward M. Hallowell, Shine: Using Brain Science to

GET THE BEST FROM YOUR PEOPLE (Harvard Business Review Press, 2011), 31.

6 Bree Buchanan et. al., THE PATH TO LAWYER WELL-BEING: PRACTICAL RECOMMENDATIONS FOR POSITIVE CHANGE (American Bar Association, 2017), 2.

7 Ibid., at 8–9.

8 Ibid., at 12.

9 Ibid., at 35–40.

10 Ibid., at 31–34.

11 IBA Presidential Task Force, MENTAL WELLBEING IN THE LEGAL PROFESSION: A GLOBAL STUDY (International Bar Association, 2021), 10, 12–17.

12 Heather Archer, THE GRIND CULTURE DETOX (Hierophant, 2022), xix–xx.

13 Ibid., at 2–10.

14 Friederike Fabritius, THE BRAIN-FRIENDLY WORKPLACE: WHY TALENTED PEOPLE QUIT AND HOW TO GET THEM TO STAY (Rowman & Littlefield, 2022), at 44–61.

15 Aaron Brooks, "7 Scientific Studies That Reveal the Secrets to Max. Productivity," *Venture Harbour*, August 12, 2020, www.ventureharbour.com/scientific-studies-productivity-secrets.

16 World Health Organization, "Burnout an 'Occupational Phenomenon': International Classification of Diseases," May 28, 2019, www.who.int/news/item/28-05-2019-burn-out-an-occupational-phenomenon-international-classification-of-diseases.

17 Paula Davis, BEATING BURNOUT AT WORK: WHY TEAMS HOLD THE SECRET TO WELL-BEING AND RESILIENCE (Wharton Digital, 2021), 10–11.

18 Adam Grant, "Preventing Burnout: The Demand-Control-Support Model," *Knowledge at Wharton*, September 27, 2022, https://knowledge.wharton.upenn.edu/article/preventing-burnout-the-demand-control-support-model/#:~:text=Demand%3A%20Make%20structural%20changes%20that,to%20request%20and%20receive%20help.

19 Igor Portoghese et al., "Job Demand-Control-Support Latent Profiles and Their Relationships with Interpersonal Stressors, Job Burnout, and Intrinsic Motivation," 17 *Int J Environ Res Public Health* (2020), 9430.

20 Ibid.

21 Ibid.; Grant, *supra* note 18.

22 Davis, *supra* note 17, at 7, 14–15; Mind Garden, "Maslach Burnout Inventory," www.mindgarden.com/117-maslach-burnout-inventory-mbi.

23 Fabritius, *supra* note 14, at 41, 82–84; Archer, *supra* note 12, at 51–55.

24 Heidi K. Brown, THE INTROVERTED LAWYER: A SEVEN-STEP JOURNEY TOWARD AUTHENTICALLY EMPOWERED ADVOCACY (American Bar Association, 2017), 33–34.

25 Ibid., at 42–43.
26 Ibid., at 41–42.
27 Susan Cain, Quiet: The Power of Introverts in a World That Can't Stop Talking (Crown, 2012), 209–210.
28 Ibid., at 219–223, 266.
29 Hana Ayoub, "Introverted or Extraverted? How to Leverage Your Energy Style," *Shine*, September 7, 2016, https://advice.theshineapp.com/articles/introverted-or-extraverted-how-to-leverage-your-energy-style; Cain, *supra* note 88, at 266; Lisa Caprelli, "Understanding Extroverted and Introverted Personalities in the Workplace," *Forbes*, March 28, 2022, www.forbes.com/sites/forbesbusinesscouncil/2022/03/28/understanding-extroverted-and-introverted-personalities-in-the-workplace/?sh=16df9b1b4f19.
30 Holley Gerth, The Powerful Purpose of Introverts (Revell, 2020), 89–90.
31 Brown, *supra* note 24, at 27–29.
32 Rebecca Knight, "How to Be Good at Managing Both Introverts and Extroverts," *Harvard Business Review*, November 16, 2015, https://hbr.org/2015/11/how-to-be-good-at-managing-both-introverts-and-extroverts.
33 Brown, *supra* note 24, at 29–32; Cain, *supra* note 27, at 348–349.
34 Fabritius, *supra* note 14, at 9–11, 13–14, 28–29, 32–39.
35 Open-Source Psychometrics Project, "Fisher Temperament Inventory," https://openpsychometrics.org/#:~:text=Fisher%20Temperament%20Inventory%3A%20The%20FTI,associated%20with%20specific%20neuro%2Dchemicals.
36 Fabritius, *supra* note 14, at 29.
37 Center for Creative Leadership, "What Is Psychological Safety at Work?" January 15, 2022, www.ccl.org/articles/leading-effectively-articles/what-is-psychological-safety-at-work/#:~:text=Psychological%20safety%20is%20the%20belief,taking%20risks%2C%20or%20soliciting%20feedback.
38 Gazala Abid Sayad, "Psychologically Safe Work Environments Matters," *LinkedIn*, November 23, 2022, www.linkedin.com/pulse/psychologically-safe-work-environment-matters-gazala-abid-sayyad.
39 Nichole Argo and Hammad Sheikh, The Belonging Barometer: The State of Belonging in America (American Immigration Council, 2023), v, https://static1.squarespace.com/static/5f7f1da1ea15cd5bef32169f/t/64074072d3daa3704b5774d0/1678196851632/The+Belonging+Barometer+%E2%80%94+The+State+of+Belonging+in+America+%281%29.pdf
40 Ibid., at v–vi.
41 Ibid., at 52; Gregory M. Walton and Shannon T. Brady, "The Many Questions of Belonging," in The Handbook of Competence and Motivation: Theory and Application (2nd ed., Guilford Press, 2017), 275–278, 283–286.
42 Ibid., at 275–287.

43 Amy C. Edmondson, THE FEARLESS ORGANIZATION: CREATING PSYCHOLOGICAL SAFETY IN THE WORKPLACE FOR LEARNING, INNOVATION, AND GROWTH (John Wiley & Sons, 2019), xiii, xix.
44 Ibid., at 26.
45 Ibid., 29–38.
46 Ibid., at xv.
47 Ibid., at 188–189.
48 Ibid., at 19, 154–182.
49 Seth Godin, "How to Change the World," March 22, 2023, https://seths.blog/2023/03/how-to-change-the-world.
50 Fabritius, *supra* note 14, at 16.
51 SHRM Foundation and Otsuka Pharmaceutical, MENTAL HEALTH IN AMERICA: A 2022 WORKPLACE REPORT EXECUTIVE SUMMARY (SHRM Foundation, 2022), 4, www.workplacementalhealth.shrm.org/wp-content/uploads/2022/04/Mental-Health-in-America-A-2022-Workplace-Report.pdf.
52 Ibid., at 18.
53 Ibid., at 13–14.
54 Ibid., at 4.
55 Ibid., at 5.
56 Ibid., at 408.
57 Michael E. McCabe, Jr., "Lawyer Alcoholism and Substance Abuse Frequent Causes for Lawyer Discipline," McCabe/Ali LLP, www.ipethicslaw.com/lawyer-alcoholism-and-substance-abuse-frequent-causes-of-discipline; D. B. Marlowe, "Alcoholism, Symptoms, Causes & Treatments," in STRESS MANAGEMENT FOR LAWYERS (Amiram Elwork, ed.; 2nd ed., Vorkell Group, 1997), 104–130 (cited in M. A. Silver, SUBSTANCE ABUSE, STRESS, MENTAL HEALTH AND THE LEGAL PROFESSION [New York State Law Assistance Trust, 2004], www.nylat.org/documents/courseinabox.pdf).
58 Craze, *supra* note 2.
59 Katy Milkman, HOW TO CHANGE (Portfolio, 2021), 7–9.
60 Ozan Varol, THINK LIKE A ROCKET SCIENTIST (PublicAffairs, 2020), 7.
61 Ibid., at 50–54.
62 Ibid., at 56–69.
63 Ibid., at 64–66.
64 Ibid., at 107.
65 Ibid., at 1.
66 Ibid., at 109.
67 Ibid., at 112.
68 Seth Godin, THE SONG OF SIGNIFICANCE (Portfolio, 2023), 1, 18–19.
69 Ibid., at 20–25.
70 Ibid., at 29.

71 Ibid., at 60–61.
72 Ibid., at 29–30, 96–97, 141–142, 163–164.
73 Ibid., at 34.
74 Ibid., at 110.
75 Ibid., at 63.
76 Ibid., at 67–71, 74, 79–80.
77 Ibid., at 34.
78 Ibid., at 110.
79 Ibid., at 63.
80 Fabritius, *supra* note 14, at 41, 82–84; Archer, *supra* note 12, at 51–55.
81 Buchanan et al., *supra* note 6, at 9.
82 Grant, *supra* note 18; Portoghese et al., *supra* note 19.
83 Edmondson, *supra* note 43, at 181–182.
84 Seth Godin, "The Maverick and the Status Quo," August 26, 2023, https://seths.blog/2023/08/the-maverick-and-the-status-quo.
85 "Maverick," *Dictionary.com*, www.dictionary.com/browse/maverick.

CONCLUSION

> Happiness comes when your work and words are of benefit to yourself and others.
>
> —Siddhartha Gautama, the Buddha[1]

> Lawyers are inevitably leaders in all positions they hold due to their privilege, power, prestige, and responsibility.
>
> —Randall Kiser[2]

> When you lead, your real job is to create more leaders, not more followers.
>
> —Kevin Kelly, founding editor of *Wired Magazine*[3]

You have completed your study of *The Legal Brain* and developed your neuro-intelligence skills and competencies. You now understand your predominant lawyering asset – the brain – and how healthy habits can empower it. You also know how chronic stress, languishing, burnout, anxiety, depression, and self-medication can harm it. You recognize the impact cultures have on brain health and mental strength.

Neuro-intelligence is important for lawyers to improve their individual well-being and enhance the capacity of legal organizations. It is also important because lawyers serve as leaders in all kinds of enterprises. President John Quincy Adams advised, "If your actions inspire others to dream more, learn more, do more and become more, you are a leader."[4]

THE SIGNIFICANCE OF THE NEURO-INTELLIGENT LAWYER AND LEGAL ORGANIZATION

Theater artist Taylor Mac reflects, "An artist's job is to dream the culture forward. To look at the things that aren't working in society and imagine how it could be better. Ultimately, for me, it's all about experiencing the full range of who you are and taking the time to actually do that."[5]

Lawyers are leaders who defend society's light. Like artists, lawyers must "dream the culture forward."

The responsibility to understand and improve your own brain health and mental strength extends to your communities because of the privilege, power, and prestige you enjoy. Neuro-intelligent lawyers and legal organizations can enlighten government, business, media, education, and philanthropic entities.

Social progress is stalled. We lack the skills to confront extreme challenges. Large swaths of people are excluded from opportunities to contribute. We are divided into tribes that are incapable of communicating with each other. We are unable to work together to create a sustainable future.

Like the failed ranking system at Microsoft, which caused employees to compete with each other instead of with their market competitors, tribes have coalesced within countries to compete against each other for what is perceived as that country's limited resources and power. People at the top of extreme hierarchies find it difficult to empathize and collaborate with the people inhabiting the vast space outside the small zone of privilege.

Extreme competition is antisocial because all the focus is on individual survival. Chronic stress reduces cognitive fitness, harms mental and physical health, and limits creativity, innovation, problem-solving, productivity, and the capacity to collaborate. Countries, governments, companies, schools, and nonprofits must work together to address challenges like climate change, food insecurity, sustainable development, equality, civil rights, gun violence, health and well-being, and conflict resolution.

Like Seth Godin's insight that work is not working for many employees, society isn't working for many people. Social structures that feature fear, scarcity, exclusion, steep hierarchy, and extreme competition are dehumanizing. And humans are suffering.

The WHO reports, "Depression is one of the leading causes of disability. Suicide is the fourth leading cause of death among 15–29-year-olds. People with severe mental health conditions die prematurely – as much as two decades early – due to preventable physical conditions."[6]

The Global Gender Gap Report has revealed that the gender gap for 2023 is 68.4% closed, with an improvement in that year of only 0.3%. If progress continues at its current rate, it will take 131 years to reach full global gender parity.[7]

The US Department of Justice has released the 2021 Hate Crime Statistics collected by the Federal Bureau of Investigation. There were 7,262 hate crimes involving 8,753 victims in the United States in that one year. The bias motivations were based on race, ethnicity, or ancestry (64.8%); sexual orientation (15.6%); religion (13.3%); gender identity (3.6%); disability (1.7%); and gender (1%).[8]

Millennials, now nearly forty years old, who don't have the time or money for a midlife crisis, yearn for safety and security because they have never experienced it,[9] and 44 percent of high school students in 2021 reported persistent sadness or hopelessness in the previous year.[10] Anxiety and depression are among the leading causes of adolescent disability, and the failure to address early mental health conditions impairs physical and mental health and limits the capacity to lead fulfilling adult lives.[11]

> Throughout childhood, children and their parents soak up a sense of pressure from American culture that they must be constantly focused on academic achievement and long-term professional success in a world with few opportunities. With this mindset, many children grow up to measure their self-worth with their number of accomplishments in school or accolades from extracurricular activities.[12]

According to the 2019 Vibrant and Healthy Kids Report by the National Academies of Sciences, Engineering, and Medicine, and the 2018 Inspiring and Powering the Future by the Robert Wood Johnson Foundation, students at high-achieving schools and those under excessive pressure to excel are at a high risk for stress, anxiety, and substance use. This extreme performance expectation category has been added to the adverse childhood experiences that negatively impact adolescent well-being along with living through trauma, living in foster care, living in poverty, living with community violence, living with a parent who is incarcerated, and living as a recent immigrant.[13]

Maverick lawyer leaders must first dream, and then act, to move the culture forward. They must make neuro-intelligence available to all people, so they can experience the full range of their identities and capabilities. We cannot afford to exclude and lose humans, and the light they could bring to the world. These lawyer leaders must educate us about the toxicity of extreme competition and cultures built on fear, scarcity, and chronic stress. These Mavericks can lead the social moonshot movement to further heal and humanize society.

WE NEED LIGHT, WE NEED LOVE

Research has shown that sad music can evoke three different kinds of emotional responses: pleasure, comfort, and pain. Older people report experiencing a comforting sadness, while younger people and women report more negative feelings when listening to sad music. But most frequent feelings associated with listening to sad music are positive.

Psychology professor Cher McGillivray explains that when musicians write and sing sad music, they are using their art to reflect, become more self-aware, and gain new perspectives, which can improve their mental health. She says that when music lovers connect with their favorite artist's stories, it can help the fan's trauma and pain become more tolerable. "Engaging with trauma in art allows us to rewrite the outcome from being victims of our circumstances to victors."

Professor McGillivray continues, "Psychologists understand that the quickest way to understanding someone is through their wounds, and musicians too understand this power of music to comfort, console, encourage and exhort themselves and other broken hearts."

Artists and athletes have been speaking out about their mental health recently, normalizing mental health conditions and treatment-seeking. Professional basketball player Kevin Love wrote about a panic attack he suffered during a game. He addressed the stigma people experience around mental health issues and the self-awareness he improved in therapy. He wrote, "It's not some magical process. It's terrifying and awkward and hard, at least in my experience so far. I know you don't just get rid of problems by talking about them, but I've learned that over time maybe you can better understand them and make them more manageable."

Perhaps Love's greatest insight was when he wrote about another player disclosing his experiences with depression. He reminded us that all humans have struggles and heartbreaks, and that while mental health issues are invisible, they are also universal. He said, "Everyone is going through something we can't see."

Professor McGillivray instructs that we need to feel safe and connected to others. The Rihanna anthem from *Black Panther: Wakanda Forever* reflects that sentiment:

> Drowning in an endless sea
> Take some time and stay with me
> Keep me safe
> We need light, we need love.[14]

We all face invisible heartbreaks and struggles. We all arrive in this world with strengths and talents to contribute. When lawyers heal themselves, they are better positioned to lead the healing of others. Neuro-intelligent leadership shines a light on each individual. It humanizes.

Neuro-intelligent leadership can enlighten the world by ensuring access to brain health and mental strength for all individuals and by spreading neuro-intelligence into policymaking in organizations of all types. Like Linkin Park's song that asks, "Who cares if one more light goes out?"[15] neuro-intelligent Maverick leaders answer, *We do!*

If lawyers want to create extraordinary change in the world, they must dance with the tension and transform the way they educate students, practice law, and lead organizations.

> *Are we brave enough to see and be the light?*
> The new dawn blooms as we free it.
> For there is always light,
> if only we're brave enough to see it,
> if only we're brave enough to be it.
>
> —Amanda Gorman[16]

NOTES

1 *Goodreads*, www.goodreads.com/quotes/22292-happiness-comes-when-your-work-and-words-are-of-benefit.

2 Randall Kiser, Soft Skills for the Effective Lawyer (Cambridge University Press, 2017), 226.

3 Kevin Kelly, "103 Bits of Advice I Wish I Had Known," *The Technium*, April 28, 2022, https://kk.org/thetechnium/103-bits-of-advice-i-wish-i-had-known.

4 *Goodreads*, www.goodreads.com/quotes/584047-if-your-actions-inspire-others-to-dream-more-learn-more.

5 Taylor Mac, "Taylor Mac's 24-Decade History of Popular Music, Official Trailer, HBO," *YouTube*, www.youtube.com/watch?v=ZwnddB4dFYk.

6 World Health Organization, "Mental Health," www.who.int/health-topics/mental-health.

7 World Economic Forum, Global Gender Gap Report 2023 (World Economic Forum, 2023).

8 US Department of Justice, "Hate Crimes: Facts and Statistics," www.justice gov/hatecrimes/hate crime statistics.

9 Jessica Grose, "Millennials Are Hitting Middle Age and It Doesn't Look Like What We Were Promised," *New York Times*, March 14, 2023, www.nytimes .com/interactive/2023/03/14/opinion/middle-age-millennials.html.

10 Centers for Disease Control and Prevention, "New CDC Data Illuminate Youth Mental Health Threats during COVID-19 Pandemic," *CDC Newsroom*, March 31, 2022, www.cdc.gov/media/releases/2022/p0331-youth-mental-health-covid-19.html.

11 World Health Organization, "Mental Health of Adolescents," November 17, 2021, www.who.int/news-room/fact-sheets/detail/adolescent-mental-health.

12 Maryam Abdullah, "Why Achievement Culture Has Become So Toxic," *Greater Good Newsletter*, August 30, 2023, https://greatergood.berkeley.edu/article/item/why_achievement_culture_has_become_so_toxic.

13 Ibid.; National Academies of Sciences, Engineering, and Medicine, Vibrant and Healthy Kids (National Academies Press, 2019); Robert Wood Johnson Foundation, "Inspiring and Powering the Future," July 1, 2018, www.rwjf.org/en/insights/our-research/2018/06/inspiring-and-powering-the-future–a-new-view-of-adolescence.html.

14 Cher McGillivray, "'I'm the Problem, It's Me': Why Do Musicians Revisit Their Pain and Doubt in Their Art," *The Conversation*, November 10, 2022, https://theconversation.com/im-the-problem-its-me-why-do-musicians-revisit-their-pain-and-doubt-in-their-art-193528; Durham University, "Music Reveals Pain, Pleasure of Sad Music," *Science Daily*, June 14, 2016, www.sciencedaily.com/releases/2016/06/160614155914.htm; Kevin

Love, "Everyone Is Going through Something," *The Players Tribune*, March 6, 2018, www.theplayerstribune.com/articles/kevin-love-everyone-is-going-through-something; Rania Anniftos, "Here Are the Lyrics to Rihanna's 'Life Me Up,'" *Billboard*, November 11, 2022, www.billboard.com/music/lyrics/rihanna-lift-me-up-lyrics-1235170173.

15 Brad Delson et al., "One More Light," Linkin Park, *One More Light album* (2017).

16 Lian Parsons, "History Has Its Eyes on Us," *The Harvard Gazette*, January 20, 2021, https://news.harvard.edu/gazette/story/2021/01/amanda-gormans-inauguration-poem-the-hill-we-climb.

SELECT BIBLIOGRAPHY

Achor, Shawn, The Happiness Advantage: The Seven Principles of Positive Psychology That Fuel Success and Performance at Work (Currency, 2010).

Adolphs, Ralph and Anderson, David J., The Neuroscience of Emotion: A New Synthesis (Princeton University Press, 2018).

Amen, Daniel G., Change Your Brain Change Your Body: Use Your Brain to Get and Keep the Body You Have Always Wanted (Harmony, 2010).

Anderson, Frank G., Transcending Trauma: Healing Complex PTSD with Internal Family Systems Therapy (PESI, 2021).

Brann, Amy, Neuroscience for Coaches: How to Use the Latest Insights for the Benefit of your Clients, 2nd ed. (Kogan Page, 2017).

Brewer, Judson, The Craving Mind: From Cigarettes to Smart Phones to Love – Why We Get Hooked & How We Can Break Bad Habits (Yale University Press, 2018).

Brewer, Judson, Unwinding Anxiety: New Science Shows How to Break the Cycles of Worry and Fear to Heal Your Mind (Vermilion, 2021).

Brown, Brene, Dare to Lead: Brave Work. Tough Conversations. Whole Hearts (Random House, 2019).

Brown, Heidi K., The Introverted Lawyer: A Seven-Step Journey toward Authentically Empowered Advocacy (American Bar Association, 2017).

Burns, David D., Feeling Great: The Revolutionary New Treatment for Depression and Anxiety (PESI, 2020).

Cain, Susan, Quiet: The Power of Introverts in a World That Can't Stop Talking (Crown, 2012).

Carter, Rita, Mapping the Mind (University of California Press, 2010).

Carter, Rita, The Human Brain Book (DK, 2019).

Clark, Taylor, Nerve: Poise under Pressure, Serenity under Stress, and the Brave New Science of Fear and Cool (Little, Brown and Company, 2011).

Cuban, Brian, The Addicted Lawyer: Tales of the Bar, Booze, Blow, and Redemption (Post Hill Press, 2017).

Davis, Paula, Beating Burnout at Work: Why Teams Hold the Secret to Well-Being and Resilience (Wharton School Press, 2021).

Devi, Gayatri, A Calm Brain: How to Relax into a Stress-Free, High-Powered Life (Plume, 2013).

Doidge, Norman, The Brain That Changes Itself (Penguin Life, 2007).

Dweck, Carol S., Mindset: The New Psychology of Success (Ballantine, 2007).

Ford, Julian and Wortmann, Jon, Hijacked By Your Brain: How to Free Yourself When Stress Takes Over (Sourcebooks, 2013).

Gibb, Barry J., The Rough Guide to the Brain (Rough Guides, 2007).

Godin, Seth, The Song of Significance (Portfolio Penguin, 2023).

Greenberg, Melanie, The Stress-Proof Brain: Master Your Emotional Response to Stress Using Mindfulness and Neuroplasticity (New Harbinger, 2017).

Grisel, Judith, Never Enough: The Neuroscience and Experience of Addiction (Doubleday, 2019).

Gupta, Sanjay, Keep Sharp: Build a Better Brain at Any Age (Simon & Schuster, 2021).

Hancock, Stephanie D. and McKim, William A., Drugs and Behavior: An Introduction to Behavioral Pharmacology, 8th ed. (Pearson, 2018).

Hanna, Heidi, The Sharp Solution: A Brain-Based Approach for Optimal Performance (Wiley, 2013).

Hanson, Rick, Buddha's Brain: The Practical Neuroscience of Happiness, Love, & Wisdom (ReadHowYouWant, 2012).

Hart, Carl L. and Ksir, Charles J., Drugs, Society & Human Behavior, 17th ed. (McGraw Hill, 2018).

Heffernan, Margaret, A Bigger Prize: How We Can Do Better Than the Competition (PublicAffairs, 2014).

Hollis, Rachel, Girl, Wash Your Face: Stop Believing the Lies about Who You Are So You Can Become Who You Were Meant to Be (Thomas Nelson, 2019).

Horstman, Judith, The Scientific American: Brave New Brain (Jossey-Bass, 2010).
Horstman, Judith, The Scientific American: Day in the Life of Your Brain (Jossey-Bass, 2009).
Kandell, Eric, Schwartz, James, Jessell, Thomas, Siegelbaum, Steven, and Hudspeth, A. J., eds., Principles of Neural Science, 5th ed. (McGraw Hill, 2015).
Kiser, Randall, Soft Skills for the Effective Lawyer (Cambridge University Press, 2017).
Ledoux, Joseph, Synaptic Self: How Our Brains Become Who We Are (Penguin, 2003).
Levit, Nancy and Linder, Douglas O., The Happy Lawyer: Making a Good Life in the Law (Oxford University Press, 2010).
Leyse-Wallace, Ruth, Nutrition and Mental Health (CRC Press, 2013).
Linden, David J., The Compass of Pleasure: How Our Brains Make Fatty Foods, Orgasm, Exercise, Marijuana, Generosity, Vodka, Learning, and Gambling Feel So Good (Penguin, 2012).
Litowitz, Douglas, The Destruction of Young Lawyers: Beyond One L (University of Akron Press, 2005).
Lustig, Robert H., The Hacking of the American Mind: The Science behind the Corporate Takeover of Our Bodies and Brains (Avery, 2017).
Martin, Nathalie, Lawyering from the Inside Out: Learning Professional Development through Mindfulness and Emotional Intelligence (Cambridge University Press, 2018).
McClurg, Andrew J., 1L of a Ride: A Well-Traveled Professor's Roadmap to Success in the First Year of Law School, 2nd ed. (West Academic, 2013).
McGonigal, Kelly, The Upside of Stress: Why Stress Is Good for You (and How to Get Good at It) (Avery, 2016).
Medina, John, Brain Rules: 12 Principles for Surviving and Thriving at Work, Home, and School (Pear Press, 2009).
Meyer, Jerrold S. and Quenzer, Linda F., Psychopharmacology: Drugs, the Brain, and Behavior, 3rd ed. (Sinauer Associates, 2019).
Morin, Amy, 13 Things Mentally Strong Women Don't Do (William Morrow Paperbacks, 2020).

Nerison, Rebecca, Lawyers, Anger, and Anxiety: Dealing with the Stresses of the Legal Profession (American Bar Association, 2010).

Pang, Alex Soojung-Kim, Rest: Why You Get More Done When You Work Less (Basic Books, 2018).

Perlmutter, David and Villoldo, Alberto, Power Up Your Brain: The Neuroscience of Enlightenment (Hay House, 2012).

Purves, Dale, LeBar, Kevin, Platt, Michael, Woldorff, Marty, Cabeza, Roberto, and Huettel, Scott, Principles of Cognitive Neuroscience, 2nd ed. (Sinauer Associates, 2012).

Ratey, John J., Spark: The Revolutionary New Science of Exercise and the Brain (Little, Brown, 2013).

Sapolsky, Robert M., Why Zebras Don't Get Ulcers (Holt Paperbacks, 2004).

Seligman, Martin E. P., Flourish: A Visionary New Understanding of Happiness and Well-Being (Atria, 2012).

Seung, Sebastian, Connectome: How the Brain's Wiring Makes Us Who We Are (Houghton Mifflin Harcourt, 2012).

Shaffer, David Williamson, How Computer Games Help Children Learn (Palgrave Macmillan, 2016).

Smith, Anne M. and Collene, Angela L., Wardlaw's Contemporary Nutrition, 10th ed. (McGraw-Hill Education, 2016).

Smith, Lisa F., Girl Walks out of a Bar: A Memoir (SelectBooks, 2016).

Squire, Larry, Berg, Darwin, Bloom, Floyd, du Lac, Sascha, Ghosh, Anirvan, and Spitzer, Nicholas, eds., Fundamental Neuroscience (Academic Press, 2012).

Sullivan, William M., Colby, Anne, Wegner, Judith, Bond, Lloyd, and Shulman, Lee, Educating Lawyers: Preparation for the Profession of Law (Jossey-Bass, 2007).

Swart, Tara, Chisholm, Kitty, and Brown, Paul, Neuroscience for Leadership: Harnessing the Brain Gain Advantage (Springer, 2015).

Sweeney, Michael S. Brain, the Complete Mind: How It Develops, How It Works, and How to Keep It Sharp (National Geographic, 2009).

Talbott, Shawn, The Cortisol Connection: Why Stress Makes You Fat and Ruins Your Health – and What You Can Do about It (Hunter House, 2007).

Tedeschi, Philip and Jenkins, Molly Anne, eds., Transforming Trauma: Resilience and Healing through Our Connections with Animals (Purdue University Press, 2019).

Van Der Kolk, Bessel, The Body Keeps the Score: Brain, Mind, and Body in the Healing of Trauma (Penguin, 2015).

Varol, Ozan, Think Like a Rocket Scientist: Simple Strategies You Can Use to Make Giant Leaps in Work and Life (PublicAffairs, 2020).

Wells, Greg, The Ripple Effect: Sleep Better, Eat Better, Move Better, Think Better (Collins, 2018).

Willeumier, Kristen, Biohack Your Brain: How to Boost Cognitive Health, Performance and Power (William Morrow, 2020).

INDEX

For EU product safety concerns, contact us at Calle de José Abascal, 56–1°,
28003 Madrid, Spain or eugpsr@cambridge.org.

www.ingramcontent.com/pod-product-compliance
Ingram Content Group UK Ltd.
Pitfield, Milton Keynes, MK11 3LW, UK
UKHW020355140625
459647UK00020B/2482

* 9 7 8 1 0 0 9 4 8 4 5 6 5 *